PRAISE FOR *LIGHT A FIRE IN THEIR HEARTS*

"This book is so much more than just another leadership book. *Light a Fire in Their Hearts* clearly articulates that what sets great people leaders apart is their ability to connect at the human level with employees and colleagues, through compassion, courage and competence. In my experience as Founder of a major and renowned North American employee assistance program, I can attest that this is essential to support the well-being and mental health of employees. This book also offers simple and practical solutions for leadership anchored in authentic and compassionate human connections at work."

— **Dr. Warren Shepell**, Founder and Past President at
Warren Shepell—The EAP Professionals

"What a wonderful leadership book with a premise I love: To ignite employees' passions and inspire them to be and do their best at work, you need to light a fire in their hearts. The world needs more of this right now."

— **Marci Shimoff**, International Speaker, Co-founder, Your Year of
Miracles, #1 *New York Times* Bestselling Author, *Happy for No
Reason, Love for No Reason, Chicken Soup for the Woman's Soul*

"As a former primetime Los Angeles talk radio host, and now as the proud owner of a successful training and consulting firm, I have come across dozens of experts in the field of employee engagement. Of them, by far the most, well…engaging is Lisa Anna Palmer. She is the perfect blend of information and inspiration. It's not just what she knows, it's who she is, and her passion and expertise come across in *Light A Fire in Their Hearts*. I have learned from her and our clients will be doing the same, as we present them with gifts of Lisa's outstanding book."

— **Joel Roberts**, Former prime time talk show host KABC Radio, Los Angeles, Owner, Joel D. Roberts and Associates

"Lisa Anna Palmer captures what sets great leaders apart in the twenty-first century: their ability to show their employees that they genuinely love and care about them, and that their work matters and makes a positive difference in the lives of others. The time has come for leaders in the world to realize that the belief that you need to act like a jerk to make money is going the way of the dinosaur. It is connecting at the human level that lights a fire in the hearts of employees, and love that drives success in business, and offers the strongest competitive advantage."

— **Steve Farber**, CEO & Founder, Extreme Leadership Institute, Bestselling Author and Renowned Leadership Expert

"If you are already a leader or are aspiring to become one, we recommend that you read *Light a Fire in Their Hearts: The Truth About Leadership*. Lisa Anna Palmer's book is filled with practical and enlightening ways to deeply connect with your employees so that they are inspired to be and do their very best to support you and help your organization succeed."

— **Janet Bray Attwood**, Co-author of the *New York Times* bestsellers, *The Passion Test* and *Your Hidden Riches*

"In *Light a Fire in Their Hearts*, Lisa Anna Palmer has provided a clear roadmap to great leadership, grounded in the knowledge that respect and motivated employees have to be earned. They cannot be purchased. If you are a corporate manager or aspire to become one, this book will provide you with the guidance you need to become a great leader."

— **Chris Attwood**, Co-author of the *New York Times* bestsellers, *The Passion* Test and *Your Hidden Riches*

"Every once in a while, one is blessed to cross paths with a human being as exceptional as Lisa Anna Palmer. A gifted researcher, writer and HR practitioner, Lisa generously shares her findings and expertise in this book that is an absolute must have for any current or aspiring leader committed to making the world a better workplace. Kudos to Lisa for having the courage to tackle this pressing and pervasive issue and for providing leaders with insights and practical tools to help them become better leaders and, by virtue of doing so, creating better workplaces."

— **Linda Caron**, M.Ed., Certified Human Resources Leader,
HR Warrior

"*Light a Fire in Their Hearts* by Lisa Anna Palmer is an easy to understand, practical manual for today's complex workplaces—a book that should be read by leaders who truly want to make a difference in this day and age where wellness, compassion and engagement are craved and sorely amiss. As an entrepreneur and seasoned Human Resources practitioner who has witnessed and experienced detrimental results from non-people centric workplaces practices, I can attest that this book is invaluable and inspiring with its meaningful guide to improving bottom line results and aligned engagement. This, through a game-changing approach that puts compassion and wellness into authentic action—with winning results that serve all."

— **Maria R. Nebres**, Author of *Love and the Highly Engaged Team*

"I have worked with leaders at all levels for over twenty years. Now, as an executive myself, I often see very high performing individuals step into people leadership roles for the wrong reasons while some new and existing people leaders struggle with the same challenges that are typically not addressed through the more traditional leadership books. How refreshing to read *Light a Fire in Their Hearts*, the book I wish I would have had when I was first starting out on my leadership journey."

— **Caterina Dattilo-Caron**, Certified Human Resources Leader,
Director, Leadership & Culture, Canada Mortgage &
Housing Corporation

"Lisa Anna Palmer is shifting the way to engage as a leader in an era where we must evolve beyond technology and ensure people are rightfully valued and provided opportunities to be the best version of themselves in a fast changing workforce. Leaders, for amazing results, use your matches wisely, aim them at their hearts instead of their tush."

— **Johanne G. Gagnon**, Assistant Director, Field Policies, Systems and Services with a Federal employer

"As the founder of the Expert Speaker Institute as well as the #1 global Trainer for Learning Tree International, I have trained thousands of leaders at all levels to enhance their communication skills and to engage with their employees so that they want to give and perform their very best. In *Light a Fire in Their Hearts*, Lisa Anna Palmer and over thirty leaders share the wisdom that sets great people leaders apart. I highly recommend her book to both existing and aspiring leaders so that they can be well equipped to connect with their employees at the human level and watch their success and productivity soar!"

— **Majeed Mogharreban**, Founder of expertspeaker.com and Author of *Expert Speaker: 5 Steps to Grow Your Business with Public Speaking*

Light a Fire in Their Hearts

LIGHT A FIRE IN
THEIR HEARTS
The Truth About Leadership

*A Guide for Igniting Engagement
Using the Wisdom that Sets
Great Leaders Apart*

LISA ANNA PALMER

NEW YORK

LONDON • NASHVILLE • MELBOURNE • VANCOUVER

Light a Fire in Their Hearts

The Truth About Leadership— A Guide for Igniting Engagement Using the Wisdom that Sets Great Leaders Apart

Published in New York, New York, by Morgan James Publishing. Morgan James is a trademark of Morgan James, LLC. www.MorganJamesPublishing.com

ISBN 9781642798272 paperback
ISBN 9781642798289 eBook
Library of Congress Control Number: 2019914377

Cover Design by:	Interior Design by:	Editor:
Rachel Lopez	Christopher Kirk	Dan Teck
www.r2cdesign.com	www.GFSstudio.com	

IMPORTANT: LIMITS OF LIABILITY AND DISCLAIMER OF WARRANTY

This book is strictly for informational and educational purposes. The purpose of this book is to share insights, information, wise practices, and stories. The various leadership approaches featured in this book are not to be considered "one size fits all" solutions, as there can be many contributing factors that need to be weighed on a case-by-case basis. As such, the author and publisher shall not be liable for the use or misuse of this material.

For greater clarity, the author and/or publisher do not guarantee that anyone following any of the approaches will become successful or transform into great people leaders. Therefore, the author and/or publisher shall have neither liability nor responsibility to anyone with respect to any loss or damage caused, or alleged to be caused, directly or indirectly by the information contained in this book.

NOTE: Some names used in case studies have been changed in order to protect identities and have been marked with an asterisk (*). In certain instances, details have been slightly altered in order to protect people's privacy. The names of those who have contributed their own pieces are accurately represented.

Morgan James is a proud partner of Habitat for Humanity Peninsula and Greater Williamsburg. Partners in building since 2006.

Get involved today! Visit
MorganJamesPublishing.com/giving-back

THE GREAT LEADER'S CREDO

I strive to connect with people at the human level and to light a fire in their hearts. I find ways to help people tap into their passions and become inspired and equipped to achieve that which is greater than themselves.

I light a fire in my own heart first so that others will be inspired to light a fire in theirs. I take time to reflect and to grow my competencies because growing as a leader requires lifelong learning.

I support and mentor people to help them reach their dreams. I help them see how their vision aligns with that of the organization so that we can create a shared one.

I strive every day to engage, motivate, coach, guide, and equip people to focus their time, effort, and resources on achieving positive results. I recognize and reward their efforts.

I foster an atmosphere where employees and other colleagues can get excited about working, growing, and accomplishing their goals. I listen attentively and learn about people. I find ways to make work more fun. I show compassion when they fail or feel hurt, or when I need to deliver difficult news.

I "walk the talk," living and working with integrity. I help all those I work with and serve feel like they belong and feel included. I treat people as they want to be treated. I hold people accountable for practicing civility and respect.

I lead myself and others to live and work purposefully. I include others in decision-making whenever I can. I make decisions in urgent situations. I explain the "Why" behind decisions.

I have the courage to take calculated risks and leaps of faith for the greater good. I encourage and equip others to stretch beyond their comfort zone so that they can build confidence and courage and step into their power.

I park my ego and show humility in my interactions, coming from a place of love for humanity and all living things. I help others tap into their power. I help them see their own gifts, realize how they matter, and how they make a difference in my life and the lives of others.

I collaborate with those who choose to join me in my quest and walk side by side. Together we create and share positive prosperity in a manner that is good for people and the planet, and that profits my organization and the community at large.

I take good care of myself so that I have the strength and energy to continue my work in the service of others.

I do my part to make the world a better workplace.

Love and Leadership

The truth about great leadership is that at its basis, it is Love. When it is mentioned in this book, it is not about romantic love. It is *agape,* the highest form of love, the love for humanity. It is about caring for and having compassion for people and all living things, recognizing that we are all connected and we are all one. It is about a powerful force that motivates us to do good work, to serve, and to accomplish something good through and for others, be they employees, clients, colleagues, society, or anyone who will be touched by the way we lead and by the fruits of our labor. It is characterised as humanity towards others: it is *ubuntu.*

DEDICATION

*L*ight a Fire in Their Hearts is a labor of love for people working around the globe. It is dedicated to my husband, Andrew, and my son, Jake, and their generation of workers and all those who will come after them.

With this book, I seek to spread the message that the state of leadership is a matter of public health: making the world a better workplace is essential for the advancement and continuation and evolution of our species, and for all living beings. Ultimately, my message to the new and future generations of leaders is that if you decide to take on a leadership role, you have a responsibility to do your part to inspire and engage employees, and to create healthier and more inclusive workplaces. As a collective, you hold the power to make the world a better workplace, which will ultimately contribute to a healthier planet for us all.

In memory of my beloved father,
Corrado Giacomo Cattelan (1933-2007)

My beloved aunt, "Zia Zinute,"
Teresina Tonini (née Vissa) (1930-2019)

Our beloved cousin, a bright light,
Wanda Christensen (née Tobin) (1967-2019)

And a great leader whose story, as told by his daughter Nadine,
is featured in this book,
John Albana Bursey (1944-2019)

CONTENTS

FOREWORD

This book gets to the heart of leadership! Whether you were born to lead, or you desire to be your best for the world, Lisa Anna Palmer uncovers the inspiration and passion that is not only possible in leadership, but which is a must.

Young or old, rich or poor, at the top of the organization in a position of power, or at the grassroots level, personal self-leadership is the starting point for leading change. Lisa takes us on a journey through the many, many, experiential stories included throughout the book. We get to learn from diverse leaders who share their stories and provide a glimpse into their mindset, their values, and the beliefs that empowered them to achieve personal success as well as success for their organizations.

An overwhelming percentage of leaders are still stuck in the Industrial Age management style of command and control, protecting their positions with hierarchy and bureaucracy. This is not the leadership style for the twenty-first century if you wish to inspire and engage millennials, who will make up 50% of the workforce by the early 2020s, not to mention the upcoming Gen-Z's, who are also known as the Digitals.

Instead, compassion, courage, competence and collaborative leadership are essential in this new era. In addition to making money, people are looking for meaning and purpose in their jobs, and they want to feel cared for as human beings, not just as human resources or as human capital.

Leadership is a calling to help others and to connect with people, rather than to simply oversee the management of work processes and the accomplishment of tasks. The key role for leaders is to serve. People don't work for the leader, the leader works for them by ensuring that jobs are secure, that goals are clear, and that they do whatever it takes to help their employees and colleagues win.

If you are looking for ways to inspire and engage your employees, this book has the answers. In it, you will find progressive approaches, tools, and strategies to boost your ability to tap into the source that unlocks and drives true human potential: The heart—the seat of all emotions and behaviors, which houses important values such as respect, loyalty, and trust.

In this book you will see that the secret to unleashing the promise of your people and help them achieve their full potential in a healthy and sustainable manner, is to light a fire in their hearts.

What a joy it was reading this book, and what magical ride you too will have. Happy reading.

Joanna Barclay,
CEO, Culture Leadership Group
Author of *Conscious Culture; How to Build a High Performing Workplace through Values, Ethics, and Leadership; Thought-leader and Equine Facilitator on Conscious Leadership and Cultural Transformation*

Introduction
FROM BEING IN KNOTS TO STARTING A MOVEMENT

"That which does not kill us, makes us stronger."
~ Friedrich Nietzsche

I was sitting at my desk, drafting an email on my computer, when I felt a cold presence at my back. The new manager, Michelle, leaned into my personal space, stretched her lanky arm over my left shoulder, and tapped her bony index finger aggressively against my monitor. "Make sure that you cc me on that!" she said with a shrill voice, using a stern and condescending tone.

"What did I do to deserve this type of treatment?" I asked myself. I had been a hard-working and dedicated employee. I had carried this division through difficult times and delivered on key files amidst the chaos and turnover at the executive level. I had compromised my health while I worked long days and even sacrificed precious time with my young son and my husband to be at the office. Now, in comes this prima donna, who just the week before had tried to take credit for a project that I had managed long before she joined the corporation. I had briefed her and brought her up to speed on key files. I had introduced her to my colleagues and had done everything I could to welcome her. And now, here she was—barely a month later—treating me like trash and undermining me in such a manner that left me feeling angry and humiliated.

I thought to myself, "Is this the thanks I get—to be demeaned and admonished like a child?" At that moment, all the stress, late nights, and lack of self-care caught up with me. Never in all my career had I felt so disrespected and devalued. But rather than confront her, I turned my anger inward. My heart beat faster, and the knot that was quickly forming in my stomach was getting tighter by the minute. From that moment, the tension between us kept on growing, as she continued to assert her dominance and disrespect everybody in the group.

My stomach had clamped down on me, and it had gone from being knotted-up to feeling like I had just swallowed a bag of rocks.

Over the next month, I ended up in the hospital three times. One of those times, I had to be transported by ambulance. As I writhed in pain on the floor, all I could think of was, "Thank God my son is in bed and didn't see his mother carried out on a stretcher." My stomach had clamped down on me, and it had gone from being knotted-up to feeling like I had just swallowed a bag of rocks. I couldn't eat, and what little I could drink was not being absorbed. I was dizzy, drained, and nauseated. I spent most of my time in the fetal position, in excruciating pain. I became severely dehydrated and needed three bags of IV within a two week period. I opened my eyes through a haze while I lay on the gurney. One moment, I saw my husband standing at my bedside with a concerned look on his face, then I would fade out again. The next time I opened my eyes, it was my sister who was at my bedside. They took shifts with my mom, who was taking care of my young son while I lay there, helplessly drifting in and out of consciousness thanks to the anti-anxiety pills and the morphine shots.

At the time, I was thirty-seven years old, and I didn't know whether I was going to make it to my thirty-eighth birthday.

In the months that followed, as I slowly recovered while I dragged myself into the office, I reflected on what had taken place. Up until that point in my career, I had been fortunate enough to have reported to good leaders.

Yes, they'd had their quirks and could sometimes get on my nerves. There were even instances when they'd made unreasonable demands and dumped volumes of work on my desk. Nevertheless, I generally got along very well with them, and there was always a great deal of mutual respect and civility in our interactions.

That day that my boss creeped up behind me and tapped on my computer screen was a turning point. I got to experience firsthand what it was like to report to someone who lacked leadership abilities and compassion. Rather than break me, this was the day I decided I was tired of seeing people suffer at the hands of poor leaders. This was the day I began transforming into an advocate for workers and for great people leaders.

During this transition, I had the opportunity to interview many amazing leaders, conduct extensive research, and reflect on my own work as a Human Resources and Organization Development (HR&OD) specialist who served employees and management teams at all levels of the organization. Today, as the Founder & CEO of the Cattelan Palmer Light Your Leadership Institute© (LYLI), I work to raise awareness about the importance of leadership. I hold up a mirror to organizations so that those in charge can see that promoting high performers into leadership roles without the proper support can actually harm them and their teams. More importantly, I share approaches that empower leaders to help their current and future employees to be happy, healthy, and productive at work.

In *Light a Fire in Their Hearts*, I'll share key insights gained in over twenty-five years of HR&OD and coaching work. You will gain knowledge about progressive leadership practices and future trends. You will read the words of seasoned people leaders who have contributed to this book so that you can also learn how to apply important leadership principles into your daily work life. Consider us your team of virtual mentors.

You'll see that—more than raises, bonuses, and perks—employees want to be acknowledged, thanked, and treated with respect. They want to know that they matter to you, and that their work is making a positive difference. They want to know and feel that you genuinely care about them.

In the pages that follow, you'll discover wise practices that go back to the basics of servant leadership and connecting with people at work at the human level. You'll see that—more than raises, bonuses, and perks—employees want to be acknowledged, thanked, and treated with respect. They want to know that they matter to you, and that their work is making a positive difference. They want to know and feel that you genuinely care about them.

Join me in the quest to make the world a better workplace.

PART I

Leadership Is Important
Because It Affects All of Us

"Leadership is not about a title or a designation. It's about impact, influence, and inspiration."

~ Robin S. Sharma

Chapter 1
THE IMPACT OF LEADERSHIP
ON PEOPLE IN THE WORKPLACE

"Great leaders harness personal courage, capture the
hearts and minds of others and empower new leaders to
make the world a better place.
~ Maxine Driscoll

This book seeks to guide those who aspire to be leaders or who are newly appointed to reflect on what they're getting into and to undertake a great deal of soul-searching and introspection before continuing to advance within leadership roles.

When it comes to leading others within an organization, leadership can be considered formal or informal. Formal leaders have a title and influence over others by virtue of their authority (by being publicly recognized and accepted by those who carry out the leader's will). Their authority is handed to them or earned—for instance, through political appointments, corporate takeovers, or promotions to higher levels within a company—or passed on, as is the case for royalty or family-run businesses. Informal leaders may not have a title, though they have a relatively strong influence over the actions of others by virtue of their character, their abilities and credibility, and perceived power. This book focuses on leaders who work in organizations and who are accountable for ensuring the desired output and behaviors of people reporting directly to them. More and more, this is being referred to as *people leadership.*

The title of this book, *Light a Fire in Their Hearts*, is a play on the old adage that in order to motivate workers you need to (pardon my language) "light a fire under their ass." If that's where the leaders of today are still lighting fires, then we're in trouble. Progressive leaders know that to motivate their employees and create healthy and wealthy workplaces, they need to learn the art of lighting a fire in people's hearts. I believe that we've entered the Passion Age, where modern workers are looking for meaning, purpose, health, and sustainability—more than just status and money.

At its core, *Light a Fire in Their Hearts* is a call to action for new and aspiring leaders to see and relate to employees as human beings. In this book, *leadership* is not a term reserved solely for CEOs; it's defined as the ability to inspire employees and colleagues to focus their passions, energy, efforts, talents, and enthusiasm toward achieving a shared vision and contributing to something greater than themselves. This can range from inspiring employees to be team players and helping the organization succeed, to making the world a better place. In my view, anyone who supervises others or has power and authority to greatly influence other people's lives at work occupies a leadership role. But merely occupying a "leadership role" does not automatically make someone a leader. Their integrity, ability to earn respect, degree of influence, and inspired actions do.

Given that virtually every person that works within an organization either reports to or is a leader with direct reports, leadership plays an important role for all of us. What happens in the workplace and how people are being treated by their leaders has an impact on society and on how we live our lives.

Employees Are Evolving

Our society and organizations need to adapt and keep pace with our evolving human consciousness and shifts in the way people view work and their relationship with employers. The Passion Age is the manifestation of a major shift in the way people think about their jobs. Just as the human consciousness is evolving, so are the expectations that people have about work. People are looking for meaning and fulfilment. They look to their leaders to inspire them, to help them grow their skill set, and to do work that makes a positive difference in the world. Just as a modern worker passionate about equity and the environment bases their choice of coffee on whether it is fair trade and organic, they also look for their prospective employers to be socially responsible.

The Different Generations

Here are terms that are widely used to define the different generations currently engaged in the workforce, as of the writing of this book.

- Traditionals (born pre-1946 or before WWII)— although proportionately, there are very few left in the workforce
- Baby boomers (born between 1946 and 1964)
- Gen X = nexus generation (born early-to-mid 1960s to the early 1980s)
- Gen Y = millennials (born early 1980s to the mid-1990s)
- Gen Z = digital generation (born mid-1990s to the mid-2000s)

Qualities and characteristics assigned to each generation can be useful to provide insights into general attitudes and behaviors. Although these can help explain shifts in attitudes toward work (and life in general), tendencies and preferences attributed to these generational cohorts may not apply to all members. Wise leaders realize that to understand their employees, they need to get to know them as individuals first so that they can get a more accurate understanding of their motivational needs and lead them accordingly.

Therefore, in this new era, a leader's capacity to motivate employees and ignite engagement hinges on their ability to connect at the human level by integrating three values that I refer to as "The 3 C's of Connection": *Compassion, Courage,* and *Competence.* Further, twenty-first-century leaders can light people's hearts through "The 8 P's of Ignition": *Profundity, Passion, Purpose, Perseverance, Professionalism, Play, Philanthropy,* and *Prosperity.*

Some may have a narrower view of work and argue that we do it solely to make money. Of course financial security remains an important reason why we work. In fact, a 2016 global study conducted by Deloitte about millennials showed that their decisions to join a company are based primarily on money. "Pay and financial benefits drive Millennials' choice of organization more than anything else. This single factor accounts for more than a fifth (22 percent) of the combined level of influence of the fourteen factors measured."[1] This likely results from the fact that many millennials don't have a lot of money because they are dealing with the pressure to pay back sizeable loans they used to fund expensive educations, mortgages, and technology.

The most recent generation to enter the workforce is Gen Z—or digitals—the generation born during a time of widespread access to digital computing technologies. This has led them to have comfort and expertise with those technologies that surpasses those of prior generations.[2] According to Gen Z Guru, a firm dedicated to helping industry connect with Gen Z:

> The question is how much value Gen Z is willing to put on things like culture, work hours or extra benefits. Companies that haven't been able to compete with cash typically ante up with something like a gym membership, work-from-home flexibility or alternative office environments. But Gen Z's walking into the interview are saying one thing: "show me the money."[3]

---

1   "The 2016 Deloitte Millennial Survey—Winning over the Next Generation of Leaders," Deloitte, 2016, p. 19, https://www2.deloitte.com/content/dam/Deloitte/global/Documents/About-Deloitte/gx-millenial-survey-2016-exec-summary.pdf

2   "What is Digital Generation," IGI Global: Disseminator of Knowledge, accessed June 24, 2019, https://www.igi-global.com/dictionary/digital-generation/7631

3   "Gen Z's Willing to Work If the Price Is Right," *Gen Z Guru,* accessed December 4, 2018, http://genzguru.com/blog/gen-zs-willing-to-work-if-the-price-is-right/(site discontinued)

I believe that this claim needs to consider context: at the writing of this book, Gen Z's are just beginning to enter the workforce and therefore have much less experience reporting to managers. I am willing to bet that in ten years, attitudes may shift so that salary drops down in the list of priorities, and the character of their leaders, the workplace culture, global impact, and the quality of their work experiences will be of greater importance than just the money. Having said that, just as with other generations of workers, what ultimately drives a person's decision to apply for a job and accept an offer is not necessarily the same thing that encourages them to stay with a company, be highly motivated, and remain productive.

In fact, studies have shown that 50-75% of people who quit their jobs, really quit their bosses.[4] The most progressive leaders are keenly in tune with this and therefore focus on growing their leadership abilities. They manage their enterprises as "3P Triple Bottom Line" companies.[5] John Elkington, founder of SustainAbility, coined the "3P" business model, which encourages companies to integrate social responsibility and sustainability into all aspects of their organizations. These companies track performance based on standards that track success with people (including their employees and the communities they serve), the impact of operations on the planet, and the profits of the organization.

The emphasis on people and planet demonstrates that contemporary leaders continually challenge themselves to ask powerful questions and listen to and engage employees in new ways so that they are happy and able to find meaning through their work. This inspires employees to do their very best to serve clients and make a positive impact on the planet. Progressive companies show proof that socially responsible values and actions grow profits. While some say there are shortfalls due to the challenges in measuring the positive financial impact of the organization on the employees and the impacts of the organization's business activities on the planet, the "3P Triple Bottom Line" business model resonates with leaders and organizations that look at success as more than just increasing revenue—those who care deeply about humanity and other living beings, and whose work extends far beyond just figuring out how to make a profit.

---

4   Voices, Valley. "Don't Be Surprised When Your Employees Quit." Forbes. October 30, 2017. Accessed December 06, 2018. https://www.forbes.com/sites/valleyvoices/2017/02/22/dont-be-surprised-when-your-employees-quit/#726688d7325e and https://www.linkedin.com/pulse/employees-dont-leave-companies-managers-brigette-hyacinth/.

5   "Small Business," Chron, accessed June 24, 2019, https://smallbusiness.chron.com/

Though paying attention to people and planet, in addition to profits, may seem obvious for progressive employers, for some reason, the message doesn't appear to be getting through to more traditional managers. That their employees want leaders who genuinely care about them and treat them with respect seems to be a foreign concept. Rather, they sit by and watch as employees rebel, disengage, burn out, or walk out the revolving door.

Those heading outdated organizations are not keeping up with modern advances. Despite investing in expensive and often ineffective talent-management and high tech solutions peddled by large consulting firms racing to create the next new buzzword and "flavor of the month" for HR interventions, the current state of the workplace is in dire need of a reboot. Outmoded employers need to realize that Industrial Age practices of commanding, controlling, and asking employees to do meaningless work in exchange for a paycheck are no longer effective means of motivating members of the contemporary workforce.

Further, leaders need to take accountability for the fact that they have an extremely important and far-reaching role to play in the lives of their employees and, by extension, their communities. To illustrate, 54% of respondents reported that work stress caused them to fight with people who are close to them. In addition, when people are stressed at work, they feel drained and this affects their ability to give back to the community. In an article written for charityvillage.com, "The changing face of volunteering in Canada," Susan Fish writes:

> In today's competitive job market, many volunteers face significant stress with volunteering being just one more task added to a busy schedule. Research studies report that individuals cite what Dr. Nora Silver calls time poverty as the biggest barrier to volunteering. Time-impoverished volunteers increasingly weigh their return on investment, assessing what is required of them and what they will get in return for their investment of time. Consequently, Filipchuk notes that volunteers report higher stress and when life becomes overwhelming, volunteers are more likely to quit than they would have in the past.[6]

---

6   "The Changing Face of Volunteering in Canada," Charity Village, Knowledge Centre, posted July 2, 2014, https://charityvillage.com/cms/content/topic/the_changing_face_of_volunteering_in_canada#.W_rUa6cZNQI.

The message here is that when leaders mistreat people and increase work stress, they're not only hurting those individuals but also their families, friends, neighbors, and other people in their lives. Leaders cause those they hurt to go home depleted of the vital energy they need to take care of their loved ones, much less the strength to give back to the community. Therefore, since leaders' behaviors have a significant impact on the stress levels of their employees, the manner in which leadership is carried out ends up affecting all of us.

Chapter 2
HOW BAD LEADERSHIP LEADS TO STRESS AT WORK

"It's gotten to the point where I am working here to pay for the
prescriptions I now require to cope with working here."
~ Quote from Greeting Card by Mini Tantrums

How many times do you hear someone say, "I am so stressed out"? Work-related stress has become a frequent topic of studies and media reports, thus raising awareness about the impact of stress on workers' health.

The current state of leadership has far-reaching implications for individual workers, teams, organizations, and communities where a significant portion of people suffer from work stress. Bad leadership affects the ability of organizations to function at full capacity—not to mention the effects on individual employees and their family members who, by extension, suffer the consequences of having to deal with one or both burned-out parents, partners, and adult children.

Gallup, a global analytics and advice firm that helps leaders and organizations solve their most pressing problems, defines engaged employees as "highly involved in and enthusiastic about their work and workplace."[7] According to

---

7   "State of the Global Workplace," Gallup, (New York, NY: Gallup Press, 2017), https://www.gallup.com/workplace/238079/state-global-workplace-2017.aspx.

the results of Gallup's *State of the Global Workplace* survey (2017), only 15% of employees are engaged. This means that 85% of employees on the planet are not engaged and are dragging themselves to work—including 18% who report being actively disengaged. Actively disengaged workers can be described as "the most damaging employees in the workplace. They are unhappy, and they let that unhappiness show in words, attitudes and actions. They undermine the performance of others by constantly voicing their displeasure and listing many reasons why they are so miserable in their jobs."[8] Gallup also found that poorly led work groups are on average 50% less productive and 44% less profitable than groups that had a good leader.

In countries like Canada and the US—where people presumably have better jobs thanks to legislated rights, minimum wage, and collective agreements—engagement levels hover at around 31%. But don't pat yourself on the back yet, US and Canada—having a workforce where 69% of the participants are disengaged is nothing to text home about. Moreover, when broken down by country, engagement levels can vary significantly, no country exceeds the 40% mark.[9] Why should organizations and nations pay attention to this? Gallup states that countries in the top 25% of highest engagement levels are 17% more productive and 21% more profitable than those that scored in the bottom 25%. The findings show that "businesses that orient performance management systems around basic human needs for psychological engagement, such as positive workplace relationships, frequent recognition, ongoing performance conversations and opportunities for personal development," will have more engaged and more productive employees.

Bad leadership affects the ability of organizations to function at full capacity—not to mention the effects on individual employees and their family members.

I believe that the high level of employee disengagement points to a massive global leadership gap. I attribute this gap primarily to the common prac-

---

8   "Engaged, Disengaged, Actively Disengaged. What's the Difference?" Executive Development Blog, UNC Kenan-Flagler Business School, posted March 17, 2016, http://execdev.kenan-flagler.unc.edu/blog/engaged-disengaged-actively-disengaged.-whats-the-difference.

9   "State of the Global Workplace," Gallup, (New York, NY: Gallup Press, 2017), https://www.gallup.com/workplace/238079/state-global-workplace-2017.aspx.

tice of promoting high performers into leadership roles even when they lack the proper skills and mindset. I've observed that once these high performers are transferred into a managerial role, they often do not get the proper mentorship and are left to figure things out on their own. In such instances, new managers are not well equipped to lead and tend to use fear and command-and-control behaviors—approaches that parents and educators used to motivate them when they were children. Since workers don't like to be treated like children, this is a recipe for conflict, workplace toxicity, loss of productivity, and disengagement.

Disengagement can manifest in many ways. For example, a disengaged person may show up to work and be disruptive or stare blankly into space for eight hours ("presenteeism"). They can become very unhappy, depressed, and physically or mentally ill. In extreme cases, some may even take their own lives or resort to violence. Beyond the socio-economic impacts of a disengaged global workforce, the current state of leadership is a matter of public health that needs to be addressed. Therefore, leadership can be viewed as a social determinant of health, which is everyone's business.

The Japanese have a word to represent death by overwork: karoshi.

Bad leadership can kill, and I don't mean a bad army general calling the wrong shots on the battlefield. For example, the impact of work stress can be so severe that the Japanese even have a word to represent death by overwork: *karoshi*. Workers in other countries are certainly not immune: The International Labour Organization (ILO) "unveiled estimates showing that, worldwide, 2.78 million workers die each year as a result of occupational injuries and illnesses. Of those, approximately 2.4 million are linked to work-related disease."[10] A *Forbes* article estimates that workplace stress contributes to at least 120,000 deaths in the US each year.[11]

---

10   "International Labour Organization (ILO): Global Cost of Work-Related Injuries and Deaths Total Almost $3 Trillion," Safety & Health: The Official Magazine of the NSC Congress and Expo, posted September 6, 2017, https://www.safetyandhealthmagazine.com/articles/16112-ilo-global-cost-of-work-related-injuries-and-deaths-totals-almost-3-trillion.

11   Michael Blanding, "Workplace Stress Responsible for up to $190B in Annual U.S. Healthcare Costs," *Forbes*, posted January 26, 2015, https://www.forbes.com/sites/hbsworkingknowledge/2015/01/26/workplace-stress-responsible-for-up-to-190-billion-in-annual-u-s-heathcare-costs/#22a4d895235a.

When it comes to mental health issues, the World Health Organization states that although "work is good for mental health, a negative working environment can lead to physical and mental health problems.... Harassment and bullying at work are commonly reported problems and can have a substantial adverse impact on mental health."[12]

Factors such as job insecurity and high work demands are also said to contribute to these deaths. An article by the ILO states that:

> ...a study from Japan that found 32.4 percent of workers reported suffering from strong anxiety, worry and stress from work in the previous year. In Chile, 2011 data shows 27.9 percent of workers and 13.8 percent of employers reported that stress and depression were present in their enterprises. Similar figures were found in practically every country we considered for this report.[13]

No one should die while trying to make a living.

Poor leadership is a contributing factor to a significant public health crisis. I find it alarming and ironic that people are so stressed by their *live*lihood that they are getting sick and dying from it. No one should die while trying to make a living.

When I interviewed Dr. Eleanor Sutherland, a renowned Canadian Physician for over six decades and recipient of the prestigious Queen's Diamond Jubilee Award, she reported a significant upswing in recent years in the number of patients coming to her with illnesses that she attributed to workplace stress. She discussed contributing factors, including patients reporting that they were being mistreated by their leaders and colleagues, being in a constant state of transition with no end in sight, and having to expend inordinate amounts of time and energy trying to adapt to a barrage of change because of new technology. Dr. Sutherland observed that many of her patients reported to leaders who demonstrated little understanding about how human beings experience change and transition. Transition is a stressful process of learning to accept the new way of being and working, while at the same time,

---

12   "Mental Health in the Workplace: Information Sheet," World Health Organization, posted May 2019, https://www.who.int/mental_health/in_the_workplace/en/.

13   "Why Workplace Stress Is a Collective Challenge and What to Do About It," International Labour Organization (ILO), posted April 27, 2016, http://www.ilo.org/global/about-the-ilo/newsroom/comment-analysis/WCMS_475077/lang--en/index.htm.

grieving and letting go of the past. Many workplaces embark upon large corporate transformations, which typically involve the implementation of a new organization structure and related workforce adjustments, a major shift in business model, a move to a new location, or the introduction of new systems—or all of the above.

Significant corporate changes often lead to increased workload, vast uncertainty, and feelings of fear and isolation. As Dr. Sutherland said:

> Communication is so important; those who occupy leadership roles don't realize their position of power and are not aware of what people are feeling. It is a problem when leadership is motivated by high-paying jobs—money, title, corner office. People feel invisible, isolated, and a lack of compassion and humanity in the workplace. There is also bullying in the workplace, and there shouldn't be.

Leaders need to take accountability for the fact that they have an extremely important and far-reaching role to play in the lives of their employees and, by extension, their communities.

Bad Leaders Are Costing Us Money

Leaders need to be equipped to communicate effectively and guide employees through transition and also create a supportive environment. Unfortunately, this is often not the case.

For those who are more bottom-line oriented, the annual global cost of illnesses, injuries, and deaths is almost $3 trillion.[14] In the US, workplace stress is costing the economy billions annually—some estimate over $300 billion per year.[15] Even in Canada, where people are thought to live in a happy bubble of über-polite kindness, stress has led to an "explosion in workplace mental health issues, which is costing the Canadian economy an estimated $33 billion a year in lost productivity, as well as billions more in medical costs."[16]

---

14   "International Labour Organization (ILO): Global Cost of Work-Related Injuries and Deaths Total Almost $3 Trillion," Safety & Health: The Official Magazine of the NSC Congress and Expo, posted September 6, 2017, https://www.safetyandhealthmagazine.com/articles/16112-ilo-global-cost-of-work-related-injuries-and-deaths-totals-almost-3-trillion.

15   "Workplace Stress," American Institute of Stress, accessed January 12, 2018, https://www.stress.org/workplace-stress.

16   John Intini, Martin Patriquin, and Ken Macqueen, "Workplace Stress Costs the Economy Billions," The Canadian Encyclopedia, updated May 27, 2014. https://www.thecanadianencyclopedia.ca/en/article/workplace-stress-costs-the-economy-billions.

Primary Causes of Workplace Stress

"You don't lead by hitting people over the head—
that's assault, not leadership."
~ Dwight Eisenhower

According to a *Business Insider* article, the primary causes of workplace stress for Americans were identified as: workload (46%), people issues (28%), juggling work/personal life (26%), and lack of job security (6%).

Leaders have a direct impact on all these factors as they are the ones accountable for managing the workload of their direct and indirect reports, fostering an inclusive and positive work environment, dealing with workplace issues, managing performance, and resolving conflicts. In addition, they have the authority to approve the team's work schedules, including leave and overtime, to address absenteeism, and create an environment where people feel safe at work. When those in leadership positions shirk their responsibilities or abuse their authority, it inevitably creates stress for employees and creates a toxic environment for all.

To demonstrate the effects of stress within a toxic work environment, here is a story about one of my coaching clients, Anisa. She wanted me to share her story to help others who are suffering at work due to major stress factors such as working with toxic managers and workplace bullies.

ANISA'S STRUGGLE

An Example of How a Toxic Manager Can Harm an Individual

Anisa came to Canada from Afghanistan. She became a client of mine in her forties. She worked for the federal government for over twelve years. Everything went very well for her for ten years. She had a great supervisor and co-workers, and the team she belonged to felt like a family. Although the work was stressful at times, up until this point in her career she had been spared the pain that can be inflicted by a toxic manager who bullies employees.

In 2012, everything changed when her organization went through what the federal government referred to as "modernization" (although in my opinion there's nothing modern or progressive about how this massive workforce adjustment was carried out). At the organization in question, this led many branches to undergo transformation, including the department in which Anisa worked. The team she belonged to was disbanded, and she and all her colleagues were declared surplus and given notice. After working with me as her coach, she applied for various positions and was delighted to land another job with the same organization.

In the following months, Anisa was bounced around from one short-term contract to the next, like many others who had been affected as part of this modernization exercise. She was tossed into another team and was suddenly reporting to an HR advisor, Marguerite.* Rather than take the time to train Anisa, Marguerite started off by being disrespectful and saying things in a huff, such as, "You don't know how to do this!"

The high degree of stress Anisa continued to endure contributed to a heart attack and mini-stroke. Though she was eventually cleared by her doctor to do office work (that is, working at a computer), her latest manager did not show empathy or good judgment when she asked Anisa, who was still recovering from cardiac events, to undertake the very physically demanding task of moving and emptying thirty heavy boxes. Fearing that her job was at risk, Anisa complied and finished up the task within two weeks. To add insult to injury, her manager didn't even bother to say thank you.

Despite the way she was being treated, Anisa wanted to continue to work. However, out of the blue, Marguerite began to grasp at straws to try to get rid of Anisa. Although Anisa brought in a second doctor's letter to prove that she could return to work, her manager manipulated the interpretation of HR policies by making ridiculous claims to get Anisa out. For instance, she declared that Anisa was now a danger to others by stating, "Anisa could endanger her co-workers. For example, if she were walking down the hall with a cup of coffee while she had a stroke, she could spill the hot drink and burn someone passing by." As a result, Anisa was ordered to stay home by a complicit HR manager who said he was not satisfied with the doctor's letter.

Anisa stayed home and cried every day for a month, was angry and depressed, and even contemplated taking her own life. She couldn't understand why she was being treated this way. In her own words, Anisa conveyed her sadness and frustration: "If something is going on and I don't understand, it stays in my heart until I cannot breathe. It brought great sadness in my life and everybody else's in my family. You need to focus on the human being first!"

Anisa's story is not uncommon. Through research, I have come across numerous studies from around the globe where results show that bad bosses can increase employees' chances of developing coronary heart disease or having a heart attack. According to the Swedish WOLF study,[17] people with less competent senior leaders have a 25% higher risk of developing a serious heart problem, and those who work for them for four years or more have a 64% higher risk.[18]

There Is Hope

There is some good news. Corporate practices are slowly beginning to shift and companies are realizing the benefits of more progressive practices, including work schedules that allow employees to rest—including in Japan. For example, a *The Washington Post* article featured a one-month experiment conducted by Microsoft Japan as part of 'Work Life Choice Challenge 2019 Summer.' Microsoft Japan introduced a four day workweek as part of this initiative and sales per employees jumped by a whopping 40%![19]

Not only was the shorter workweek healthier for employees, it was extremely good for the bottom-line. Hopefully, the results of studies and experiments such

17   A Nyberg, L Alfredsson, T Theorell, H Westerlund, J Vahtera, M Kivimäki, "Managerial Leadership and Ischaemic Heart Disease Among Employees: The Swedish WOLF Study," *Occupational & Environmental Medicine* 66, no. 1 (2009): 51-55.

18   John Intini, Martin Patriquin, and Ken Macqueen, "Workplace Stress Costs the Economy Billions," *The Canadian Encyclopedia*, updated May 27, 2014. https://www.thecanadianencyclopedia.ca/en/article/workplace-stress-costs-the-economy-billions.

19   Jena McGregor, "In overworked Japan, Microsoft tested a four-day workweek. Productivity soared 40 percent," *The Washington Post*, November 4, 2019. Retrieved from https://www.washingtonpost.com/business/2019/11/04/overworked-japan-microsoft-tested-four-day-workweek-productivity-soared-percent/

as this will finally convince leaders within organizations that their key to success is ensuring their people have what they need to succeed, including a reasonable work schedule with plenty of time to rest and take care of themselves. Though we are not quite there yet, there are indications that leaders on the global scene are slowly beginning to shift their attitudes in the right direction.

Given the major impact and influence that you have as a leader, if you're considering the formal leadership path, it's crucial that you ask yourself, How do I want to show up as a leader? and What steps do I need to continue to grow my leadership competencies?

If the burden of responsibility of being a leader hasn't scared you off yet and you want to continue growing your leadership abilities, then read on to learn the tools and strategies I call the "Light Your Leadership© Approach." You'll gain greater insights from progressive leaders on how to ignite engagement. You will learn the ins and outs to ensure that employees remain happy and healthy, want to contribute their very best at work, and still have enough juice at the end of the day to engage in positive relationships with their loved ones and to become involved in their communities.

At its core, Light a Fire in Their Hearts is a call to action for twenty-first-century leaders to break free from Industrial Age practices, drop the mask that keeps them from being humane and authentic, and evolve the way they interact with and motivate the contemporary worker. It is my belief that the adoption of progressive, purpose-based leadership practices will uplift our society and make the world a better place for all of humanity.

Summary of Part I

Part I discussed the importance of great leadership as well as the effects of bad leadership. I provided you with an overview of how employee expectations of their leaders are evolving during the Passion Age. In addition, you read about how bad leadership leads to workplace stress and how leaders can be key contributors to the primary causes of workplace stress.

Indeed, leadership is important. Not only does it affect the bottom line of the company, it also affects the lives of workers and their families, and it has an impact on the community. I've seen this first-hand. Over the course of my twenty-five year career, I've been a coach and a trusted advisor for countless leaders—

including team leaders, managers, directors, vice presidents, and CEOs—in the private, public, and non-profit sectors. I've supported, advised, and coached great leaders and witnessed how they engage and inspire employees to achieve excellent results. In contrast, I've also had to pick up the pieces, clean up the messes, and handle the trails of casualties left behind by destructive, ego-driven, leaders—those who abuse and burn out staff to realize short-term gains and make themselves look good in the eyes of senior management and shareholders.

My hope is that Part I provided context to demonstrate that leadership can make or break an organization, its employees, and the community.

Now, let's turn the focus onto you. Part II will help you reflect on and answer the questions, *How do I want to show-up as a leader?* and *Is formal leadership really for me?*

PART II

How Do You Want to Show Up as a Leader?

"My advice for new and aspiring managers is simple: Have fun and listen to your heart, and you will go a long way as a leader. Realize that you will never know it all and that you can learn something new every moment of your life. You are better and stronger when you work as a team. What is most important is to take care of yourself—great leaders will never compromise on this, and it is never too late to start, even if you've hit a rough patch. Energize yourself and you will energize the world."

~ Marc André Sirois

Chapter 3
CONNECTING WITH YOUR INNER LEADER

"When we change, the world changes. The key to all change is in our inner transformation—a change of our hearts and minds. This is human revolution. We all have the power to change. When we realize this truth, we can bring forth that power anywhere, anytime, and in any situation."
~ Daisaku Ikeda

Before delving in too deep to help you to connect with your inner leader, let's define *leadership*, a broad term that has been interpreted and defined in many ways.

While conducting research to identify the standard definition of leadership, I consulted many sources—including dictionaries, textbooks, scholarly articles, blogs and vlogs. The standard definition, "to lead," merely states the obvious. Other definitions relate to notions regarding the ability to get others to follow you toward a common goal or vision.

One of my biggest findings is that there are countless definitions and interpretations of the term leadership.

One of my biggest findings is that there are countless definitions and interpretations of the term *leadership*. In a 2003 study, Bruce E. Winston and Kathleen Patterson at Regent University conducted a search of the Expanded Academic database of published articles that use the word *leadership*. The search yielded 26,000 hits and uncovered that there were ninety discrete variables to define leadership.[20] I highly recommend that leaders read through the results of this fascinating study featured in an article published in the *International Journal of Leadership Studies* (vol. 1, Issue 2) entitled "An Integrative Definition of Leadership."

However, trying to wrap your head around ninety discrete variables to define leadership isn't practical when you're a busy manager or director. Therefore, for simplicity's sake, I decided to take into account the results of the research, my own observations, and what I've learned from others in the business, and defined leadership from my own experience and perspective—as a witness of how leadership plays out in the day-to-day management of organizations. Given that this book focuses mainly on the workplace, here is a more focused definition: *If you demonstrate leadership, you have the ability to get people to work toward the goal you envision, at the speed you aim for, with the quality you need to succeed, while securing, leveraging, maximizing, and increasing available resources and assets for the organization.* In my view, this can be accomplished best by connecting with employees at the human level, through compassion, courage, and competence.

> *Great leaders put employees first, and they consider the well-being of people at work a top priority. Such types have social influence, and they inspire through passion and shared vision.*

At its most basic level, our inner leader is that part of us that springs forth the ability to get others to take action and contribute to the goal you envision in order to manifest your will and intentions. If the person who is manifesting your intentions is you, it can be referred to as self-leadership. If it is someone else who is working to manifest your intention, it is leading others.

It's important to distinguish between the different types of leadership, as

---

20   Bruce E. Winston and Kathleen Patterson, "An Integrative Definition of Leadership," *International Journal of Leadership Studies* 1, no. 2 (2006): 6-66, https://www.regent.edu/acad/global/publications/ijls/new/vol1iss2/winston_patterson.doc/winston_patterson.pdf.

some leaders just want to wield power and amass resources, while others feel the pull and call of duty to improve lives or to make the world a better place. Let's explore some of the behaviors that can be portrayed as bad, good, and great leadership.

Bad leaders seek to command, control, and motivate through fear and manipulation. They are authoritative and dictate "solutions" without involving their employees. Bad leaders play games, care primarily for themselves, and only take care of their favorites. Favoritism is the scourge of the workplace. Such leaders get results at all costs, even if it harms colleagues, employees, and the company. These types typically lack trust and micromanage employees. Their demands and expectations are unrealistic, and their chronic lack of compassion and understanding drive their employees nuts or out the door.

Good leaders seek to understand, empower, and equip their employees. They communicate priorities and get results that meet expectations. Such leaders work toward clear objectives, involve others in generating solutions, manage work effectively, and are well organized. They're very good at managing processes and resources, and they know how to lead day-to-day operations and improve the workplace by streamlining work processes.

Great leaders inspire workers and colleagues to focus their passions, energy, efforts, talents, and enthusiasm toward achieving a shared vision and contributing to something greater than themselves. They do everything good leaders do plus seek to inspire and engage employees, colleagues, senior management, clients, and community members for mutual benefit and for the greater good.

Great leaders put employees first, and they consider the well-being of people at work a top priority. Such types have social influence, and they inspire through passion and shared vision. They engage others in designing the desired future. These individuals deftly manage change, create a safe space to foster innovation, and support employees and other colleagues through periods of transition. They give and share rewards and recognition, demonstrate compassion, and have high levels of emotional intelligence. Those who fall into this category know how to guide and empower others to manage their own work to achieve desired results. They help others see their gifts and understand how their work can make a difference. They explain the rationale behind their decisions. They have the courage to escalate issues and respectfully defend the ideas of their team before management. Great leaders are role models for how they practice self-care and healthy work practices, and they encourage employees to take good care of themselves. They foster collaborative and inclusive work environments. The teams they lead thrive and consistently surpass expected results and are able to sustain success through healthy organizations. Great leaders celebrate success with genuine gratitude and know how to have appropriate fun at work. They have a high degree of integrity and earn respect at all levels. They have high expectations of others and help them be and do their very best.

Management vs. Leadership

People often ask me, "What's the difference between managing and leading?" The simplest way to sum it up is that you manage with your head, and you lead with your heart. In other words, managing is about organizing resources and processes while ensuring that tasks are carried out to align with and achieve a common goal. Leadership is more about connecting with and engaging people and inspiring them to tap into their passions, talents, and intuition, motivating them to consistently give (and be) their very best to achieve a shared vision.

Both management and leadership are important. Those responsible for heading a team or a company need to demonstrate aptitude in both areas. Though the terms are often used interchangeably, there is a vast difference between the responsibilities tied to management and leadership. According to Business Dictionary, "Management consists of the interlocking functions of creating corporate policy and organizing, planning, controlling, and directing an organization's resources in order to achieve the objectives of that policy."[21] The definition goes on to explain that management is about decision-making. In contrast, the Business Dictionary defines leadership as:

> The activity of leading a group of people or an organization or the ability to do this. Leadership involves:
> 1. establishing a clear vision,
> 2. sharing that vision with others so that they will follow willingly,

---

21   "Management," Business Dictionary, accessed June 24, 2019, http://www.business dictionary.com/definition/management.html.

3. providing the information, knowledge, and methods to realize that vision, and

4. coordinating and balancing the conflicting interests of all members and stakeholders.

A leader steps up in times of crisis and is able to think and act creatively in difficult situations.[22]

If you decide to step into a leadership role, it's crucial that you understand the difference between management and leadership.

If you decide to step into a leadership role, it's crucial that you understand the difference between management and leadership. Those who do not take this advice seriously and never learn the difference may try to take the same approaches with their employees as they do with their financial processes and information-technology systems. Contemporary workers don't want to be viewed as just another piece of office equipment; they want leaders who can help them find meaning and be inspired, valued, and engaged.

People are not systems and usually don't respond well to being commanded and controlled. In fact, analysis by Gallup underlines that:

> One of the most important ways in which command-and-control leadership can stifle productivity is by denying employees the flexibility to gravitate toward roles and responsibilities that play to their inherent abilities. Strategies that allow individuals to identify, develop and use their natural talents so they become strengths have the potential to dramatically improve workforce productivity.[23]

Beyond this, great leaders help employees to stretch and tap into their own strengths and talents and to exercise their free will when it comes to managing their own work and making decisions. They understand that their role is to train, guide, coach, engage, and inspire.

---

22 See more: "Leadership," Business Dictionary, accessed June 24, 2019, http://www.businessdictionary. com/definition/leadership.html.

23 "State of the Global Workplace," Gallup, New York, (NY: Gallup Press, 2017), https://www.gallup.com/ workplace/238079/state-global-workplace-2017.aspx.

Management is an important skill set that is complementary to leadership. However, leadership is more like a state of being, as it emerges from the inside out. When those with direct reports, known as people leaders, confuse management and leadership, it can result in employees feeling like they are being micromanaged and undervalued—they feel like they are just a number.

Individuals who are in tune with human nature and occupy roles where they must engage others to succeed, learn that in order to motivate employees to do their very best, they must shift their mindset and way of being from mostly managing to mostly leading.

The following diagram demonstrates how early in their career as people leaders—those occupying positions as supervisors, team leaders, or assistant managers—tend to devote more time to managing to keep the team organized and moving forward. As leaders get promoted into roles of increasing responsibility, they need to draw upon leadership abilities to engage larger and larger groups and ensure they are all rowing in the right direction.

Formal Leadership: The Shift from Manager to Leader©

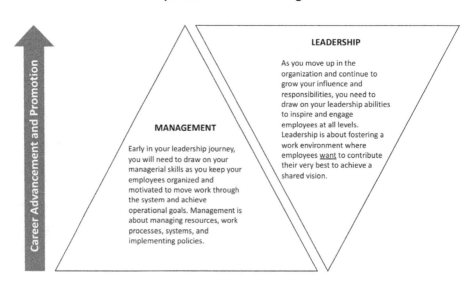

Career Advancement and Promotion

LEADERSHIP

As you move up in the organization and continue to grow your influence and responsibilities, you need to draw on your leadership abilities to inspire and engage employees at all levels. Leadership is about fostering a work environment where employees want to contribute their very best to achieve a shared vision.

MANAGEMENT

Early in your leadership journey, you will need to draw on your managerial skills as you keep your employees organized and motivated to move work through the system and achieve operational goals. Management is about managing resources, work processes, systems, and implementing policies.

A leader's continued growth depends on their commitment to keep on increasing their leadership abilities throughout their career and understanding that people don't want to be managed—they realize that employees want to be treated as valued members of the organization, to be heard, and to be recognized for their contributions. It also involves letting go of the need to control others, which requires a commitment to raising self-awareness as well as deepening one's empathy.

As they continue to advance their career, a great leader refines their competencies and professionalism, and becomes more polished. For instance, they learn to communicate more clearly, upgrade their ability to influence senior management decision-making, as well as their ability to build healthy and collaborative working relationships across the organization. As the leader matures, their desire to leave a legacy expands and they begin to dedicate more time to developing and mentoring the next generation of leaders.

How to Connect with Our Inner leader

"There is one art of which people should
be masters—the art of reflection."
~ Samuel Taylor Coleridge

I love to engage others in conversations about what leadership is, where it comes from, whether it's a thing or a state of being, and how we connect with it. I really appreciated discussing leadership with Lisa J. Weiss.

I met Lisa J. several years ago when we were both asked to present at an event for women enrolled in the STEM programs (Science, Technology, Engineering, and Mathematics) at two local universities. The first thing that struck me about Lisa is her radiance—her beautiful and calming presence. Through her work (including her coaching business, which she calls "I of the Storm Coaching"), Lisa reminds us to go within and connect with our truth. Here is what Lisa said about connecting with our Inner Leader, or what she refers to as the LeaderSELF©.

CONNECTING WITH YOUR INNER LEADER
By Lisa J. Weiss, I of the Storm Coaching & Consulting[24]

The truth about being a leader is, it begins in the womb. Even before we're conceived our perceived beliefs, values and attitudes around what a leader is, is encoded in our DNA. And we are so much more! In my work, I believe we are in a process of reawakening the leader that lives deep within us, our LeaderSELF©.

I speak of LeaderSELF instead of Leadership because on a ship there is only ever one captain. We are seeing more and more the old way of leading is no longer working.

To lead differently, we must first come to know how we have defined leader, beyond the cultural conditioning of our early family systems, and reimagine a new way of leading. Imagine being able to access the leader that lives within, through the sensory cues in your body. Relaxing into each wave as an invitation to become more. With this in hand, we become the invitation for others to access their LeaderSELF.

Like everything else, leading is a process that ebbs and flows from one state to another as we evolve, shift, change, and grow. It all begins with the willingness to hear our breath, specifically the exhale, to know that each of us is unique in our expression and have something to share. Connecting with your breath, your capital-S SELF, is the pathway to knowing, being, and living as a leader, differently.

Like Lisa J., I believe that leadership comes from a place deep within us. What we do with our state of leadership is influenced by our internal environment (our mental, physiological, emotional, and spiritual state) and external environment (all our interactions outside ourselves). Therefore, one person may

---

24   Lisa J. Weiss, "I of the Storm Coaching & Consulting," accessed September 20, 2019, http://iof thestormcoaching.com/.

decide to be the leader of their own life (something we should all aspire to) while another may feel the burning desire to lead others.

In order to gain greater clarity on the type of leader that is best aligned with you, ask yourself, "What am I called to do in life?" "What is my 'Why'?" "What is my burning desire?" There is no right or wrong when it comes to choosing between self-leadership, informal leadership, or formal leadership. What matters most is that you choose a path that aligns with your truth.

Let's examine this a little further. First you need to get quiet and go within to connect with that part of you that decides how you want to show up in your life. Ask yourself, "Does my calling involve being a leader of others?" "Does the thought of leading others feel joyful and aligned with my passions and my values?" This will help you to determine whether formal leadership is your true desire.

If you're having trouble answering these questions, think back to your first memory of when you first thought about becoming a leader. What were your first thoughts about leadership? Where does your desire to lead stem from? From the inside (i.e., do you feel like you were born with it) from the outside (i.e., it's what you were taught or inspired to do), or a bit of both?

Sit with these questions to gain greater clarity. If you need help to sort it out, a leadership coach or someone with a counseling background can help you navigate this process. For your answers to be truthful, they need to come from within you. Once you have your answers and you've connected with your inner leader, next comes time to gain greater clarity and make decisions about how you want to show up as a leader.

"Understand that the right to choose
your own path is a sacred privilege. Use it.
Dwell in possibility."

~ Oprah Winfrey

Chapter 4
"To Lead or Not to Lead"
That's Your Decision

"It is in your moments of decision that your destiny is shaped."
~ Tony Robbins

F ar too many people base their decision to take on formal leadership roles on the wrong reasons, such as financial gain and increased power and status. The decision to seek and accept formal leadership roles should not be taken lightly. It is one of the most important decisions you will make—a decision that will shape your life and that of your prospective employees, a decision that can have important implications not only for your direct reports, but for the culture and success of the entire organization. The ramifications extend far beyond the office walls. Formal leadership carries with it major responsibility that can have an impact on all important aspects of the leader's, employees', and co-workers' lives.

If you choose the formal leadership path for the right reasons, you will be more likely to have a positive impact. Your actions will have an enduring ripple effect that can extend beyond the confines of the organization and result in a lasting legacy.

If you choose the formal leadership path for the right reasons, you will be more likely to have a positive impact. Your actions will have an enduring ripple effect that can extend beyond the confines of the organization and result in a lasting legacy. On the other hand, if you choose formal leadership for the wrong reasons, you will have a far-reaching negative impact. You will cause suffering for employees, and by extension, the lives of their loved ones, and affect the members of their community. In extreme cases, bad leaders ruin lives! Is this how you want to be remembered?

The truth is that your employees will remember how you treated them for decades. To illustrate, in January 2018, I met one of my friends and former colleagues for a coffee. Danielle* had been a brilliant high performer and an excellent manager during her lengthy career as a federal government employee. Her colleagues and employees recall that she had a very positive attitude. Her laugh was contagious and could cut the tension that was so prevalent in our workplace.

I was sad to see that stage 4 cancer had taken away Danielle's zest for life and her vitality. The disease had ravaged her physically, and she had trouble walking and breathing. It was difficult to watch and to be in her presence, knowing that the end of her life was imminent. I wanted to see her one last time before she transitioned, so we met in her favorite coffee shop.

Saddened and feeling awkward, I was at a loss about how to start the conversation; I waited for Danielle to take the lead. It did not take long for her to start sharing about how badly she had been treated by one of her former directors. The irony of it all struck me like a ton of bricks: Although she had endured years of chemotherapy and multiple surgeries, Danielle felt compelled to vent about the emotional and mental pain that she had endured being constantly undermined at the hands of an overbearing and micromanaging director—after over a decade since she had reported to her!

My heart broke for Danielle. As she kept talking through labored breaths, I wondered to myself, "How many more people are there out there, staring death in the face, while at the same time trying to process the pain from being emotionally abused by their current or former bosses?"

A month later, at her funeral, among the sea of people who had come to celebrate Danielle's life, I ran into the director in question. There she stood paying her respects, completely unaware of the pain she had caused. When she said hello to me, I could barely look her in the eye as I recalled my last conversation with Danielle. My resolve to complete this book and raise awareness about the effects of leadership was further strengthened that day.

If you are considering formal leadership as your chosen path, I implore you to reflect on the reasons why. Is your desire to lead motivated by ego or by a desire to be of service to others?

If you are considering formal leadership as your chosen path, I implore you to reflect on the reasons why. Is your desire to lead motivated by ego or by a desire to be of service to others? Think about how you want to show up as a leader and ask yourself how you want to be remembered.

Getting Clear: "What Is My True Motivation for Taking on a Formal Leadership Role?"

My experience working with leaders at all levels for over twenty-five years is that the decision to take on a formal leadership role with direct reports is often embarked upon without the necessary degree of conscious decision-making or mindfulness. Rather, leadership roles are offered and accepted based on superficial matters related to the real or perceived perks, or beliefs about it being "the next logical career move for me."

In many cases, individuals who are excellent at what they do, or who are considered subject matter experts (SMEs), are the ones approached for potential promotion. Therefore, if you are a high performer and are likely to be offered a promotion to a formal leadership role, be mindful of your decisions and reflect on your motive for applying for or accepting a promotion in the first place. Ask yourself the following questions to assess whether formal leadership is a part of your calling:

♦ Do I love inspiring, engaging, appreciating, growing, and motivating others to do their very best?

♦ Do I see leadership as an opportunity to be of service to employees and my organization?

◆ Am I able to help others shine and help them get the recognition they deserve?

◆ Am I prepared to invest the time, effort, and resources to continue to grow as a leader?

◆ Do I have a strong desire to leave a legacy of things being better than when I first took on the role?

If you answered yes to these questions, you may be choosing to pursue formal leadership for the right reasons. However, if you are approaching leadership from the perspective of "I *have* to do this; it's my duty to step up," "My boss told me to," "It's the natural progression," or, worse, "It's a great way to get a corner office and afford my dream vacation"—and nowhere in the equation are you thinking, "I cannot wait to get in there to inspire and engage others, help them grow to be their best selves, and make a difference"—you may want to reconsider and stick with becoming the best advisor or specialist you can be or start a business as a solopreneur.

What Type of Leader Are You?

There is a tendency in business to want to organize things or people into neat categories. There are leadership assessments, leadership styles, and leadership approaches. Psychometric tests and personality assessments—such as the DiSC, MBTI, Insights, StrengthsFinder, and a slew of others—ask you to respond to a questionnaire and then generate a report that will place you into categories. These assessments can provide interesting insights and can be very useful tools to raise your awareness about your leadership preferences and tendencies. They can also inform your leadership-development plan, provided that you keep the results in perspective: when you are a leader, almost everything you are and do falls into a gray area with no quick answers, no clear path, and no easy decisions. It's the nature of leadership.

Given that there are reams of information about leadership assessments, I will not go into detail other than to say, use them as a guide rather than as sacred text. Regardless of your type or preferences, it's important to continue to grow your leadership abilities, building on your current strengths and improving in areas of weakness. This will help you to become more resilient, adaptable, and better equipped to tackle anything that's thrown your way.

Leaders who are self-aware are generally better equipped to meet the motivational needs of their employees.

Leaders who are self-aware are generally better equipped to meet the motivational needs of their employees. Paul Hersey and Ken Blanchard, authors of the classic Situational Leadership Theory,[25] maintain that skilled leaders adapt their style based on the maturity of their employees. They posit four main leadership behavior types: Directive, Coaching, Supporting, and Delegating. For instance, if you are the manager of a new and inexperienced analyst, you may need to be more directive and do a little more hand-holding at first while they ramp up, as compared to an employee who has one year of experience and responds better to coaching.

Continuing along the same vein, an intermediate employee with several years of experience is able to handle day-to-day work fairly autonomously and is looking for support when they encounter new tasks or complex situations, while a more seasoned employee who has been in the same or similar role for years is more likely to be self-directed. By the time your employee gets to this stage, you can delegate just about anything to them and they have the experience, skills, and competence to handle it. In fact, you would be wise to view them as one of your key advisors.

The number of months or years someone moves along in their maturity is influenced by numerous factors. As a leader, you will need to gauge the maturity level of each one of your direct reports. Too much or too little supervision can result in a mismatch between the employee's growth and motivational needs and the manager's leadership behaviors and can influence how tasks get accomplished. Inexperienced employees left to their own devices may feel lost and abandoned and become disengaged. Conversely, more experienced high performers may feel micromanaged and also become disengaged if they are not given a sufficient degree of autonomy.

Innate vs. Accidental Leaders

Jean-François Pinsonnault is the owner of SoGesPin Inc., a leadership trainer, facilitator extraordinaire, and one of my longtime friends and collaborators. He is an experienced learning and development expert who has presented

25   "Situational Leadership II," Ken Blanchard Companies, accessed June 24, 2019, https://www.kenblanchard.com/Products-Services/Situational-Leadership-II.

on leadership at international conferences and worked with leaders for over four decades. Over the years, he has designed and facilitated several hundred programs for all levels of management, employee categories, and professionals. He also works closely with Françoise Morissette, author of *Made in Canada Leadership*, a book based on empirical research that she co-authored with Hamal Henein. In a recent interview, Jean-François shared the following with me:

> The *Made in Canada Leadership*[26] research uncovered an interesting new pattern. When asked "When you want or have to provide leadership, what process takes place internally?" respondents identified two avenues for embarking on the leadership path: "innates" dive in right away, while "accidentals" think about it first before committing. Innate leaders, about a third of those who lead, have the desire and drive to lead, often starting at a very young age. They constantly seek opportunities to lead throughout life. The other two-thirds of leaders are considered "accidental leaders." They are the people who take on leadership roles and step up only when there is a situation, an event, or a cause that they are passionate about that presents itself.
>
> Innate leaders (those born to lead) demonstrate an early disposition for, and strong interest in, leadership. In their own words, they "burn to lead" and tend to do so in a variety of situations from a very young age—it is part of their identity. They prefer to lead rather than to follow.
>
> In contrast, accidentals tend to connect with leadership later, through circumstances or conviction. The impetus comes from the outside world—for instance, a crisis or a situation they feel motivated to do something about. However, once they connect with the leader within, they are surprised to find a genuine connection to leadership.

---

26   Amal Henein and Francoise Morisette. Made in Canada Leadership: Wisdom from the Nation's Best and Brightest on the Art and Practice of Leadership. (San Francisco, CA: Jossey-Bass, 2012).

According to Françoise Morissette, the good news is that there is no right or wrong way to embark on the leadership path.[27] "It's only the doorway that gets you into the 'leadership house.' Both types have positive leadership attributes and excel in certain areas. At the same time, both need to take steps to develop in areas outside of their preference."

When I asked Jean-François about his views on the leadership journey, he offered additional insights and demonstrated that leadership is from the inside out. He shared how he associates his first experience within a leadership role with the time that he stepped up to care for his mother even though he was the youngest in the family. Here is his story.

TAPPING INTO MY LEADERSHIP FROM THE INSIDE OUT
By Jean-François Pinsonnault

I believe that for most people, a leadership role is daunting. Unfortunately, when I received my education (in the '70's and '80s), leadership characteristics were maybe 5 percent of the curriculum; and based on my observations, I fear that not much has changed. The belief that leadership is being a "manager" was strongly forced into our heads, and only many years later in the workforce did I discover I was wrong.

While working with Françoise Morissette I discovered that leadership skills are available to all and tend to fall into two categories: "innate" and "accidental."

I will share my personal story to illustrate the emergence of an accidental leader. In my book, Lasting Touch,[28] I share how in 1982, following my mother's hospitalization, the medical experts and my siblings wanted to put my mother in a home (a seniors' residence). I knew my mother very well and

---

27   Ibid., p. 66.

28   Jean-François Pinsonnault, *Lasting Touch*. Accessed July 05, 2018. http://www.lastingtouchbook.com/.

was aware of her guilt over having done that to her own father (though he was nearly 100), as he died soon after. She regretted putting my grandfather in a home, and her greatest fear was that someone would do the same to her. So, as an "accidental leader," I found my voice and stepped up to announce that, "No, we are not putting Mother in a home." I then arranged a comfortable and efficient infrastructure including a live-in companion so that she could continue to live in her own home—something she did for ten more years. In 1992, she accepted my long-standing invitation and came to live with me for another four years until her heart gave up.

An authentic leadership role is not for everyone. To hold such a position, you need a comprehensive understanding of what drives you. You need to understand the reasons why you want to take on a leadership role and be clear about the positive impact that you want to make. You need to respect others and leave the world a better place than when you found it.

Continuing to grow in my leadership journey in the years following my mother's death, I decided to voice my concerns and take action while I worked at a major federal department. This time, I felt strongly that the manner in which conflict was handled by managers and HR within the organization was unacceptable. The only option available to employees was to make formal complaints—for instance, to file a grievance or make a human-rights complaint. There was no alternative dispute-resolution process in place. I thought that there must be a better way. That is when I set out to change how conflict was handled within government departments.

I conducted research and became a certified mediator. I then began offering my services as a mediator and showed others how to negotiate. Within two years, the deputy minister of the department I worked at learned about the conflict-resolution processes I was putting in place. I was asked to provide negotiation and mediation support across the department. Although I received a great deal of pushback from HR, I persevered. Today that approach is now common process throughout the entire federal government of Canada.

Jean-François recommends that accidental leaders start small and begin to step up as a leader within their own families or communities first, and then continue to build their skills and confidence to take on more formal leadership roles, just as he did.

Another example of accidental leadership is Anna-Karina Tabuñar, an international advocate for employees with disabilities. She works full-time as Director of Corporate Affairs and Communications for Sodexo Canada and sits on Sodexo's Global Disability Task Force.

She shares her story of how she made the documentary film Talent Untapped, which premiered December 3, 2015, the International Day of Persons with Disabilities, and which she presented to dozens of organizations in Canada and the US. She also explains how she became the contributing editor of the award-winning TV show *Canada in Perspective*, which looked at current issues through the lens of aging and disability. Here is how Anna-Karina describes stepping into her leadership.

FROM JOURNALIST TO ACCIDENTAL LEADER
By Anna-Karina Tabuñar

Journalists are trained to uncover the truth and share stories. I made my living by telling other people's stories. As a broadcast journalist, presentation coach, and corporate spokesperson, I could frame and tell a compelling story.

My own truth was no one's business. My story was mine and mine alone. Why would anyone care to hear it? Especially the truth about my disability.

In the spring of 2009, I was diagnosed with a rare neurological illness, Miller-Fisher variant of Guillain Barré Syndrome. My doctors wrote me off as "completely disabled for any occupation."

My entire career hinged on my ability to think, write, and speak. Now, my brain was failing me. My peripheral nervous system was shot. I didn't have the fine motor skills to use a keyboard or hold a pen. My muscles were weak. I had no sensation in my face, arms, and lower legs. I couldn't feel heat or cold, pressure, or pain. I couldn't experience taste or smell. Visually, I couldn't make sense of the world around me. My vision was terribly distorted.

My disabled body was my shame. I questioned my worth and whether I could ever make a meaningful contribution.

It took me nearly three years to recover. As part of my recovery, I wanted to dust off a familiar skill—video storytelling. I felt compelled to share the stories of my new network: my friends with vision impairment and hearing loss, those who use wheelchairs or prosthetic limbs, and my friends who manage neurological conditions and chronic illness. They are extraordinary problem-solvers and innovators because they navigate physical barriers every day.

They taught me simple hacks, like how to use my foot to read the road, how to count the steps by knocking the risers with my hard-toe shoes, and how to use the accessibility features on my smart phone. They showed me that planning and preparation are a by-product of disability. It's not enough to know your bus route and an alternate route; you also need a backup accessible walking route because you do not want to be stranded.

I made it my mission to shine a light on the ingenuity and tenacity of people with disabilities. And so, the documentary film *Talent Untapped* was born.

Scriptwriting and financing a film are stressful. There are disappointments throughout the journey, and many times I asked myself, "Why am doing this? How am I going to get to the finish line?"

Two pieces of advice kept coming back to me. My close friend, another former journalist, urged me, "You have to include your own story to be able to sell this. Your story will make your film real and relatable."

Another friend advised me, "You won't get people to believe you until you own your disability. Disability is not a source of shame. It's a source of strength."

It took many months to reframe my self-perception and summon the courage to be able to share my story.

The responses, to this day, overwhelm me. At one of the film's fundraising events, I was approached by a mom and her sixteen-year-old daughter who was sitting in her wheelchair. The teenager had a wide grin as she told me, "You're my hero." The tearful mom said, "Your film gives me hope for my daughter and her future. Thank you."

Several business owners have approached me to find out how they can hire someone with a disability.

When I finally shared my story, I opened the doors to supporters who made my success their business. I owned it: I finally stepped into my power and into my leadership.

Jean-François and Anna-Karina are both inspiring role models for accidental leaders who stepped up to the plate to make a positive difference. They connected with their inner leader and their passions. They dedicated their time and their talents for something they believe in.

Some people have personality types and preferences that point toward leadership at a young age, but these are not the only people who are destined to lead. Whether you are introverted or extroverted, whether you feel comfortable or uncomfortable speaking in public, you too can become a leader. What is most important is a sense of purpose and the desire to engage people to achieve a vision. When you treat those who help you to achieve your vision with respect, help them to grow, and motivate them to do their best work, then you will be a true leader.

My Early Exposure to Examples of Innate Leadership

I see many examples of innate leadership in my family, including in myself. In fact, my mother and my aunt recount the story about how some of my very first words were "Me boss." I don't know who taught me to say it, but the thought of me as a toddler walking around pointing my index finger to my chest saying, "Me boss, me boss," makes the whole family chuckle. All through school, I somehow always ended up captain of sports teams and even President of the School Council. I don't even remember why or how it came to be that I wrote and produced the Christmas play on my own initiative in grade six, but there I was at 11 years old giving instructions to the rest of the class about who was going to do what in what scene, and when. At work, though I was younger than my peers for most of my career, I often ended up either in informal or formal leadership situations at the office. I wasn't necessarily chasing leadership, it's just something that kept following me around and now I no longer question it.

The apple doesn't fall far from the tree. Almost all my family members held some version of a leadership position at work or in the community. My late father, Corrado Cattelan, and all five of my paternal and maternal uncles held senior leadership roles. If you knew the women in my family, you would notice very strong character traits for innate leadership. For instance, my sister, Emily, managed over twenty people and was responsible for the national QA function at a large travel agency in her early to mid-thirties. Moreover, had my grandmothers, my mom Elvia, and my aunts been born a few generations later, I'm convinced that they would have also been formal leaders and perhaps even CEOs, given the chance.

My uncle Claudio Vissa is also a paradigm of innate leadership. He is an engineer who has literally lit up the world. He is so passionate about his work that although he's in his mid-seventies, he still travels to all corners to bring electricity to remote locations in developing countries around the globe. He spent most of his career moving up the ranks at Aecom, a large multinational that now employs over 100,000 people and is the biggest engineering consultancy company in the world.

I hear stories about how my uncle used to be a natural leader even as a child. He brought justice to the school yard and stepped up to defend others when he saw there was injustice. As an adult, Claudio became a master at building relationships with clients, colleagues, and collaborators from diverse cultures. When high-ranking dignitaries and foreign government representatives want electricity brought into remote places in their countries, they ask for Claudio. Here, in his own words, Claudio gives us a glimpse into his journey as an innate leader and shares his wisdom about what sets great leaders apart.

THE STORY OF AN INNATE LEADER WITH GLOBAL IMPACT
By Claudio Vissa

It was during my humble beginnings as a young child, born during World War II in Italy, that my leadership qualities began to emerge. During my formative years, I would sit and listen to WWII veterans tell their stories and so I learned a lot about leadership, teamwork, and care for each other.

My family then emigrated to Canada, where I continued to develop my leadership abilities. An important milestone is that at eighteen years of age, I went to work for a company and was given the opportunity to hire forty people and complete a big job at one of the Canadian air bases. It was not easy to gain the trust of people who were that much older than me and for them to accept me as their leader in such an important role. However, based on the philosophy of togetherness and achieving common goals that I had learned from the WWII veterans, I brought the people of this large team together and was able to gain their trust. Together we achieved excellent results.

Soon after that, I enrolled in school. At nineteen, I started English night school at the seventh-grade level, and by the age of thirty, I graduated with distinction in the engineering field. While listening to my peers and after completing a master's degree in engineering, I requested a chance to open affiliate hydro companies in India, Pakistan, Costa Rica, Algeria, and elsewhere.

These countries are very different from one another, yet I was able to build highly interactive teams that performed well in all of them. By building trust with employees, clients, and government officials in those countries, we were able to work on most of the major projects in the hydro power sector. Moreover, the teams were so motivated and so conscientious that the quality of work was second to none. This is no easy feat, but again we did it by creating trust within the team and pride in our work.

Being a leader is not easy, but with the proper preparation and actions to motivate and build trust, one can succeed. Great leaders realize that listening to people is the greatest talent they have. When you listen to people, you learn a lot about them, and you tap into their talents. That way you help them draw upon their strengths to support their visions and ambitions. Moreover, a leader will always put forth goals that the team will *want* to achieve.

As we can see, Claudio began demonstrating his innate leadership abilities at a very young age and continued to expand his formal and informal leadership. Formally, Claudio made it to the position of Vice President in Hydro Power and Dams at Aecom. There, he was given the title of fellow being chosen the top engineer in the energy sector out of 50 000 engineers and technicians. Claudio was one of the Aecom engineers who was fortunate enough to have led in some of the largest projects in the world to produce electricity and light the homes and communities of millions of people living in different countries around the globe.

Informally, Claudio continues to be a mentor to many engineers who seek his leadership and advice, as well as to clients who look up to him and reach out to seek his expertise. His innate leadership has truly shaped his journey and made an important impact in the field he loves.

Leadership Is In Our DNA

An interesting aspect of innate leadership is that it appears to have genetic origins. Research conducted by the University College London (UCL) has identified a genetic sequence for leadership. The international research team—including academics from UCL, Harvard, NYU, and the University of California—studied a large twin sample and estimated that 25% of the observed variation in leadership behavior between individuals can be explained by genes passed down from their parents. The discovery is summarized as follows: "We have identified a genotype, called *rs4950*, which appears to be associated with the passing of leadership ability down through generations," said lead author Dr. Jan-Emmanuel De Neve (UCL School of Public Policy). "The conventional wisdom—that leadership is a skill—remains largely true, but we show it is also, in part, a genetic trait."[29]

---

29   "Born to Lead? Leadership Can Be an Inherited Trait, Study Finds," University College London, posted January 15, 2013, https://www.ucl.ac.uk/news/2013/jan/born-lead-leadership-can-be-inherited-trait-study-finds.

Although genetic predisposition may play a role in innate leadership, it certainly isn't destiny—there is still a great deal about leadership that is a learned skill. Both innate and accidental leaders need to build on their strengths and work on their growth areas. For example, one strength of innate leaders is that they feel comfortable communicating their goals and their vision to others in a compelling way and have a certain ease of making decisions. In my experience, innate leaders typically need to learn to become better listeners and involve others in the decision-making process—to create space for others to shine and grow as leaders. Innate leaders need to learn to trust that others also have talents, competencies, and leadership abilities and keep themselves in check so that they are not viewed as "taking over." It is beneficial for them to learn how to go within to self-reflect and manage their impulses and risk-taking behaviors. Further, innate leaders need to ensure that they keep their expectations of others grounded in reality and remember that employees operate at different levels. They need to realize that it is their job to help employees grow their skill set so that the innate leader is not left picking up the pieces while others sit idly by in boredom or frustration.

From what I've observed, accidental leaders are typically excellent listeners and like to reflect before they jump in with both feet. This trait is beneficial when it's necessary to undertake analytical thinking. However, reflection left unchecked could lead to analysis paralysis. Accidental leaders need to get better at communicating their ideas with confidence and become more comfortable with the notion that, as a leader, they sometimes have to make decisions on the spot. The tendency is for accidental leaders to be more introverted. Thanks to their preference for going within, they may forget to share what they're thinking and are surprised when their employees and colleagues can't read their mind. As such, accidental leaders need to learn to communicate their vision and their thoughts outwardly, speak in an inspiring way, build the courage to get out of their comfort zone, and take more calculated risks to avoid becoming a bottleneck.

If you're considering formal leadership as a career choice, I beseech you to become informed and take this decision seriously.

If you're considering formal leadership as a career choice, I beseech you to become informed and take this decision seriously. Take the time you need to go within and reflect so that you may gain greater clarity about your "Why," and let these insights guide you on how to step up as a leader.

Chapter 5
STEPPING UP AND ADVANCING YOUR CAREER AS A LEADER

"Leadership is not about a title or a designation. It's about impact, influence and inspiration. Impact involves getting results, influence is about spreading the passion you have for your work, and you have to inspire team-mates and customers."
~ Robin S. Sharma

S elf-leadership is all about connecting with your inner leader, directing that power to following your heart, and manifesting the life you truly desire rather than living the way you think you should or living your life according to other people's expectations. It's about digging for your gifts and bringing them out into the light as an offering to the world. It's finding and expressing your voice with courage and conviction.

Self-leadership is also about stepping up to advance your career in alignment with your leadership vision. Though you can't control everything, you can control your own actions and choices, and you can use that to influence many things. Stepping into your leadership is a journey of expanding your degree of influence in all aspects of your life and realizing that every moment of every day, you are making decisions that impact yourself and others.

In order to manifest the life and the career you want, you must clarify your passions and tap into your heart's desire. To help my clients do this, I recommend a tool called The Passion Test.™ This powerful tool, created by Janet Bray Attwood and Chris Attwood, helps people get clear on their top five passions in life, the five things that are most important to them. Your passions will point to your purpose, also referred to as your calling or your "Why." When people tell me they're searching for their purpose, I say that they need look no further than inside themselves—in their own heart.

If you choose to follow your passions, your purpose will reveal itself to you one inspired decision and one inspired action at a time. The good news is that you don't have to figure it all out at once; as multidimensional and complex beings, we can have more than one purpose or calling in our lives.

If your calling is to lead others, I encourage you to step into your power and fully accept responsibility as a leader. Do what you need to allow your leadership to flow from within outward into your external environment. A vital part of this process is to get clear about your leadership intentions: Ask yourself, "How do I want to show up as a leader?" and "What kind of impact do I want to have on others—be it at home, at work, throughout the community, or throughout the world?"

Once you figure this out, don't be surprised if feelings of overwhelm and fear surface, and you begin to doubt yourself: "Who do I think I am?" "Who am I to lead others?" "What if I fail and don't live up to the expectations?" These are all symptoms which could be linked to Imposter Syndrome.

Struggling with "Impostor Syndrome"

As progressive leaders, we must make a conscious decision to face self-doubts every single day—it's part of the battle with the nagging voices in our heads that challenge and question us at every turn. The truth is that being a highly capable, talented, and brilliant leader will not insulate you from self-doubt, as illustrated by the story of Craig Szelestowski, a thought leader who helps organizations work better at every level. Szelestowski teaches about Lean Management through his company Lean Agility. Even though Craig was a former VPHR, taught in university, and is accomplished in many ways, he is completely raw and authentic when he shares about how he felt like an impostor as he advanced his career to the executive ranks.

"I'M A FRAUD": IMPOSTOR SYNDROME
By Craig Szelestowski

The Introduction

[8:30 on a sunny Monday June morning in a bright conference room overlooking the city]

The twenty-something trainer rose from his seat at the back of the room and strode with a deliberate air of confidence to the podium. He was about to deliver an orientation workshop to a group of new hires. He looked out over the audience; some of them were students, fresh out of school, here to work for the summer. And some, it appeared, were diplomats, senior executives and distinguished experts in their fields, who recently joined the organization to write the next chapters in their high-achieving careers. As he straightened his notes at the podium and prepared to speak, he thought, "Wow. These people are pretty important. And pretty smart."

He cleared his throat, and with all the confidence he could muster, in an authoritative voice, said "Welcome to our organization and to your orientation training!"

As he said this, a thought draped itself over his mind, darkening it like a black cloud blocking the sunlight: "I wonder if they can tell that I really don't know what I'm talking about." He quickly rebutted this thought: "But I prepared so much for this workshop! And it is a really strong design!"

He continued addressing the audience: "We have planned a great day of interactive learning to help you find your way around here and to get you off to a running start!"

Another dark thought descended: "But you've never done this before. And you're not a professionally certified trainer with years of experience. They'll know that." Then another: "And you're the first person in your family to work in a corporate job like this, with people this important and this much smarter than you." His vision narrowed, and his breathing became shallower.

"I'd like to start by introducing myself," he said aloud. Noticing that he was running out of air, he took a breath, but there wasn't much air coming into his lungs.

Another thought descended: "Do you think they know that you got hired only because you were in the right place at the right time?"

"My name is…Craig…Szelestowski"

Yet another thought: "If they didn't know before that you don't belong here, they definitely will know now."

Fighting for breath, each word struggling to emerge, he said, "Let's go… around the room…and…introduce…ourselves….Your name…your new job… where you come from…and…what you would like…to learn…today."

The first participant began speaking.

The trainer slumped down at a table, defeated after only a few sentences. He took a deep breath. A few minutes to get back on track. "That was a close one."

I Only Got Here Because of Luck!

That was one of my most vivid of a great number of experiences with "impostor syndrome." While speaking in front of experts, senior executives, boards of directors, and unfamiliar but high-achieving audiences, again and again impostor syndrome reinserted itself into my world. Or I should say, I allowed impostor syndrome to reinsert itself into my world.

Despite clear evidence of achievement, accreditations, and validation by peers, a person with impostor syndrome perceives themselves as being fraudulent and, accordingly, fears being found out. It often appears at, or just before, a moment when one is called on to perform. But it can also remain in the background, persistently reminding a person that they are not good enough—often manifested in the thought that "I only got here because of…" [fill in the blank]:

- "I just happened to be in the right place at the right time."
- "Other people put me in this job, but they didn't really know that I am not good enough—or just haven't found out yet."
- "I am only here because I was lucky—I'm not really qualified."
- And so on.

Why Don't We Talk About It?

It has been estimated that nearly 70% of individuals will experience signs and symptoms of impostor syndrome at least once in their life.[30] So why don't we talk about it? I suspect it's because if you suffer from it, you perceive (almost by definition) that you'll be found out as a fraud or a phony! What I've found, though, is that as soon as you talk about it, the most unlikely people start saying, "I get that too!"—doctors, academics, experts, artists—it does not discriminate by job title or place in the hierarchy.

♦ The effects include:
♦ Spending so much effort pretending not to be a fraud in key situations, that one misses out on making important contributions, and perhaps fulfilling the perception that one is not good enough
♦ Avoiding opportunities for fear of being found out
♦ Limiting the contribution you offer to others

The reason why it's important to talk about impostor syndrome in a book about igniting employee engagement is that it's difficult to ignite others if you are limiting your own contribution. Imagine how much more you could contribute if you could just put this annoying and sometimes crippling nuisance to bed for good.

I initially learned to live with impostor syndrome and managed to thrive in spite of it. In my early thirties, I became a vice president at a multi-billion-dollar corporation where I contributed to a remarkable financial turnaround and an increase in employee engagement, which resulted in our being named one of the top companies to work for in my country. Later, I started my own professional services firm that has helped other organizations implement dramatic turnarounds and built a solid reputation at or near the top of its field—all while maintaining a very happy home life.

Despite the measurable (and often obvious) evidence of success and aptitude, I began each new level with self-doubt, worrying, "What if I get found out?" But along the way, by trial and error, I increasingly learned how to deal with it. And now, I've effectively immunized myself against it.

---

30   Sandeep Ravindran, "Feeling Like A Fraud: The Impostor Phenomenon in Science Writing," *The Open Notebook*, posted November 15, 2016, https://www.theopennotebook.com/2016/11/15/feeling-like-a-fraud-the-impostor-phenomenon-in-science-writing/.

How Do You Get Past Impostor Syndrome?

1. Learn more about it.
2. Recognize it and name it.
3. List your evidence against it.
4. Talk to your mentors who helped you get this far.
5. Take charge of it.
6. Mentor others.
7. Over-prepare.

Implement these strategies and then get out of your own way! You will find that you will be even more effective at igniting others. You belong here. You earned it. Now go out there and make a difference!

The lesson from Craig's story is that feelings of self-doubt are normal as you gain more and more responsibility as a leader. The good news is that you're not alone and there's no need to let these feelings define you. If you have a strong desire to lead people, you can focus on your passions and find the courage in your heart to transcend normal feelings of inadequacy. In fact, I believe that going through such a process will help you become a more compassionate and understanding leader who knows how to support and encourage employees when they experience a lack of confidence at work.

Creating a Personal Vision for Leadership

"When you are clear, what you want will show up in your life,
and only to the extent that you are clear."
~ Janet Bray Attwood and Chris Attwood

Visualisation is a powerful tool we can use to manifest the life and career we want. For instance, my brother, Roger, began envisioning himself as a professional football player from a very young age—he was super-focused and crystal clear about his goal. He watched and listened to every football game he could, he played football every chance he got; he literally lived and breathed football. He ended up winning a full scholarship at Boston College, and then was picked up by a CFL team, the Ottawa Rough Riders, in 1983.

Once you're clear about your passions and your calling, you too can use the power of visualization to create your personal vision for leadership. This is different from being a leader at work and creating a shared vision for your team or organization. That is extremely important within the corporate context. However, self-leadership is somewhat different from you as a leader in the workplace or in your own business.

You can create your self-leadership vision on your own, with the help of a coach or counselor, or by using one of the numerous visioning exercises available. However you proceed, be sure to write down your vision in as much detail as possible, including all your senses—that is, what you see, hear, taste, smell, and feel. Here's an example to give you an idea of how to use all your senses to make your vision a powerful one. Say that at the moment, I am occupying a frontline engineering position and dreaming of becoming a director at my firm. My vision is to one day lead a team of engineers and marine biologists to invent a machine that will save the oceans. I'd also love to be stationed in France and to be the type of leader who celebrates wins with her team. If this is how I want to show up as a leader, my visioning journey might be as follows:

> I am sitting at a café in Paris with my team of international engineers and marine biologists. I can smell the fragrant coffee and taste the delicious chocolate-filled croissant. The members of the team and I feel happy and energized about our latest project. I hear the pride in the project manager's voice as she gives a status report to the team. We are celebrating the successful launch of a new machine that will help clean microplastics contaminating our oceans. We are making expansion plans. The members of my team are grinning from ear to ear when I thank them and recognize them for their work; they are proud to be making such a positive impact. We are overjoyed to be pioneers in the ocean clean-up, creating a healthier and more sustainable environment for marine life and for all living beings.

After your visioning exercise, sit in silence as you write down all the fine details to make your vision as vivid as possible.

Making it Happen

Once you have a clearer vision of what you want to achieve, it's time to develop a plan and implement it—to make your next career move to advance your leadership. Rather than think, "How do I get from here to there?" (which can feel overwhelming), stay anchored in your vision as though it's already happening and reverse engineer it. Imagine that you have already achieved the apex of your career as a leader, and ask yourself, "What steps did I take to be able to achieve this?" and work backward to identify what you had to do to get there. Write everything down. Next, look at your list of activities and determine how you can leverage your strengths to accomplish your vision. In addition, identify any skill gaps or other missing pieces needed to make it happen. Think of what you'll need to learn, what resources you need, and who can support you in the process. Be sure to include skills related to advancing your career. For instance, learn how to successfully compete for leadership positions.

When I teach career advancement at My Next Career Move workshops or when I do one-on-one career coaching, I focus on three areas:
- ♦ Personal and Leadership Branding
- ♦ Strategic Networking
- ♦ Up-to-Date Job-Search Tools and Strategies

Let's look at each of these areas right now, one at a time.

Personal and Leadership Branding

Developing and communicating your personal and leadership brand requires you to clarify your promise to employers and employees. What will you bring to the table in terms of personal suitability, skills, and competencies? Be able to state at the drop of a hat what sets you apart from other leaders and how are you going to help the organization succeed. It's key that you become clear and comfortable about your personal and leadership brand because in order for you to land a promotion or a lateral move that's a good fit for you, you'll need to communicate it confidently and concisely.

One of my bosses, Art, taught me the old saying, "You have two ears and one mouth, so listen twice as much as you speak."

A good way to look at communicating your brand and networking is that you're on a mission to learn more about prospective employers' needs. One of my bosses, Art, taught me the old saying, "You have two ears and one mouth, so listen twice as much as you speak." People will remember how you made them feel more than what you said.

Prepare great questions that will get the conversation going. Focus on getting to know people and then figure out what you could offer them. When there's a good match, ask permission to follow up. As you develop these types of relationships and continue to plant seeds in the minds of senior managers, HR professionals, or recruiters about how you would be as a leader, state your intention about how you plan to apply for a position with their organization. They may even offer to keep you posted or refer you to another person within the organization.

Strategic Networking

"When you project your authentic self, people will respond to and connect with it."
~ Michelle Tillis Lederman

An initial step is to take inventory of the people and organizations that are already part of your existing network. Next, find ways to leverage and grow it. Here's a simple exercise to help you do this: make a list of everyone you have a good connection with. Think about the people or type of people they can introduce you to and how (e.g., introducing you to their co-worker via email, LinkedIn, or other social media; meeting for coffee; or a video chat). Connect with the people and follow up to schedule a meeting. If the person I want to speak with is in the same city, I always request a coffee meeting as a first option. If they live far away or are pressed for time (which is very common for executives), I give them the option of a quick phone call or video meeting. I also suggest that rather than coming on too strong and asking for a job right off the bat, you instead conduct an informal information interview to learn more about the organization, what they value, and what type of skill sets they are seeking. Ask to learn more about how their staffing processes work (or talent-acquisition processes, to use the latest buzzword).

At some point during the conversation, the person you are speaking with will surely ask what it is you do. This is your cue to communicate your personal and leadership brand, beginning with your elevator pitch (how you'd quickly explain what you do so that if you were in an elevator, you'd be able to convey your brand in the time it takes to go from the ground floor to your destination).

When it comes to networking or making an elevator pitch, clients often tell me, "Lisa, I don't like having to sell or market my skills. I feel uncomfortable talking about myself to people I've just met. I feel like I'm bragging." My advice is to look at branding and networking from a different perspective, which is more aligned with twenty-first-century leaders. That is, you are providing valuable information about how you can be of service. When you're preparing to go out and expand your network, outline some elevator pitches. The clearer and more confident you are in answering the "What do you do?" question, the better the impression you will make while networking and with potential hiring managers. A good formula goes something like this:

"I lead (or help/specialize in) _____ (name target audience) by providing _____ (product/service) so that they can _____ (state what can the target audience can achieve thanks to your help or products and services)."

Example: *"I coach high performers and help them transform into great people leaders. I do this by providing them with tools, strategies, and approaches that help them to shift their mindset and connect with their employees at the human level, so they can: boost team morale, engagement, and productivity. I also help them learn how to advance their career while they stay true to themselves."*

Learn the formula, then forget the formula.

Be sure not to memorize your pitch; for you to be authentic, it needs to come from the heart. For this reason, I encourage my clients to "learn the formula, then forget the formula." In other words, practice and practice some more, until it feels comfortable, like it's second nature and easily rolls off your tongue. If after a few minutes of conversation you find that the person you are speaking with might be a good contact for you, ask to exchange information. Follow up and make a connection through LinkedIn or send them an email to stay in touch and begin laying the foundation for relationship building.

If your new contact works with a prospective employer, if and when you do apply for a job in their company, or if your name is being put forward to the company by a search firm, then circle back to your contact and advise them that you've applied for a position. Then see what their reaction is, as they may even put in a good word for you if the position reports to one of their colleagues.

Rather than look at each person you meet as a prospect, focus on making connections and establishing relationships to broaden your network. You'll find that you feel less pressure. Your contacts will pick up on that and see you as more of an equal and tend to open up to you more than they would if you come across as a needy job-seeker. Just as in other aspects of leadership, think of connecting at the human level first, and then evolve the relationships that resonate the most with you through the spirit of reciprocity and collaboration.

Up-to-Date Job-Search Tools and Strategies

As you expand your network, be sure to update your job-search tools and strategies. Always keep your resume up to date and remember to adapt it to each targeted job and employer so that you can increase your chances of being called for an interview.

When searching for higher level jobs, consider contacting executive search firms and staffing firms. If they find that you're a good match for one or more of their clients, then they'll put your name forward to potential employers. Begin prepping for interviews way ahead of time to give yourself a chance to think through your potential responses so that you're on top of your game by the time you get called for an interview. Be sure to prepare for both technical questions and for competency-based questions.

Once you land your job, then the real work begins and it's time to light your leadership in your new role.

Chapter 6
GETTING OFF TO A GREAT
START AS A PEOPLE LEADER

"If your actions inspire others to dream more, learn more,
do more and become more, you are a leader."
~ John Quincy Adams

There's no more exciting and frightening experience at work than that moment of your first day as a leader, when it dawns on you that you're now responsible for leading others to success. Unless you're launching a start-up or stepping into a newly minted position, chances are that when you're promoted, you'll be replacing another leader within an organization.

When you're appointed to a role with leadership responsibilities within an organization, you may or may not know the members of your new team. If you're starting with a new organization and don't know them, you need to build trust from the ground up. If you're promoted from within, you need to navigate the murky waters of a change in relationship, which often involves (re)building trust.

In either of these scenarios, you'll be exposed to a number of risks related to what Dan Ciampa and Michael D. Watkins coined "Successor Syndrome." To paraphrase Ciampa and Watkins, the symptoms of Successor Syndrome include:

falling behind the learning curve and not knowing enough before you begin, becoming isolated from the people on your new team and your colleagues, coming in and acting as though you have all the answers and acting as though your mind is already made up, sticking with under-performing team members for too long, taking on too much at once, and giving too much of your attention to the wrong people on the team or from other parts of the organization.[31]

Always keep in mind that even though people may be assigned to follow you on paper, they have free will and can decide not to follow you in practice.

To avoid these and other pitfalls when you take on roles of increasing leadership responsibility, it's important that you take stock of how you wish to show up as a leader. Be deliberate in how you build trust and relationships and get to know the people you need to engage in following your lead. Always keep in mind that even though people may be assigned to follow you on paper, they have free will and can decide not to follow you in practice. For instance, if you're not able to effectively establish yourself as a leader, people may still show up to work; however, they decide whether or not they're going to give it their all to support you and the team.

Making It Magical

I met Carol Novello at a course about crafting our message. I found her to be a brilliant, heart-centered, accomplished, and compassionate leader and an absolutely inspiring person. Carol went from serving as a senior executive at Intuit to leading the organization at Humane Society Silicon Valley.

One evening, after a long and fun day of training, Carol and I went to grab dinner. I asked if I could interview her for my book, as I was very intrigued by what she had shared about her leadership journey. In the few hours over dinner, she gave me so much great information that I could write an entire book based just on her interview! Here are a few highlights from that memorable conversation:

---

31   Dan Ciampa and Michael D. Watkins, "Right from the Start," *Working Knowledge: Business Research for Business Leaders*, Harvard Business School, posted December 10, 1999, https://hbswk.hbs.edu/archive/right-from-the-start.

IT'S JUST LIKE BEING A CONDUCTOR OF AN ORCHESTRA
An Interview with Carol Novello, President of Humane Society Silicon Valley

Humane Society Silicon Valley (HSSV) is making a significant impact by launching a national initiative called Mutual Rescue,™ and Carol Novello has played a major role in this effort. The idea behind Mutual Rescue is that when you rescue animals, they rescue you back by giving you unconditional love and companionship that can transform your life. As president of HSSV, she's mobilized a team of passionate employees, volunteers, and partners—in the US and around the globe—who are spreading this message, transforming the conversation about animal rescue and the importance of supporting local animal shelters, and saving lives.

When I spoke with Carol, her team had recently created a moving series of short films. The first film was about a man named Eric and a rescue dog named Peety. The launch of this first film was so successful that it got over 50,000 Facebook shares from one post alone. At the writing of this piece, Eric and Peety's' film had been viewed over 100 million times around the globe across various social media platforms! Collectively, all their short films released to date have been viewed 153 million times. She is also author of the book *Mutual Rescue: How Adopting a Homeless Animal Can Save You, Too* which came about from the astounding response to the short films.

Inspired by all this success, I asked Carol how she defines her role as a leader. "I model my approach based on leading as a conductor of an orchestra," she told me. Elaborating on this analogy, she continued:

> As the conductor, you need to figure out how to put all the pieces together so that you can have a harmonious output. You need to ask yourself, collectively, how is the music playing and how does it sound? You need to ask yourself whether the sounds of the different musicians and the instruments they

play are integrating properly to make beautiful music. You need to know the different roles that people play. You need to reward and acknowledge each person because the kettle drums are not more or less important than the violin. And it's not just all about the violin either—you need to value all the different roles. You also need to help the members of the orchestra understand why all the other roles are valuable to be able to make beautiful music.

This leadership philosophy helped Carol create a movement for Mutual Rescue so that the organization could change the perception of animal shelters. "As a charitable cause, animal welfare is sometimes considered second-class," she said. "There can be pushback [with some people] asking, 'why are you helping animals rather than helping people?'"

Carol led her team by creating an environment that fostered creativity. She called a brainstorming session with her team. One of the members had the idea to seek out stories that could be featured in short films that show what's at the heart of mutual rescue. Eric submitted the "before" and "after" of how Peety helped him regain his health. As a result of the team's efforts and creativity, HSSV was able to shift the conversation so that potential donors no longer had to feel torn because they had to choose between giving to people or animals—now they could feel good knowing that giving to animals was also supporting people, too!

Coming back to Carol's analogy, she was able to lead the orchestra to see the bigger picture—together they created a symphony that changed the conversation. Carol presented their new approach to the board of directors, and one board member personally committed to funding this particular effort.

Carol said, "I recognized that creating this type of video content for social media was not my expertise." She needed to expand the orchestra to bring in the skills that would be necessary to implement the vision. She brought in award-winning executive producer and animal lover, David Whitman. When asked if he could make the concept "magical," he came up with the phrase "Mutual Rescue."

Carol made sure they had all the talent on hand necessary to make this initiative a success by supporting the team in soliciting stories from adopters about mutual rescue, retaining a film company renowned for being extraordinary storytellers, and bringing in celebrity judges and community volunteers to review the stories.

During our interview, Carol reflected on how each of these people contributed to the success and vision of Mutual Rescue and Humane Society Silicon Valley. "At meetings, we often share stories of mutual rescue. This is how we operationalize our values to make things concrete for everyone. We created a culture of philanthropy, where every person feels responsible for both the mission and financial success of the organization. It is important to create a sense of ownership and impact no matter what level an employee is in the organization so that they can see that *you see* the impact of their work."

When I asked Carol about what advice she would give to a newly appointed leader, she said, "You need to spend your first hundred days doing a whole lot of listening and reflecting while you meet with your new employees—whether through town-hall style gatherings, small 'focus' groups, or one on one meetings."

When I asked her, "What is your role as a leader?" Carol named the three key things a leader has to do:

1. Remove obstacles.
2. Resolve conflicts.
3. Drive clarity.

Leadership is also about appropriately allocating resources to drive organizational results and instilling operating values. "At Intuit, we did a tremendous [job of] living, breathing, and teaching values. Sometimes values are thrown around as ideas, and you need to recognize that as a leader, you are responsible for inspiring people in the organization to want to strive to live up to them. As leaders, we have to spark better conversations and dialogue. We need to discuss why operating values matter, and values need to be made real."

Visit https://mutualrescue.org and get inspired by seeing what is possible when you are a great leader.

Through her approach, Carol was able to successfully overcome the high degree of skepticism that is often encountered by newly appointed leaders at any level. More often than not, a new leader assigned to an existing group will encounter a certain degree of resistance—they will size you up, test your boundaries, and try to figure out how they will work with you. Some will vie for your attention and favor. Others will try to assert their own dominance to remind you that they were there first. The sooner you recognize all this posturing as part of human nature, the better you will be to integrate and build a unified team that trusts you and looks to you as their leader.

In addition to connecting with your employees, you must also establish relationships and build trust with management, key colleagues from the organization, your clients, and other key stakeholders who will impact your work and vice versa. Be prepared for meeting with many people, asking great questions, and accelerated learning. This can be at once overwhelming and exciting. Be sure to set aside some of your pocket change to invest in a coffee (or green tea) budget. You'll be glad you did!

Starting Off Right While Working in a Manufacturing Plant

It is important to note that that the principles in this book can be applied within all work environments, be they be in an office environment or at a manufacturing plant. Although there may be adaptations to suit the context, by and large the principles of great leadership stay the same. For instance, my cousin Carlo, an engineer and Operations Manager for a reputable heavy civil contractor/precaster in North America, to this day applies lessons that were passed down to him by his father, my uncle Rinaldo Cattelan, a revered leader who worked in the construction industry for over sixty years. At a spry eighty-five years of age, Uncle Rino is the semi-retired founder and former owner of the very successful Fana Terrazzo, in Sherbrooke, Quebec. Here are excerpts from a list of basic leadership principles that are based on these lessons, which Carlo and his management colleagues now share with new leaders in the manufacturing plant.

CATTELAN'S TOP TEN TIPS FOR NEW LEADERS IN THE PLANT
Adapted from a list by Carlo Cattelan, Operations Manager

1. *Be a Leader, Listener, and Teacher*—We expect you to be a leader and a teacher, where you will transfer skills and knowledge to your fellow workers. Be excited at the prospect of seeing people evolve and better themselves. It all starts with being a good listener and being responsive. You are oftentimes a servant to your team.

2. *You are Both a Student and a Follower*—Mature workers can learn from new workers, and new workers learn from mature workers. Allow constructive dissent, have reasoned discussions, and adopt the best solution.

3. *Uphold Fairness and Integrity*—Fellow employees must be treated equally and fairly with no favoritism.

4. *Be Collegial*—Promote a collegial style and foster an atmosphere where you and your employees all work together to solve problems.

5. *Exhibit Proper Conduct and Ensure Proper Safety Practices*—Ensure that people are working safely, that they are safe, and that they feel safe.

6. *Respect All*—Treat people with respect and dignity: Respect every job and position in the company; every position is crucial to the success of the operations, and everyone is equally important.

7. *Respect Confidentiality*—Learn to keep quiet when people confide in you; people will respect you. (This one is truly important.)

8. *Act Professionally*—There is no room to hold grudges or make personal attacks. If there is an issue, it is best to take someone aside in most situations and discuss one-on-one rather than creating a spectacle in front of the whole crew.

9. *Take Accountability and Avoid Blame*—If you make a mistake, own up to it and ensure that you (we) can learn from it. You will be

respected for this. Hiding errors or, worse, blaming others for them, is unacceptable. Stay honest and truthful and show humility.

10. *Stay Positive*—If you have an issue, talk and share with others. We all have issues to deal with. It is much easier to deal with them when we help each other out.

These clear and easy to grasp tips for new leaders help them to understand what is expected of them and their employees. This facilitates their onboarding, benefits them and their team, and helps to ensure the good functioning of the plant.

Building Relationships Beyond The Team

Although many leadership courses focus on ways to lead employees and manage all aspects of the operations, the following diagram illustrates that when you step into a leadership role, you need to build and manage multiple degrees of relationships—up, down, and all around. Going in with this mindset will help you build credibility with all the key players.

MORE THAN JUST BUILDING RELATIONSHIPS WITH EMPLOYEES

Leadership Is About Building Relationships
Both Inside and Outside the Organization

While you are establishing your credibility, it is of utmost importance that you approach your new role by balancing confidence in your abilities with humility and recognition for the people who came before you, as well as those who have been assigned to be part of your team. Simply put, be gracious and avoid coming across as a know-it-all. We've all seen the type of person who comes in, is condescending with "the old guard," and wants to change everything without first learning the ropes. Avoid saying things like, "Back where I used to work, we did things like this" or using a condescending tone as you say, "Why do you do things like this? It doesn't make any sense! We have to change that, pronto!"

Drop the "back in the day" spiel. When introducing new ideas, use more engaging and respectful language that recognizes the value of your current team and all the work they've done.

Drop the "Back in the day," spiel. When introducing new ideas, use more engaging and respectful language that recognizes the value of your current team and all the work they've done. For instance, consider saying something along these lines: "I can see that you have all worked really hard on this well-run initiative. I have a few suggestions to build on all the great work and help take the results to the next level so that we can increase our revenues."

Summary of Part II

In Part II of this book, we reviewed what leadership is as well as its origins, and you had an opportunity to self-reflect on whether you are called to be a formal or informal leader. You had an opportunity to connect with your inner leader to explore whether you have calling for people leadership. These important insights can assist you in making informed decisions about whether or not pursuing formal leadership roles is right for you. In addition, you learned how to create a leadership vision and establish your leadership brand. You also read about tips and tools that you can use to advance your career and received guidance on what to do during your first few months as a leader to connect with your employees and colleagues, begin to build trusting relationships, and establish a solid foundation for making a positive impact.

In Part III, you will learn about formal leadership challenges that they typically don't teach you about in school. Each chapter will discuss one of eleven common challenges in plain language, provide scenarios for how these challenges can play out in the workplace, and offer solutions and approaches to address them.

PART III

Facing Your Challenges as a People Leader

"Servant leadership is all about making the goals clear and then rolling your sleeves up and doing whatever it takes to help people win. In that situation, they don't work for you, you work for them."

~ Ken Blanchard

Chapter 7
TO BE A GREAT LEADER
IS TO SERVE

"True leaders understand that leadership is not about
them but about those they serve. It is not about exalting
themselves but about lifting others up."
~ Sheri L. Dew

The use of Industrial Age management practices is way passed its expiration date. The expectations of the evolved modern worker are much higher and more complex than those of eighteenth- and nineteenth-century workers. The problem is that some managers still try to use the command-and-control, rules-based practices of the past to motivate employees—practices that no longer work. Instead, compassionate, courageous, and competent leadership is essential for twenty-first-century employers. The challenge for current and aspiring leaders is to keep up with a fundamental shift that is happening in workers' needs and attitudes in the Passion Age. People are seeking meaning in addition to money, and they want to know that their managers and employers care about them as human beings.

In 1970, Robert K. Greenleaf coined the term "servant leadership," the fundamental characteristic of which is the desire to lead with a "servant's heart."[32] Servant leadership is not about being subservient; it's about a calling to help others. It's about identifying and meeting the needs of employees/colleagues, customers, and communities.

Greenleaf says that servant leadership "begins with the natural feeling that one wants to serve, to serve first. Then conscious choice brings one to aspire to lead. That person is sharply different from one who is a leader first, perhaps because of the need to assuage an unusual power drive or to acquire material possessions." Greenleaf goes on to say that the difference between servant leaders versus other types of leaders is that servant leaders make sure that other people's highest-priority needs are being met. He says that the best test is to ask the following questions about those being served:

- ♦ Are they growing as people?
- ♦ Are they becoming healthier, wiser, freer, and more autonomous?
- ♦ Are they more likely to become servants as a result?

Simply put, servant leadership is based on one's desire to serve, do good for others, and watch them grow—rather than to wield power over them. When applied to the workplace, servant leadership is about identifying and meeting the needs of employees and other colleagues, as well as meeting the needs of clients and communities.

Paradoxically, the way to meet the needs of the modern worker is to go back in time and examine a philosophy espoused by ancient sacred teachings.[33]

The Ancient Roots of Servant Leadership

"Leaders eat last."
~ Simon Sinek

As with many anthropological quests, it is difficult to pinpoint the exact moment in history when human beings began to practice servant leadership.

---

32 Robert K. Greenleaf, "The Servant as Leader (1970)," accessed November 25, 2019, http:// https://www. greenleaf.org/servant-first-servant-heart/.

33 While the idea of servant leadership goes back at least two thousand years, the modern servant leadership movement was launched by Robert K. Greenleaf in 1970 with the publication of his classic essay, "The Servant as Leader." In that essay, he coined the terms "servant leader" and "servant leadership." Greenleaf defined the servant leader as follows: http://toservefirst.com/definition-of-servant leadership.html

While conducting research, I realized that many ancient traditions, religions, and worldviews emphasize the need for servant leadership. This is certainly the case with the Indigenous Peoples of North America; servant leadership has been an important part of their philosophical and spiritual teachings for thousands of years. The book *The Sacred Tree: Reflections on Native American Spirituality*[34] makes it clear that, according to Native American spiritual teachings, the essence of true leadership is service to people:

> To serve others, to be of some use to family, community, nation or the world, is one of the main purposes for which human beings have been created. Do not fill yourself with your own affairs and forget your most important task. True happiness comes only to those who dedicate their lives to the service of others.

I had the opportunity to experience these teachings firsthand when I was asked to assist with the development and delivery of a one-week session of the Aboriginal Leadership Development Initiative hosted by Crown-Indigenous Relations and Northern Affairs Canada. It was such a blessing and a privilege to learn about Indigenous culture and the sacred teachings directly from the Elders, the faculty of the Banff Centre for Arts and Creativity, participants from numerous federal government departments, and my friend and colleague Nathalie Bloskie, *Dancing Star Sparkles Through Water Woman*, a Pipe Carrier[35] of Algonquin and Huron Ancestry, and adopted into the Red Mountain Goat Clan of the Navajo Nation through ceremonialist Ron Yellowman. Through working on this program, I learned more about the Seven Sacred Teachings.

I share the following not as a teacher but as a non-Indigenous witness of the beauty of the Seven Sacred Teachings, which have made a profound impact on the way I see leadership and life in general. These principles, also known as the Seven Grandfathers Teachings, are at the heart of several First Nations' (such as

---

34   A collaboration between Phil Lane Jr., Judie Bopp, Michael Bopp, Lee Brown, and elders (1984, 4th ed. 2014).

35   "Pipe Carriers are individuals who have been acknowledged by one or more individuals from the community as healers with spiritual gifts. The community recognizes these individuals by offering them a pipe. If the individual accepts the pipe and its inherent responsibilities, then he or she is a Pipe Carrier." Source: J. M. Sander, *The Sharing of Traditional Aboriginal Knowledge of Pipe Carriers from Winnipeg, Manitoba and the Implications for the Health of Aboriginal Peoples Living in Urban Centers* (Ontario, Canada, 2012).

the Algonquins) way of life in its purest form. The Seven Sacred Teachings are: Love, Respect, Truth, Honesty, Courage/Bravery, Wisdom, and Humility.

Though I was told that these teachings "take many lifetimes to fully grasp and learn," I was deeply moved and inspired by just one glimpse of what they are and what they mean. As I reflected on these powerful precepts, I saw an important link to servant leadership. I felt like I had finally found what could help heal organizational trauma[36] that is at the basis of chronically low morale, poor leadership, and workplaces where not everyone feels engaged and like they belong. I believe that the Seven Sacred teachings can address what employees really want from their leaders:

- ♦ *Love*—People at work want to be loved, appreciated, and recognized. They want you to know they exist. They want to feel included and feel like they belong. They want to be seen as human beings rather than as mere cogs in the organizational wheel.

- ♦ *Respect*—Employees want to be respected and to be treated fairly and equitably. They want you to recognize their intelligence rather than insult it. They want you to listen to them and acknowledge that what they bring to the table has value. They want to feel safe at work and that you have their back.

- ♦ *Truth*—They want you to be yourself and let go of pretense. They want to know the true purpose of the work and of your team. They want to know how their work makes a positive difference and how they are contributing to something greater than themselves. They want to see and hear that their work, knowledge, and views truly matter to you and that you see their truth (their essence and humanity) and help them to connect with it at the human level.

- ♦ *Honesty*—They have a strong desire for you to be transparent. They want to know and understand the rationale behind decisions. They want you to be a great communicator so they don't have to guess what is going on or get left in the dark about changes or decisions that affect them, their colleagues, and their work.

---

36 "Organizational trauma is a collective experience that overwhelms the organization's defensive and protective structures and leaves the entity temporarily vulnerable and helpless or permanently damaged. Traumatic events can be sudden and shocking and can throw the organization into turmoil." Source: Pat Vivian and Shana Hormann, *Organizational Trauma and Healing* (North Charleston, SC: CreateSpace, 2013).

♦ *Courage/Bravery*—They want you to stand up for employees. They want you to model healthy boundaries and demonstrate the courage to manage upward and push back to defend or challenge ideas on behalf of your team. They need you to negotiate reasonable timelines, as it is important to their health and to long-term success. They are inspired when they watch you struggle and persevere and leap out of your comfort zone. They need you to believe in them, help them tap into their own courage and support them as they learn and stretch out their comfort zone. They want you to have the courage to be vulnerable and to be your genuine and authentic self.

♦ *Wisdom*—They want you to recognize that they have talent and expertise and to tap into their wisdom as well as yours. They want to continually learn and grow. They want to be mentored and for you to be mentored by more experienced leaders. They want to see you make wise decisions and to share your knowledge.

♦ *Humility*—They want you to be humble and open to learning and feedback. They want to see you as part of the group, not lording the hierarchy above them. They appreciate when you periodically have informal chats or go to lunch with them so that you get to know them as human beings of equal value. They need to see you take accountability and acknowledge mistakes or gaps in your abilities and to have the humility to ask for forgiveness and to ask for help when you need it. They will respect you for it and learn that it is okay to make and learn from mistakes and to ask for help.

Servant Leadership Is Universal

Spiritual leaders of many faiths have spoken of servant leadership as a spiritual practice and a way of being. Lao Tzu (a sixth-century BCE philosopher to whom the philosophy of Taoism is commonly attributed) said, "A leader is best when people barely know he exists; when his work is done, his aim fulfilled, they will say: we did it ourselves." Judaism also supports the well-being of workers; for instance, the Talmud states that the master (i.e., leader) is to provide the needed tools, schedules, pay, and other resources necessary for the worker to complete his task with specific attention given to the welfare of the worker.[37]

37   A. Cohen, *Everyman's Talmud*, (New York: Schocken Books, 1949).

Jesus said that "whoever desires to become great among you shall be your servant. And whoever of you desires to be first shall be slave of all. For even the Son of Man did not come to be served, but to serve."[38]

In Islam, it is demanded that leaders pay attention to their followers' needs as demonstrated through the Prophet's words: "If Allah puts anyone in the position of authority over the Muslims' affairs and *he secludes himself*, not fulfilling their needs and wants, Allah will keep Himself away from him, not fulfilling his need, want, and poverty."[39] The Bhagavad Gita (a central book of Hindu philosophy)[40] states that "Leaders achieve lasting power and glory by exercising compassion and selfless service." And Mahatma Gandhi said, "The best way to find yourself is to lose yourself in the service of others."

> *Though the servant leadership construct has been around since time immemorial, it has yet to go mainstream in today's corporate world.*

Though the servant leadership construct has been around since time immemorial, it has yet to go mainstream in today's corporate world. Mainstream leadership authors and thought leaders have just recently begun to examine it more closely as a viable progressive leadership practice to help twenty-first-century organizations succeed. Those who believe that servant leadership is the answer to the global engagement crisis are part of a movement to create the body of knowledge and the practical tools necessary to fully integrate it into applied leadership and organizational development. Thought leaders such as Simon Sinek, Deepak Chopra, Beth Lefevre, and Karin Lubin are getting the word out about purpose-based, enlightened leadership, which has servant leadership as the underlying theme.

Having spent over twenty-five years in Human Resources and Organizational Development roles and now as a leadership trainer, coach, and consultant, I've had the opportunity to see firsthand what happens to organizational culture when servant leadership is not practiced. When those occupying lead-

---

38   Mark 10:42-45 (New King James Version).

39   Rafik Beekun, "Leadership and Islam: Effective Leadership Steps for Strategy Implementation in Islamic Organizations," *The Islamic Workplace*, updated September 9, 2012. https://theislamicworkplace.com/leadership-and-islam/.

40   "Uncovering the Leadership Lessons of the Bhagavad Gita," Chief Executive, posted August 29, 2006, https://chiefexecutive.net/uncovering-the-leadership-lessons-of-the-bhagavad-gita__trashed/.

ership roles lose sight of their duty to make the well-being of their employees a priority, things can begin to spiral out of control. In these situations, managers become so preoccupied with looking good—and with their own advancement and greed—that they treat their employees as commodities to be exploited. The result is that those who decide to pursue leadership roles for their own selfish reasons end up ruining organizations, the lives of the people who worked for them, and by extension, the lives of workers' families and communities. The irony is that they often ruin their own lives too, as they burn out and have to deal with disengagement, HR complaints, and a lack of collegial relationships at work.

If you aspire to land a formal leadership role, it is crucial that you examine your own belief system. Depending on your upbringing, you may need to reconcile what you've been taught about leadership with the reality that true leadership is not all about glamour, power, and money. It is about empowering, equipping, and ensuring that the needs of those who report to you are met and that they have what they need to do their work within a positive work environment. This in turn leads to better customer service and increased ROI (return on investment) for shareholders. For you as the formal leader, the great intrinsic reward is the satisfaction one gets for caring and watching others grow thanks to your decision to be of service to your team, colleagues, clients, and organization.

Benefits of Adopting a Servant Leader Mindset to Attract and Retain Employees

Outdated leadership practices and the lack of servant leadership qualities are driving many people to turn to self-employment. In 2015, the finance and accounting software firm Intuit conducted a study that predicted that by 2020, 40–50% of the American workforce will consist of freelancers.[41] A 2017 *Forbes* article states that "If freelancing continues to grow at its current rate, the majority of US workers will be freelancing by 2027."[42]

---

41   "Intuit 2020 Report," Intuit, posted October 2010, https://http-download.intuit.com/http.intuit/CMO/intuit/futureofsmallbusiness/intuit_2020_report.pdf.

42   According to projections in the Freelancing in America Survey, released by the Freelancers Union and the giant freelance platform Upwork. Source: Elaine Pofeldt, "Are We Ready for a Workforce That Is 50% Freelance?" *Forbes*, posted October 17, 2017, https://www.forbes.com/sites/elainepofeldt/2017/10/17/are-we-ready-for-a-workforce-that-is-50-freelance/#5f2997853f82 referenced SlideShare, "Freelancing in America, 2017," posted September 28, 2017, http://www.slideshare.net/upwork/freelancing-in-america-2017/1.)

Corporations will therefore need to focus on creating organizational cultures that attract a shrinking pool of talented workers with very loose ties compared to prior "job security" obsessed generations. The effect will be that workers will no longer feel stuck or continue to follow leaders who mistreat them. Rather, they will gravitate toward organizations that can benefit from what they have to offer, so long as they can inspire and engage them with vision and meaningful work (with fair pay, of course).

Pay attention, because the writing is on the wall: as a twenty-first-century leader, not only will you be competing for talent against other companies, the public sector, social enterprises, and innovative start-ups, you will be contending with the fact that an increasing number of individuals will choose to bypass working for a steady employer and go into business for themselves.

Pay attention, because the writing is on the wall: as a twenty-first-century leader, not only will you be competing for talent against other companies, the public sector, social enterprises, and innovative start-ups, you will be contending with the fact that an increasing number of individuals will choose to bypass working for a steady employer and go into business for themselves.[43] You will be challenged to retain high-potential employees as the next generation is well on its way to finding creative and personal freedom through more modest and sustainable lifestyle choices and a strong desire to truly experience life. Minimalism is a growing trend, as is the emergence of the micro-housing craze, as shown by Kirsten Dirksen's documentary We The Tiny House People.

Increasingly, members of Gen Y and Gen Z are paving the way for future generations via these environmentally responsible movements. In growing numbers, they're choosing to live in smaller and more economical houses so that they can achieve a better balanced and more harmonious lifestyle. Millennials spend twice as much time with their families as parents did fifty years ago

---

43   "Gen X Parents Support Gen Z's Exploration of Alternative Education," Gen Z Guru, accessed November 25, 2018. http://genzguru.com/blog/gen-x-parents-support-gen-zs-exploration-of-alternative-education (site discontinued).

and experience life with more meaning rather than jumping into the rat race to amass material goods.[44]

I work and interact with many millennials and digitals, and I've learned that they're adopting a more sustainable lifestyle and reviving lost arts such as sewing, knitting, slow cooking, and growing their own food. (Urban chicken coops have even begun popping up in the suburbs!) Contrast that with Boomers and Gen-Xers toiling away at jobs they hate so that they can pay off what they owe because of unaffordable mortgages and a pervasive debt addiction, as well as an over-reliance on highly processed fast-food because they are too tired to cook when they get home late at night.

The newfound freedom of emerging and future generations from over-the-top materialism will put pressure on organizations that can no longer count on employees to stay at corporate jobs that support their high-debt lifestyles but offer little personal satisfaction. Given the rise of a mindset that rejects the shackles of high mortgages and credit card debt, organizations need to offer more than just fair pay and benefits to attract and retain top-talent and high-potential workers. Employers need a new approach to leadership. As human consciousness continues to evolve and workers' attention shifts increasingly from materialism to meaningfulness, compassionate servant leaders are the ones who are better equipped to engage workers. They can help them to gain greater clarity and connect with their passions and with the overall vision of the organization. Employees will expect to connect with a company not only in terms of financial compensation but also at the emotional level.

Many modern employees are motivated by a desire to contribute to a mission and vision bigger than themselves. A leader's job then becomes to help employees identify and ignite their passions from within so that they are intrinsically motivated to contribute their talents and have a more positive attitude toward a shared goal. I predict that by the third decade of the twenty-first century, servant leadership will once again be considered central to great leadership, and leaders will recognize that love will be a competitive advantage and become mainstream.

---

44   "Parents Now Spend Twice as Much Time with Their Children as 50 Years Ago," *Economist,* posted November 27, 2017, https://www.economist.com/graphic-detail/2017/11/27/parents-now-spend-twice-as-much-time-with-their-children-as-50-years-ago.

Why Love Needs to Become More Present Within Organizations

Steve Farber is truly a thought leader of our times. He is a *Wall Street Journal* and *USA Today* bestselling author and one of the top 100 best-selling business authors of all time. He has coached and advised leaders of some of the biggest and most renowned companies around the globe. When I interviewed Steve in 2015, I asked him for the top advice that he could give to new and aspiring leaders, and he told me that "love is just damn good business"!

LOVE IS JUST DAMN GOOD BUSINESS
Interview with Steve Farber, Bestselling Author and Renowned Leadership Expert

Steve's top piece of advice to leaders is to resist the temptation to talk too much and tell people "what's what." It's important to listen to people and to learn from them, he said.

> Spend the first bit of time as a manager with as many employees as you can, one on one. Be a student. Ask them to tell you about themselves and the company, including: their opportunities, their frustrations, their hopes and dreams, and their accomplishments, so that you can learn what skills they have. This will help you build relationships of trust and really help you get the answers you will need as their new manager. This is how you will get the material to help you learn what your employees need to succeed.

> At the same time, employees want to learn more about who you are. Share your philosophy, your expectations, and your values. Engage employees in a dialogue and learn about them from the standpoint that emphasizes what they have to say.

He also advised managers about the importance of presenting employees with opportunities to accomplish things that are "greater than themselves."

When I asked Steve about managers who don't enjoy working with others, he offered the following insight: "People who don't like people shouldn't be in leadership roles."

During our interview, Steve shared an important exercise he uses to help leaders reflect on how they show up as a leader. He recounted that the first time he used this exercise, he was in Dubai. He asked the group of participants at a conference the following, "Have you ever had someone in your life that had a greater belief in you than you did? What effect did they have on you?"

He continued, "If I were asking that question to people in your life, would they say that about you? Wouldn't you want to be that kind of person?"

He underlined that the role of a leader is to coach and develop superstars and that when you focus on this, you can get any help you want. He called this the "goodwill camp."

He went on to explain that true leaders view all employees as leaders and reminds them, "Make no mistake about the fact that you have an impact on the workplace, even if at first it is that you show up every day. What can you do or say to have a positive impact and to make a positive difference?"

According to Steve, it is important that leaders help all employees understand that they have an influence, even if they are an individual contributor, and that leadership is "not about your position and title."

Everybody lives within a hierarchy. Even the president of a company must answer to the board of directors. To feel powerful, he suggested that leaders and employees ask themselves this question: "What can I do regardless of what anybody else is doing to change the organization and make it better?"

"If the answer is 'nothing'—leave!"

When I asked Steve if he had any parting thoughts, he answered: "Love is at the foundation of good business," and it is a hard-core business principle. If you want your customers to love what you create—and to love your products and services—you need to love your people. It will give your company the competitive advantage. Then it follows that, as a leader, you need to create an environment that people love.

Steve shares more wisdom in his latest book entitled, *Love Is Just Damn Good Business: Do What You Love in the Service of People Who Love What You Do.*

What I admire most about Steve's work is his bravery in speaking truth to power about what true leadership is about. At the end of the day, what matters most is that human beings need to feel loved and that they matter. Therefore, as a leader, you need to convey to your employees that you truly care for them and that you have their best interest in mind. When your employees feel safe and cared for, they will almost always make sure they do their best work for the client.

A Great Leader's Formula for Success

When I speak about the responsibility of leaders to serve employees and ensure they are well treated, one common reaction I get is: "The primary responsibility of the CEO and senior management team is to the shareholder." To which I respond, "Fine—sure it is. So, tell me, how do you go about getting the highest and best possible value for your shareholders? Could it be by investing your time and effort in growing and strengthening the company's most important asset—its people?" Here is my simple equation:

Workers Led by a Great Leader

=

Happy + Healthy + Engaged + Equipped Employees

=

Happy Clients

=

Great for Business & Excellent ROI for Shareholders

I often wonder: "Why on earth is this simple concept so hard for so many to grasp?"

As mentioned earlier, even in Canada, stress has contributed to an increase in health issues in the workplace now costing the Canadian economy an estimated $33 billion dollars a year."[45] That's a lot of money, especially for a country with a relatively small population (under 40 million) and a GDP of $1.7 trillion dollars.[46]

Is it that difficult to conceive that this phenomenon can't be good for shareholders? Further, grumpy, frustrated, low-energy employees who work on your frontlines will be less likely to have positive interactions with clients. Bad client service presents a reputational, operational, and financial risk for your company.

> *What is good for shareholders is for your company to have employees who are happy, healthy, engaged, and well equipped to do their work.*

What is good for shareholders is for your company to have employees who are happy, healthy, engaged, and well equipped to do their work. When leaders foster a work culture that can produce an environment that supports these conditions, then your employees will not only be much more productive, they will be much more pleasant and more likely to create a positive client experience. This will boost your brand and help position your company as a market leader.

---

45   Ken MacQueen, "Dealing with the Stressed." Macleans.ca. March 18, 2014. Accessed July 01, 2019. https://www.macleans.ca/work/dealing-with-the-stressed/.

46   "Canada—Gross Domestic Product (GDP) 2024: Statistic." Statista. Accessed July 01, 2019. https://www.statista.com/statistics/263574/gross-domestic-product-gdp-in-canada/.

Chapter 8
From SME to We: Shifting Your Mindset from Individual Contributor to Leader

"It is literally true that you can succeed best and
quickest by helping others to succeed."
~ Napoleon Hill

As discussed earlier, managing is more about planning, processes, and strategies to realize the most efficient and effective way to complete the work; leading is about connecting at the human level to inspire and engage others to want to work and do their best and continue to grow and to contribute to something greater than themselves—to make a difference in the lives of clients, colleagues, and stakeholders, which happens to be in the interest of shareholders. The skilled leader will strike the right balance between management and leadership that is needed to engage their team.

Through my work, I've observed that talented subject matter experts (SMEs) and other high-performing individual contributors and team members (employees who contribute individually and do not have direct reports) are often promoted to managerial roles because they are exceptionally good at what they do in their field. However, without proper preparation, training, and mentoring, they find they are ill-equipped to do what matters most as a leader: connect with employees, colleagues, and management at the human level.

Without the ability to connect at the human level, managers and directors lead employees to become disengaged, resentment and animosity among colleagues grows, and members of senior management become frustrated because teams led by ill-equipped managers and directors are not able to properly serve clients and deliver the desired financial results. In other words, managers and directors who are technical specialists who are exceptional at what they do, do not necessarily have what they need to become a good leader.

Typically, people get promoted to managerial and leadership roles because they are very good at their job. Whether they are aspiring managers or have been in the role for several years, SMEs and individual contributors must transform into people leaders to be effective and engaging middle- and senior-level managers. They need to shift from thinking as an SME ("How am I going to do my very best?") to thinking as a great people leader ("Now that I'm responsible for ensuring that *others* do their very best, how am I going to help every one of us to ensure that *we* will all succeed? More than ever, I realize that it's not just about *me*."). In other words, to be effective and engaging as people leaders, individual contributors and other specialists need to make the personal transition and shift their mindset from SME to "We."

Whenever I bring up this subject, consensus is that at the heart of why the state of leadership has gone sideways, lies the common assumption that an individual contributor who consistently delivers high technical performance and exceeds every goal can *automatically* become a great leader. This is a terrible fallacy and a major factor contributing to the widening leadership gap. In an article for the Center for Creative Leadership, Jean Leslie defines "leadership gap" as a situation in which "crucial leadership skills in organizations are insufficient for meeting current and future needs" and describes two possible causes of this global phenomenon:

A leadership gap or deficit may have one of 2 causes: lack of mastery of the required competencies or lack of focus on necessary skills. The first is a matter of degree; the second is a matter of substance. Either can be a problem in both the short and long term…Today's leadership capacity is insufficient to meet future leadership requirements. The 4 most important future skills—inspiring commitment, leading employees, strategic planning, and change management—are among the weakest competencies for today's leaders.[47]

Based on my direct observation and research, I contend that the root of these causes is that those who are typically offered leadership roles are high-performing SMEs who have yet to go through the necessary transformation to become great people leaders. Individual contributors are seldom promoted to managerial roles based on their ability to effectively lead, ignite employees' passions, and ensure high engagement levels.

Passionate and engaged employees tend to produce the best results and remain healthy and happy at work. Unfortunately, many new leaders are often left to their own devices and fail to understand what it means to lead. They are not properly mentored or equipped to make the transition from individual contributor or team member to become the leader of a team or an organization. They fall short when they struggle to shift their mindset and behaviors from SME to We. As a result, they fall back on the same archaic command-and-control management methods that were modeled for them. They don't realize that in the twenty-first century, the primary focus is to inspire their employees and to ignite and grow engagement. To be successful contemporary leaders, managers and directors will need to do a very important job even before they reach the senior management ranks: stoke the fires of passion, purpose, and enthusiasm in their employees. These are the secret ingredients to driving success and engagement.

To illustrate how high-performing SMEs and other "go-to" people run the risk of becoming misfit leaders, imagine a thirty-something fellow named

47   Jean Leslie, "The Leadership Gap: How to Fix What your Organization Lacks," *Center for Creative Leadership*, posted September 2015, https://www.ccl.org/articles/white-papers/leadership-gap-what-you-still-need/.

Brendan who is promoted and appointed to a leadership role.

Jim the CFO: "Brendan, you're our best accountant, and you saved the company $500,000 last fiscal year. To recognize your efforts and hard work, we're offering you a big raise, a corner office, and your own division. Congratulations!"

Brendan (excitedly): "Wow! Thank you. I'm truly honored that you recognized my hard work. Those 80-hour weeks are paying off after all!"

Jim the CFO: "Oh, and by the way—small detail—you're now going to be responsible for leading the financial analysis division, a group with fifteen finance professionals, two reporting analysts, and two office administration professionals."

Brendan (gulps): "Oh…isn't that the largest group in the finance sector? Uh, but the biggest team I managed in the past was a team of two co-op students last summer. And I organized the golf tournament last year. Oh, and I was the informal lead on my MBA project."

Jim the CFO (lets out a big corporate laugh and pats Brendan on the back): "Ha-ha-ha! Oh, don't worry Brendan, even if you've never managed a formal team before, we'll send you on a three-day management workshop, and you'll be good to go. That's what I did, and in management you either sink or swim. We saw how good your spreadsheets and balance statements are—we trust you'll do a great job as a senior manager too."

Brendan (feeling reassured, takes the plunge): "Thanks, Jim. I'll make you proud."

Does this sound familiar? Perhaps this is how things happened for you or for your manager. Now, this is not to say that SMEs can't be good leaders. On the contrary, they could become brilliant leaders provided they focus on making decisions that are aligned with their passions and answer the leadership call for the right reasons. If you're an SME and do the proper amount of self-reflection and internal work to get clear and remove your personal blocks, then you can transform from high-performing individual contributor and/or SME into a great people leader.

You can accomplish this by focusing on continually growing as a leader. Find a mentor, hire a coach, take courses, and take on special assignments that can help you to grow your leadership competencies. Learn to communicate clearly and build trusting relationships. Make concerted efforts to connect at the human level with your employees and colleagues so that you can make a very strong, authentic, and well-respected leader, and you'll successfully move forward with your transformation from SME to We.

In response to a post regarding this scenario in my Light Your Leadership Community on Facebook, one of the members, Stephen, commented that it reminded him of the "Peter Principle," which claims that "In a hierarchy people tend to rise to their level of incompetence."[48] According to this notion, as people are promoted, they become progressively less effective in carrying out their work at higher and higher levels within their organizations. Good performance in one job does not guarantee similar performance in another. For instance, just because one might be high performing in their profession, it doesn't mean that they will be good managers and leaders.

Fifty years after the term was coined by Dr. Laurence J. Peter, *Forbes* reports that the Peter Principle still holds true.[49] *Forbes'* contributing author Rodd Wagner recounts that three professors—Alan Benson of the University of Minnesota, Danielle Li of MIT, and Kelly Shue of Yale—have analyzed the performance of 53,035 sales employees at 214 American companies from 2005 to 2011. The data show that the best salespeople were more likely to be promoted, but they often performed poorly as managers, supporting the idea that the Peter Principle actually exists.

This research shows that promoting your best technical performers without any consideration given to whether they can lead people results in a decline in competence. Wagner states that the research concluded that, "Consistent with the Peter Principle, we find that promotion decisions place more weight on current performance than would be justified if firms only tried to promote the best potential managers," and that, "The most productive worker is not always the best candidate for manager, and yet firms are significantly more likely to promote top frontline sales workers into managerial positions." Further, the study found that when a high-performing salesperson becomes a manager, their direct reports' performance also tends to decline.

---

48   Dr. Laurence J. Peter (1910-1990) popularized this observation in his 1969 book, *The Peter Principle*. "Peter Principle," Business Dictionary, accessed November 19, 2018, http:// www.businessdictionary. com/definition/Peter-principle.html.

49   Rod Wagner, "New Evidence the Peter Principle Is Real—And What to Do About It," posted April 10, 2018, https://www.Forbes.com/sites/roddwagner/2018/04/10/new-evidence-the-peter-principle-is-real-and-what-to-do-about-it/#6ce6ce2b1809

The moral of the story is that just because someone is a high performer in their profession, it doesn't automatically make them a great people leader.

The moral of the story is that just because someone is a high performer in their profession, it doesn't automatically make them a great people leader. In other words, using promotion as a reward for top performance can lead to a decline in overall results of the organization. I would add that promoting high performers without the proper support to help them expand their leadership abilities and management skills can actually hurt them and, by extension, hurt members of their team—and the company too.

I cannot stress enough the importance of promoting high performers while also taking into consideration their ability to effectively lead people; or at the very least, consider whether they have both the potential and openness to learn to do so. In addition, there is a need to assess their ability to masterfully manage processes, systems, and budgets; to navigate approvals processes; and to establish and maintain positive relationships with colleagues, clients, and key stakeholders.

If you're preparing to transition from high-performing individual contributor and/or SME into a great people leader, chances are that it will require you to make a significant shift in mindset accompanied by a personal transformation.

When we see the Peter Principle play out within organizations, we can see why there's an engagement crisis and why organizations are not performing at their highest potential. After all, the predominant practice is to promote high performers to recognize their hard work and results. I believe that the challenge for high-performers-turned-managers lies within them.

If you're preparing to transition from high-performing individual contributor and/or SME into a great people leader, chances are that it will require you to make a significant shift in mindset accompanied by a personal transformation.

Suit Syndrome

A visual representation of this shift in mindset and personal transformation is that our wardrobes tend to change as we climb the ranks. For example, commissioned corporals will exchange their army fatigues for an officer's uniform, workers on the assembly line may begin to wear a tie when they are promoted to manager, and an SME fast-tracked to an executive role at a tech start-up might hang up their hoodie in exchange for a black turtleneck and a blazer or a shift dress (with some exceptions, such as Facebook founder Mark Zuckerberg, who still wears plain T-shirts). I call this phenomenon the "Suit Syndrome."

The shifts and transformations are particularly challenging for those who advance within the same company. It is more difficult still for those promoted to lead a team composed of their former peers, some of whom may have become good friends. I've seen this scenario time and again, both when I was an internal HR representative and as an external leadership coach and consultant.

It is just like the stories we hear about people who win Power Ball or Lotto Max. The newly minted multi-millionaires say that they still feel the same toward their friends and family and often want to share the wealth. However, there may be a change in dynamics with friends and family. Although the winner might feel the same about them, the family and friends may experience a change in the way they perceive the winner, and the sudden shift in power structure has an impact on their relationships. The same thing happens to a person when they suddenly shift from individual contributor to manager, from manager to director, or from director to vice president.

The perception of people you work with may change, and colleagues who used to be comfortable around you and treat you as an equal may begin to place a subtle distance between you.

The perception of people you work with may change, and colleagues who used to be comfortable around you and treat you as an equal may begin to place a subtle distance between you. Often, these changes in relationship are more about the way colleagues and your new direct reports see you in your new role than they are about you. This was the case with Mark* and Jerry,* two assembly-line workers who found that being promoted to manager brought some unexpected negative side effects.

THE AFTERSHOCK OF MOVING FROM "JUST TWO OF THE GUYS" TO "BIG CHEESE" MANAGERS

By the time they were in their thirties, Mark and Jerry had spent over a decade working on an assembly line within a manufacturing environment. During that time, they'd forged very strong ties with their colleagues, many of whom had started working at the same time. They were both funny, charming and well-respected, and they emerged as natural leaders among their peers. As time passed, they both became lead hands (unionized team leaders within a manufacturing environment) and enjoyed these roles for several years. While working in these positions, they often advocated on behalf of their colleagues if ever there were grievances or disagreements with management. Mark and Jerry both enjoyed the additional responsibilities, and though they were able to show leadership, each of them was still viewed by their peers as "one of the guys."

When two manager jobs became available at the same time, they both applied and won the positions. It seemed like becoming managers would be a natural fit for them. As their HR representative, I was assigned to coach and support them to transition from lead hand to non-unionized managers. Soon after they started as managers, they noticed that their former peers who were now their direct reports started treating them differently. We were having a weekly check-in to touch base when Mark said to me, "Lisa, it's so weird. I've worked with the guys on this team for years. We were good friends; we used to go out for a beer after work once a week and hang out. Now, we don't get invited to go along anymore, and no one comes to talk to us or even says hi to us anymore. It's like we're strangers to them."

Mark and Jerry were really taken aback by this sudden change in behavior and had difficulty reconciling what was going on. They felt alone and isolated.

Thank goodness they had each other. I felt bad for them because they were no longer being included in their team, which left them both hurt and confused. I tried to find a way to explain what was happening to them. Up until they became managers, Mark and Jerry had worn plant-issued uniforms. As soon as they crossed over to non-unionized manager roles, they had to begin wearing suits to work.

I decided to use this easily observable matter as a platform. I proceeded to explain that what they were experiencing was the "Suit Syndrome." I invited them to think about what it must be like for their former peers. "One day you're their colleague and advocating for them as lead hands, and now you're part of management—you come in wearing suits, telling them what to do, and holding them accountable for their work." They reflected on this, and I could see the lights go on as it began to sink in that their colleagues now viewed them in a much different light. I explained to them that they were not alone and that this was a normal part of the process of shifting from being a team member to manager. In effect, they had now shifted peer groups and were beginning to realize the impact. This process was not easy for them, but eventually they began to form stronger relationships with other managers, while figuring out how to fully transition into the managerial role, rebuild trust, and reconnect with their direct reports.

This cycle repeats every time someone from the team gets promoted to head that team or another team within the company. I saw it again a few years later within a financial institution where a longtime manager in an IT department was promoted to director of a closely related area within the same company. He was no longer invited for social activities with the IT managers, and it really bothered him.

When you get promoted, although you may continue to feel like the same person, others will likely see you in a different light and behave differently with you. Keep this in mind as you climb the hierarchy.

I took him through the same explanation, and he began the process of shifting his identity from manager to that of director and all that would entail. You see, when you get promoted, although you may continue to feel like the same person, others will likely see you in a different light and behave differently with you. Keep this in mind as you climb the hierarchy.

Learning to Delegate and to Share the Spotlight

Another potentially confusing aspect of leadership is that to feel good as a leader, you need to be able to shift your perspective on how you experience reward and recognition, and to re-examine your source of work satisfaction. Up until the point where you were promoted to a managerial role, you likely gained a great deal of job satisfaction from being recognized for doing an excellent job as a high-performing individual contributor or team member. Chances are, that's why you were promoted—because you were very good at producing a high standard of quality work, on time, and within budget and management took note of your potential.

As a new leader, you may start to notice that you're no longer getting the same amount of praise as you did as an individual contributor. You may also begin to feel the difference between being responsible for your own work and performance and being responsible for the output of others. This may leave you feeling underappreciated and like you are a fish out of water in your new role. Furthermore, the simple fact of moving away from everyday busy work to carrying out more visionary and strategic work might play mind games with you. For instance, one of my coaching clients, a director, shared with me that she felt like she wasn't doing anything important because a manager whom she had trained to be her backup was now thriving and able to prepare for all the important key stakeholder meetings on her own—without my client's help. I said, "Hang on a second… I know it may feel like you're not accomplishing as much as when you were knee deep in the day-to-day. However, transferring your knowledge, clearing the way for your employee to build her own relationships with key stakeholders, mentoring her, and helping her to boost her confidence and to shine means that you are in fact doing a very good job at being a leader." After a few moments of sitting quietly to process, she told me that she had just experienced a powerful insight.

HOW TO TRANSFORM FROM INDIVIDUAL CONTRIBUTOR TO LEADER
An Interview with Steve Kanellakos, City Manager of Ottawa

Steve Kanellakos, City Manager of Ottawa (the capital of Canada), shared with me a very important insight during his interview that led me to examine this phenomenon more closely. When I asked Steve to share his best piece of advice for a new leader, he told me, "You have to start to see yourself as a leader rather than as an individual contributor." He said that a common issue is that when you change roles from SME to leader, you lose the biggest source of approval and job satisfaction: getting recognition for the excellent work that you do. He went on to explain why he sees many SMEs crash and burn in the first six months of being a manager:

> They try to take on all the work that should be done by their team and do it themselves rather than delegating. Then their team becomes frustrated with their new manager because they feel like they're being micromanaged. This is when new managers begin to question what gives them work satisfaction. Ultimately, those that go on to become engaging leaders realize that the answer to the question of "What will feel satisfying to me at work?" shifts as you move from being a SME to becoming a leader.

> To feel good about work and continue to feel engaged, you will need to shift what motivates you: Strong leaders realize that they can receive immense satisfaction by helping and watching others succeed rather than by being the principal *doers*. As a manager, you will need to have enough courage and self-confidence to feel rewarded when you help others to succeed. You can grow and experience a fundamental shift when you begin

to define your personal success not through your own work but through the work of growing others who look to you for coaching, support, guidance, and inspiration. As a leader, once you're able to shift what finding satisfaction through your work means to you, it feels amazing!

In other words, the more you allow your employees to shine, the better off they, the organization, and you will be. Seek out top talent and help create opportunities for them to grow to their full potential—even if that potential exceeds your own. Rather than feel envy or resentment at seemingly being outshone, a true leader will feel their heart bursting with pride for each one of their followers' successes.

As Harvey S. Firestone once said, "The growth and development of people is the highest calling of leadership."

This sentiment was echoed by another leader, Giulietta (Juliet) Tonini, a longtime and highly sought-after head nurse. She added that "there is no better feeling than when your employees recognize that you've played an important role in their success and come and thank you for having been a good leader for them." As Harvey S. Firestone once said, "The growth and development of people is the highest calling of leadership."

Learning to delegate and building trust go hand in hand. Micromanaging and lack of delegation come from fear of failure, of being upstaged, of losing power and control. A way to stem your fears as a manager is to first become aware of them. Next, realize that the more you are able to trust your employees, the more you will feel comfortable delegating.

As a leader you will need to trust and let go of trying to control all the details. Micromanagement can be largely attributed to a lack of trust in the ability and reliability of your employees to get the job done. There is a fear that employees may not deliver or understand the inner workings of the organization. It is also one of this biggest morale busters and reasons why people lose their motivation at work.

Building and Engaging Teams

One of the most crucial tasks that managers at all levels face is to build a cohesive and highly productive team. Each team consists of people with diverse motivational needs, wants, working styles, and perspectives. It's your job to figure out how to piece all these together.

Over the years, there has been a great deal of research and information about team development, such as the "Team Development Wheel." Developed by Bruce Tuckman in 1965, it's still one of the simplest and most straightforward illustrations of team development. It originally included four formation stages that teams go through—*forming, storming, norming,* and *performing*—but in 1977, Tuckman (together with Mary Ann Conover Jensen) added another stage, *adjourning.*[50]

Myriad other team-development models have been developed and implemented in the last half century, including Japanese models such as ZD activities, QC circles, and *Jisyu-kanri-katudou* (self-managing groups),[51] which have been viewed as best practices in managing teams beginning in the 1970s and '80s and have inspired team-management approaches in western countries since that time. When I first started working as a management consultant at one of the "Big 4" accounting firms, I was involved in Total Quality Management (TQM), which was based on the Japanese style of creating and managing high-performing teams striving to continually improve their work processes. Many of these approaches underpin how workplaces operate.

I find it interesting (though not altogether surprising) that while the Japanese innovate, research, develop, and produce efficiently and effectively through lean processes, they are also the nation that coined the term *karoshi,* or "death by work" (as mentioned in the introduction). If companies worldwide are adopting these practices, should we be surprised that workers all

---

50   Denise A. Bonebright, "40 Years of Storming: A Historical Review of Tuckman's Model of Small Group Development," *Human Resource Development International* 13, no. 1 (2010): 111-120. Retrieved from https://www.tandfonline.com/doi/abs/10.1080/13678861003589099?src=recsys&journalCode=rhrd20

51   Koji Okubayashi, "Japanese Style of Teamworking," in *Corporate Governance,* ed. H. Albach, ZfB-Ergänzungshefte, vol 1, (Wiesbaden: Gabler Verlag, 2000).

around the globe are burning out? Fortunately, employers are starting to shift their practices even in Japan.

While it is important for companies to examine their team and work processes, focusing on human dynamics and human connection needs to take precedence over process analysis. At the end of the day, teams consist of individuals who are trying to work together, get along, feel like they belong, and contribute to something that is greater than themselves.

Solid teams build on their strengths and figure out how to work together to achieve a common goal, while seeking to gain a greater understanding of what each individual brings to the table, including their strengths and growth areas. Strong teams establish respectful norms to work through differences in perception and opinion in a constructive manner. Great teams help each individual feel like they belong and are valued. As a result, employees are happier, healthier, and more engaged, and they form more productive teams.

Conversely, ineffective teams are not cohesive and are the breeding ground for toxicity, backstabbing, and infighting. Team members demean one another, play games, gossip, form cliques, and are not inclusive. When team members feel isolated and do not get along, productivity suffers. Although ensuring good team dynamics is a joint effort, it's the leader's job to figure out how to lead teams to become more cohesive, inclusive, cooperative, and effective.

Conducting research and taking courses to learn more about popular team-management theories and approaches can be very useful to you as you grow your leaderships skills. In addition, here are some tips:

- Learn to tap into the humanity and motivational needs of each team member.
- Help individuals connect and engage with one another at the human level so they can form close bonds and transform into a true team rather than just a group of independent workers.
- Be a model for your team members to establish relationships and collaborate with other teams across the organization.
- Find a mentor and tap into other support available to first work on yourself to get ready to lead teams.

If every manager and every other leader within the organization focused on creating a spirit of inclusion and collaboration, then the entire organization could become a "super team" where everyone is operating as one and is engaged in moving toward achieving a shared vision.

Fostering Happy Teams

Stephen Whiteley is a speaker, author, mentor, coach, consultant, former president of the Canadian Association of Neuro-Linguistic Programming (NLP), and the author of *Happiness Works! Get Yours Here!* Renowned for his work about happiness, Stephen leads numerous live events, where he offers attendees his big welcoming smile, a hug, and a loud infectious guffaw that can raise anybody's spirits. He is also a retired member of the Royal Canadian Air Force, where he was rated as the Top Major while he served and led several hundred troops. By the time he retired, he had was a high-ranking Lieutenant-Colonel. He describes himself as follows: "I used to be a 'Master of Destruction' as a fighter pilot. Now I am a 'Master of Happiness and Harmony' and spend my days helping others achieve true and lasting happiness, no matter where they are starting from." He sets himself goals and has worked himself up to running marathons and triathlons—he is a model of "mind over matter" and pushing through pain thanks to a strong mindset.

A few years ago, I sat down with Stephen and asked him to share his wise insights and advice for new and aspiring leaders on how to build a team.

"MAJOR" GOOD ADVICE
An Interview with Stephen Whiteley, Former Lieutenant-Colonel, Royal Canadian Air Force, and Author of *Happiness Works! Get Yours Here!*

When I asked Stephen, "What does leadership mean to you?" he began by stating that leaders help others motivate themselves to accomplish goals. Leadership is about painting a vision of your team and your organization as "being more," he told me. When you paint a clear and inspiring vision, your team members can connect to it with their heart. That sense of deep connection "can enable you as the leader of the team to optimally resource your vision and strengthen your social skills so employees know that they are valued, appreciated, and supported." It is important to use "I can," and "We can" phrases and to pay attention to what is working and what isn't working for your team.

Stephen suggests that leaders use the 5 Rs to build a team:

1. *Reasons*—You need to explain to your team members "Why are we doing it?" Your team needs to understand the reason behind projects, goals, actions and decisions. Stephen emphasizes that the team should be motivated beyond money. While money is important, it is not a great motivator. What we are really about is helping others solve their problems.

2. *Results*—It is really important for you to be clear with the team members and to ask, "What results do we want?" and "What do we want customers to say and feel about us?" It is also key to track and share the results achieved and to hold team members accountable for achieving results. "Accountability is huge for productivity." It is also important to think about the results we want in relationships, which are our most critical asset.

3. *Relationships*—There are many different forms of relationships. The most important one is the relationship with self. You need to model to your team what it means to have a positive relationship with oneself and with others. If leaders criticize themselves or others, their team members will follow suit. It is important for you to lead the team to build positive relationships with their employer, colleagues, suppliers, clients, collaborators, and others. Ingrain in your team that the more positive relationships we have, both internally and externally, the more successful we will be as individuals and as a team.

4. *Resources*—As a manager, it is your job to impart that "we must manage resources, or the resources will manage us." Resources in terms of time, money, energy, and relationships—at both the personal and team levels—must be managed appropriately. It is also important to help team members continue to grow their skill set so that each individual can contribute their very best talents

and work as a resource for the team and also to help secure and increase other types of resources for the team.

5. *Routines*—Having routines allows us to repeat success, which will provide a platform for projects to improve. It is easier to lead a team where everyone knows what to expect and what is expected of them. This helps to build better trusting relationships.

Stephen emphasized that leadership is about growth and not about judgment. It is not about the leader solving all the problems either. Rather, communicate to team members that when they come to you with a problem to solve, they also need to bring you possible solutions to discuss. In summary, Stephen shared the following wisdom with aspiring leaders:

♦ Be a learning person: Learn to do and then get it done (rather than just learning about it!).

♦ Learn both about people and about productivity.

♦ Connect with meaning and establish meaningful relationships.

♦ Make difficult conversations easy: instead of *telling* an employee what's wrong, *ask* them to share their perspective about the situation first.

During the interview, Stephen reinforced that it is important to engage your team with a balanced approach so that they are happy. You need to do your very best to inspire your employees so that they want to follow in your footsteps and be a model and a teacher for how your team members can be of service. And remember: "Happiness is an energy that will boost productivity and engagement."

Chapter 9
ESTABLISHING AND MANAGING RELATIONSHIPS UP, DOWN, AND ALL AROUND

"The most important part of being a great boss is focusing on the people who work for you. Perhaps the second most important element is learning to effectively manage upward. Doing this well can be a great help to the people that work for you."
~ Karl Moore

When you begin to think of yourself as a leader, you may envision yourself managing a team or group of teams and figuring out ways to motivate direct reports to get them all working toward a common goal. But to be a truly successful leader, you not only need to manage your team, but also manage upwardly, horizontally, and outwardly. This means that you not only need to build relationships with and motivate your direct reports, but you also need to figure out how to build and maintain solid working relationships with senior management, colleagues, clients, shareholders and suppliers—all stakeholders in the success of your organization. Leadership requires a 360-degree effort, so it's no wonder that there's a popular assessment tool called 360-degree feedback.

Many books and courses cover how to lead with employees. However, relatively little time is spent on topics related to "managing upward" and "managing horizontally."

Each group of stakeholders you encounter at work requires its own strategy. There's a vast body of knowledge and resources for developing business and building relationships with clients. Many books and courses cover how to lead with employees. However, relatively little time is spent on topics related to "managing upward" and "managing horizontally." Managing upward means establishing trust with senior management and successfully influencing their decision-making so that ideas and project put forward by you and your team get approved, are properly resourced, and can be implemented with top-down support from executives. Managing horizontally means establishing trusting and collaborative relationships with other managers and peers within your division as well as in other parts of the organization. As you learn to gain greater support from colleagues and their teams, your positive interactions with them will help to foster a spirit of reciprocity, support, and mutual respect.

Ideally, knowing how to establish positive and collaborative relationships up, down, and all around the organization will facilitate the work of you and your team, institute a true spirit of collaboration, and help you succeed. However, a major challenge is that fostering a spirit of reciprocity doesn't always happen smoothly when there are competing agendas. What takes place instead are insidious political games. This topic is often overlooked until new leaders get their first whiff of organizational politics, which leave them scratching their heads until someone more experienced says to them knowingly, "Ah yes, you need to learn to play 'the game.'" "What game?" you might ask. "The games that people play to get to the top of the organization." The following section will give you a sense of what is meant when people talk about "Playing the Game" within an organizational context.

Taking the High Road: Advancing Your Career While Staying True to Yourself

If you're like many of the genuinely good people I've coached who are aspiring leaders, the fact that "The Game" even exists may make you uncomfortable and leave a bitter taste in your mouth. I have heard this type of advice myself when I was on a career fast-track. Mentors and former bosses would tell me: "To get ahead in an organization, you need to 'Play the Game'!" Presently, I don't agree with this narrow and traditional view.

To be clear, "playing the game" within this context is not about fairness and following honorable rules of engagement—it's about organizational politics. Rather than being promoted fairly and getting ahead based on merit and solid leadership abilities, it would be more accurate to categorize it as "playing the M.E.A.N. game"—i.e., being:

♦ Manipulative
♦ Egotistical
♦ Awful
♦ Narcissistic

People who play the game use strategies to intentionally hurt and manipulate people at work, be they colleagues or members of senior management, to win their favor by using underhanded schemes. These toxic and hypocritical types are quite comfortable advancing their career at all costs, even when it's to the detriment of others. In practice, playing the game can take the form of an overly competitive employee propping up and complimenting colleagues they perceive as a threat to their advancement and then turning around and undermining them behind their backs. It can be about taking credit for other people's work, while at the same time attempting to discredit them with influencers and decision-makers in order to ruin their reputation.

People who play the game set up win-lose situations, act with ill intent toward co-workers, usurp others' power, and step on their backs in order to get ahead. If this is the path you are on, then know that there is a better way to advance your career.

If you're an honest person, there's no reason for you to play along with unscrupulous and shameless people, such as those who get ahead by "sucking up" and manipulating senior leaders while trying to make colleagues look bad. The truth is that there is another way for you to you get ahead while you uphold integrity and maintain your dignity.

I advise my clients to take a different approach to advance their career, one that aligns better with their values. If you're an honest person, there's no reason for you to play along with unscrupulous and shameless people, such as those who get ahead by "sucking up" and manipulating senior leaders while trying to make colleagues look bad. The truth is that there is another way for you to you get ahead while you uphold integrity and maintain your dignity.

To those who have high leadership potential but don't feel right about playing the game, the good news is that you don't have to. You only need to *understand* the game so that you know when someone is trying to play you. That way you can choose to stop them in their tracks by taking the high road. Your best strategy is to imagine that you are gathering intelligence. Become very aware of the different players involved, the key relationships, and the benefits that each of the parties derives from playing the game. Realize that some may not even be aware that they're part of a game—they play along and follow the lead of puppet masters.

GENUINE AND HONEST PEOPLE BEWARE: Never ever try to play the game of those who have a weak moral compass or little remorse for their actions. It's not that they are better or more intelligent than you, it's that they will stop at nothing to step on others and get ahead, whereas your conscience will stop you from sinking to their level and retaliating. To beat manipulators at their game, you need to behave in awful ways and make power plays that leave you feeling like a horrible person—so even if you "win," you'll likely get little or no joy or satisfaction from it.

My advice regarding the game is:

1. Understand the games people play in the higher echelons of organizations.
2. Shift your focus back to your vision, your goals, and your team.
3. Build your own relationships with management and work on your communication skills.
4. Stay neutral with the person trying to get a rise out of you and stay the course. Do not take the bait and do not feed their drama.
5. Be very good at what you do, get out of your comfort zone, and learn to influence decision-making by preparing and presenting excellent business cases for your ideas and those of your team.

6. Be the best leader you can be with members of your team and form positive relationships with colleagues throughout the organization.

If your nemesis tries to drag you into a conflict or a competition, then you need to rise above it and keep focused on your goals. Become skilled at helping your leaders succeed and look good, and they'll appreciate you. Become an expert at supporting your team and making sure to give them what they need and empower them to do excellent work.

If your nemesis tries to drag you into a conflict or a competition, then you need to rise above it and keep focused on your goals. Become skilled at helping your leaders succeed and look good, and they'll appreciate you. Become an expert at supporting your team and making sure to give them what they need and empower them to do excellent work. Always show them your appreciation for their efforts and guide them in their own growth. Your employees will appreciate you when you help them shine. In return, they will always have your back and let you know if someone is trying to sabotage you.

Instead of playing the game and being mean, B.E. T.R.U.E. to yourself by being:

♦ Bold
♦ Enthusiastic
♦ Trustworthy
♦ Respectful and Resourceful
♦ Uplifting
♦ Engaging

In addition, learn how to put forward well-reasoned and well-researched business cases in support of you and your team's ideas. In comparison, those playing the M.E.A.N. game will look like scheming whiners and will eventually implode all on their own. If you opt out of playing games and focus on your people, your goal, and your leader, you'll eventually have good results and your nemesis will lose credibility in the eyes of senior management. If this doesn't work, then you may want to consider changing employer. Be sure to seek a potential employer where honesty, integrity, and ethics are recognized and encouraged in real life, not just on paper or on their website.

Here is an illustration of how to take the high road even when others are trying to drag you into the game (based on a true story, with names and minor details changed to protect confidentiality).

UNDERSTAND THE GAME AND TAKE THE HIGH ROAD ANYWAY

I had a coaching client, Samantha.* She was a new director and a very good leader. Her people loved her, and she was building a high-performing team. Samantha quickly noticed that her colleague Vivian* was the favorite of the vice president they both reported to and that Vivian got everything she asked for. Vivian was busy empire-building and was known for trying to take human and financial resources away from other divisions so they could be assigned to hers. Samantha came to me and had no idea where to begin to secure her position with the vice president and at the same time avoid becoming Vivian's next victim. She shared that although she saw the games Vivian was playing, she was not interested in playing games and just wanted to get on with her job.

Sure enough, before long, Vivian trained her sights on Samantha's social media strategist and the accompanying social media budget. She began mounting an attack and started recommending to the vice president that social media was a better fit for her policy shop than for operations. Samantha was scratching her head and began to panic when the vice president started to buy in to Vivian's perspective.

Samantha asked me for help: "Lisa, I don't know what to do. Do I have to play the game?"

I told her, "Promise me you won't because if you do, you're going to lose! Vivian has been playing the game her whole career, and you are a person of honesty and integrity. You do what you're good at and take the high road. You don't need to play the game; you just need to understand it, so that you can be strategic. You need to begin to form a closer bond with the vice president and make well-reasoned business cases outlining the benefits to the organization and the VP's sector for allowing the social media strategist to stay in your group.

You also need to observe the dynamics during meetings and learn to step up when necessary to clearly state your position. Don't wait for the VP to come to you and call a meeting with just the two of you. When you meet, focus on clearly communicating your proposition and its benefits, and avoid mentioning Vivian. Remain professional—always! Build relationships with your other director colleagues. Also, be sure to respect Vivian and see her for all her insecurities."

The result was that Samantha came across as much more professional, polished, confident, focused, and solutions oriented than Vivian. Vivian's arguments started to sound childish and more like complaints than solutions in comparison. Samantha was able to convince the VP of the benefit of keeping both the social media strategist and the budget in her division. When Vivian found out that she didn't get her way, she pouted, was visibly frustrated, and started to disparage Samantha behind her back.

The VP appreciated Samantha's professionalism, did not appreciate Vivian's pouting, and began to have doubts about her true intentions. Vivian's resistance and behavior got worse, and eventually the VP lost total respect for her. Samantha kept her employee and the accompanying budget and won favor as a respected leader. Vivian went off on sick leave and stayed out until she landed a job elsewhere.

Samantha's experience demonstrates that decent, honest people can get ahead without compromising their values or becoming mean.

The Art of Communication and Authenticity

Dan Duguay and his family are our awesome neighbors. Ask anyone in the neighborhood and they'll vouch for the fact that Dan is an excellent, authentic communicator and an expert at building positive relationships. He's the first to welcome new people who move into the neighborhood. He always smiles, never gossips, and will even clear your driveway when Old Man Winter dumps two feet of snow onto our street.

Everybody loves Dan; he's the heart of our neighborhood. In his youth, Dan worked in the logging industry, where he held various roles that ranged from cutting trees and operating heavy equipment to driving trucks; now he works as an arbitrator, which can be very challenging as he renders decisions about people's workplace injuries or illness files. As a result, he encounters a great deal of tension, as conflict resolution is an inherent part of his role. Throughout his career, Dan held a number of formal leadership roles. While we grabbed a coffee at the nearest Tim Hortons coffee shop, he shared the following important insights and I learned a little more about how my neighbor manages to remain so positive and build lasting relationships both at work and in the community.

"DAN'S THE MAN"
An Interview with Dan Duguay, an Expert in Building Relationships in the Workplace

Dan says that in order to light a fire in people's hearts, you need to communicate in such a way that they can see the vision. It's also important to be authentic because "When a leader puts up a façade 100% of the time and does not let their real personality shine through, it hurts passion and engagement." Here's what Dan shared:

> When it comes to communication, I always make sure that I listen carefully. When there is a conflict between two people, I help them to clarify each of their concerns. Then I help them find common ground. It is important to go deeper during difficult conversations and ensure that what is being put forward are the true concerns. You need to observe and analyze interactions and people's reactions to gauge whether they are being authentic, and keep in mind that communication is both verbal and non-verbal.

In addition, there needs to be appropriate humor to relieve tension at the office. It helps employees deal with the challenges related to their job and work environment. I tend to also effectively use humour to bring focus back after a challenging meeting.

During our interview, I asked Dan his opinion on various topics:

Lisa: "In your opinion, what are the top ineffective leadership behaviors?"

Dan: "Lack of vision, breaking of trust, lack of commitment, lack of follow-through, and an uncaring attitude. Ignoring concerns raised by others. Providing limited or no information about why decisions are being made."

Lisa: "What are the most effective leadership behaviors and engagement boosters?"

Dan: "Having vision, interaction, and listening. Maintaining commitment and analyzing the situation and then acting on it. Being flexible to adjust your approach when needed. The ability to accept responsibility when things do not work out as desired."

Lisa: "What are the characteristics of your best leader?"

Dan: "Sharing of information to provide rationale for why the change is being implemented. Being trustworthy, honest, and approachable."

Lisa: "What kinds of things do you do to become a better leader? What would you recommend to aspiring leaders?"

Dan: "Read about other leaders and best practices, find a mentor that you can trust, and listen to and associate with people who ask questions and believe in continuous learning."

Lisa: "What is your advice for new and aspiring leaders?"

Dan: "My top advice for leaders is to:

- ◆ Make a point and ensure that everyone knows that they are important. Grow your interpersonal skills and make an effort to greet everyone on your team. Say hello, smile, and be in the moment. Everyone in the organization is important and they want to feel like they belong and are valued.

- ◆ Great leaders are grateful, so you need to practice an attitude of gratitude. Thank people for all their hard work.

- ◆ Cultivate mutual respect and believe that people are good until proven otherwise. Point out with kindness when another person is being offensive.

♦ Build trust by treating people with respect, and then you get it back. Follow through on commitments.

♦ If you're in a conflict, be straightforward and honest with the other person. You may not be friends, but you still need to be civil and respectful with each other.

♦ Make yourself available when someone needs to talk. If you are really busy, ask them to come back in an hour or to book an appointment.

♦ Be transparent and tell employees upfront about decisions and the rationale for your decision. Even if they may not agree with the outcome, they will be glad to get closure.

♦ Make it fun! Leaders can't take themselves too seriously."

Dan is an excellent role model who teaches us that it's important to focus on the human being, to be authentic and kind, and to show respect for the other party when you are in conflict with someone. Communicating authentically to build and maintain relationships goes a long way to smooth the waters during charged situations.

Chapter 10
BUILDING TRUST

"People buy into the leader before they buy into the vision."
~ John Maxwell

Low-trust organizations tend to have too many approval levels, are highly bureaucratic, and are slow at responding to changes. In these types of workplace cultures, micromanaged employees are unhappy, disengaged, unhealthy, and less productive because management doesn't trust them to make the right decisions or achieve goals without being scrutinized.

L ow-trust organizations tend to have too many approval levels, are highly bureaucratic, and are slow at responding to changes. In these types of workplace cultures, micromanaged employees are unhappy, disengaged, unhealthy, and less productive because management doesn't trust them to make the right decisions or achieve goals without being scrutinized. Multiple layers of approvals create bottlenecks and highly convoluted processes. By the same token, employees don't trust management with anything.

In an article for Treasure Holders International,[52] Clifton Anderson highlights the nine warning signs of low-trust organizations:

1. Excessive consensus building
2. More backstabbing than an Agatha Christie novel
3. "Cover Your Butt" language runs rampant
4. No scenario left unexplored (so you get analysis paralysis)
5. Small decisions are run up the pole
6. Monday morning quarterbacking
7. Functional silos
8. Severe risk-aversion
9. Behind-the-back feedback

By contrast, high-trust organizations allow employees to keep their power and give them authority to make decisions. These employees find more meaning in their work and feel like valued members of the team, working together toward a greater goal. People across the organization feel like they matter and are therefore more engaged. This leads to higher morale, higher productivity levels, greater innovation, and better relationships between management and employees.

Build Trust by Articulating a Clear Vision

Lack of clarity leads to a lack of trust. If people don't know the truth about what is happening, they'll be sure to make one up—and it won't necessarily be the right one. One of the biggest complaints I hear from employees is that their leaders don't clearly communicate their vision, direction, roles, and responsibilities. When team members aren't clear about the vision or their roles, it can impact morale and cause major conflicts. When individuals don't have clarity about how they fit into the big picture and how their contribution makes a difference in the organization, it affects their performance and interferes with their job satisfaction. Your challenge as a leader is to provide clarity, even when you don't have all the answers yourself.

If you're a CEO or team leader, keep in mind that many people in your organization may not share your ability to envision the future and see the big picture. What is clear in your mind may not be for those you are trying to

---

52   "9 Warning Signs That Your Organization Is Low-Trust." Discover the Treasure You Seek. Accessed July 05, 2019. http://treasureholders.com/9-warning-signs-that-your-organization-is-low-trust/.

involve in your vision. That is, you may feel excitement while they experience fear of the unknown. Rev. T. D. Jakes, a spiritual teacher and internationally renowned motivational speaker, illustrates this type of difference in perspective with the story of a giraffe and a turtle, which I've adapted below to fit the leadership context.

THE GIRAFFE AND THE TEAM

Imagine that you're a leader who happens to be a giraffe in the Serengeti plains in Africa. As a giraffe, you can see your mountain destination from dozens of miles away. The path there seems fairly straightforward, except for a few bumps along the road. In addition, what you can't see firsthand, you feel confident that you and your team will be able to figure out as you get closer. With a couple of calculated risks and the right moves, you'll all get there in record time. You see your vision clearly, you know what to do to get there, and it's obvious that everyone will win, so they'll definitely want to come along.

Or so you thought.

The team you recruit to accompany you on your journey are not other giraffes—instead, they are of all shapes and sizes, and they're all closer to the ground than you are. They each have talent and wisdom to complement yours. They can band together to do the heavy lifting, as they have all the resources and supplies strapped onto their strong backs. They also have an ear close to the ground to listen for and avoid being trampled by the herd of wildebeests that took out a giraffe-only expedition last week—they came from the back, and those poor giraffes never heard or saw them coming, given that their heads are so high, up above the all the action. In the past, your team members have come up with great ideas about how things can work better in your daily operations. Plus, you like to have them with you because they are your people—you love them and enjoy their company and want to help make their lives better. You know in your heart that working together, you'll be able to make it to the lush valley at the foot of the mountains—a place where there's plenty of food, water, and prosperity for everyone.

As you begin the journey, you grow more and more excited about the amazing adventure you're embarking upon. Soon, however, you notice that the team is starting to lose steam as fatigue and fear of the unknown take hold. Some are slowing down, others are working twice as hard to pick up the slack, and some are grumbling and beginning to doubt that you're on the right path. There are even a few that are digging in their heels and all out resisting, while others are hiding in the bushes a few meters back because all this change makes them feel sick and stressed out.

You quickly realize that to get to the mountains, you need to find a way to motivate your team to accompany you because you need their help as much as they need yours. But you're frustrated that they aren't as excited as you, and their actions seem to point to the fact that they're not committed to achieving this fantastic vision that will make you all succeed. You shout in your mind, "Why can't they see that this will be great for them too?"

The problem is, whereas you can see the mountains from miles away and have a fairly clear view of the path to reach your destination, your team can only see a few inches above the ground directly in front of them—and even that view is obstructed by shrubs, rocks, tall grass, and trees. Further, they can't move as quickly as you can. They feel vulnerable and afraid. They can't see where they're going and are picturing the worst-case scenarios, such as being eaten by lions or trampled by wildebeests. Now more than ever, they're looking to you for answers and guidance.

Finally, when you look closely into their wide, questioning eyes, you have a sudden insight: They're not able to see things the same way you do, and you will have to clearly communicate with them, guiding and coaching them through the journey with patience, perseverance, and compassion.

As illustrated by this fable, your challenge as a leader is to inspire and engage your team to move forward and excel despite their fear and waning trust using the following approaches:

- *Build trust* so that they can buy into the vision you can see, communicate, and interpret for them. Hear them out and listen to their fears, some of which may be well-founded concerns that require close attention and a contingency plan.

♦ *Help them feel safe* along the journey. Reassure them that you'll do whatever you can to keep them safe along the way, even if issues arise and some team members need to be left behind.

♦ *Make sure they're well equipped* and help them build the knowledge they need to navigate new terrain. This will help them speed up their pace so that they can keep up with you.

♦ *Elevate them and give them a boost* so that they too can get a clear view of the vision. Describe this vision in vivid detail so that they can share in it. Help them get excited and see if they have ideas that can help the team get there faster while maintaining their good health.

♦ *Invite them to contribute to a shared vision* based on their strengths. This can be accomplished by describing your vision, asking questions, listening to their concerns based on a frontline view, and then helping them see how their contributions fit into the bigger picture. You also need to keep reminding them that they're valued and they matter.

♦ *Guide them* by describing the next steps and getting their input. Check in with them on a regular basis and adjust the course when necessary.

♦ *Clearly communicate* your expectations for them to ensure that you all stay on the same page. Let them know how and when to brief you in a useful way.

♦ *Say goodbye to some team members.* Some will drop out. You will also need to take stock and notice those who are losing interest, are no longer contributing, and whose negative attitude is having a negative impact on the herd. Although it may sadden you, you may need to ask some team members to leave the team. Release them and help them get ready and equipped so they can join another herd and continue their journey elsewhere. Make sure they're treated with integrity so they can keep their dignity and land in a safe spot with enough food and water to keep them afloat during their transition. Though they will likely be upset with you for a while, wish them well. They may even thank you for it one day.

♦ *Keep them motivated,* even through the droughts, storms, and rainy seasons.

Building Trust Through Respect and Civility

Respect and civility are essential ingredients for building trust and fostering inclusion. Read what Dominique Dennery, President of Dennery Resources, an accomplished coach, facilitator, and management consultant with over twenty years of experience, says in one of her blogs about respect in the workplace.

R-E-S-P-E-C-T in the Workplace[53]
By Dominique Dennery

I've had many opportunities over the years to facilitate conversations between leaders and their teams on the topic of respect. We then get to the heart of the matter: the actual behaviors that demonstrate respect, those deemed disrespectful, and what to do about them.

"What does respect look like, feel, or sound like to you?"—Top 5 Responses:

1. *First of all, please say hello.* Courtesy, after all, is still important to most people. Even this simple act of recognition can make a person feel valued. Let's not take it for granted. And, as many meeting participants pointed out, respect is more than just common courtesy.

2. *Share your expectations of me, clearly.* A lack of clarity is often equated to a lack of respect. Many team members have felt: "If

---

only they took the time to explain…" By "taking the time," a leader makes room for another person's perspective and questions.

3. *Are you listening?* Active listening means paying full attention to the speaker, without judgment. It's also listening without checking your phone or letting your mind wander. The goal of active listening is to gain greater understanding of a situation rather than waiting for an opening to interject or contradict.

4. *Keep an open mind. You might learn something about my talent you didn't know before.* Once a researcher, always a researcher; once a clerk, always a clerk, right? Wrong! A narrow view of a person's skills means that you will miss out on the hidden talent in your organization.

5. *Say thank you.* More than courtesy, an attitude of gratitude is also a demonstration of appreciation for work well done, notable skills, new ideas, commitment…and the list goes on.

A simple recipe, right? So, what's in the way of saying hello or thank you or engaging in any of the practices listed above? Some of the most common reasons include excuses and false beliefs such as:

♦ "I didn't even notice this person. Why didn't *they* say hello if it's that important to them?"

♦ "Why say thank you if they're just doing their job?"

♦ "Once you start providing a sympathetic ear, you'll have folks parading into your office all the time."

♦ "There are already objectives associated with the job; why would an employee also need expectations?"

♦ "I'm too busy."

Dominique's blog underlines the importance of respect in the workplace. Leaders play an important role in setting the tone by expecting, fostering, and modeling respect and civility for employees. In other words, a respectful leader plays a critical role in *showing* the way. They don't make excuses, and they bust through false beliefs, which insinuate that being civil and respectful will create more work or be detrimental in any way.

The Spirit of Inclusion is Essential to Building Trust

An essential ingredient to building trust and employee engagement is to help people at work feel like they truly belong to the group, the team, and the organization. Adopting a solid Diversity, Equity, and Inclusion (DEI) mindset and integrating it into every aspect of the business is key to building a high-trust organization where every employee feels that they belong, that they are important, and that their differences are appreciated and considered assets to be proud of rather than feared. Organizations that truly embrace DEI understand that it's also a business advantage rather than a "nice to have" for organizations. We'll delve deeper into this topic in Chapter 12.

Chapter 11
LEAPING OUT OF YOUR COMFORT ZONE AND INSPIRING OTHERS TO STRETCH

"In an instant, everything changed. I stopped fighting the fear. I became present to my anxiety, nervousness, ego—everything. I breathed it all in and became one with it.... Fear is never the problem. It's the fear of fear that cripples us."
~ Akshay Nanavati

Being a leader doesn't mean that you feel brave all the time; it means that you face your fears every day and help others do the same. It means that you persevere and push ahead to make a positive difference in your life and the lives of others. It means answering your true calling and not buckling under the weight of the task of being yourself.

Being a leader takes courage. If you lack courage, then your growth area is to focus on growing your courage and confidence because if you don't, both you and your employees will suffer because of it.

Being a leader takes courage. If you lack courage, then your growth area is to focus on growing your courage and confidence because if you don't, both you and your employees will suffer because of it.

Managerial Courage

Today, managerial courage is yet another broadly defined term, just like leadership. However, it was Mike Lombardo and Bob Eichinger, the creators of the Lominger competency framework, that featured managerial courage as a key skill and defined it as "saying what needs to be said at the right time, to the right person, in the right way."[54] While I researched the various aspect of managerial courage, I came across the following list (in a blog by Judy Mackenzie that was featured on the JKS Talent Network) that effectively represented the behaviors demonstrated by courageous leaders in day-to-day operations—leaders who demonstrated the courage to:

- Face reality
- Speak the truth
- Rely on others
- Weed out those who can't succeed
- Question the status quo
- Make decisions in risky or uncertain situations
- Work outside their comfort zones
- Live by and enforce values
- Uphold rigorous standards
- Be themselves[55]

I would add the courage to:

- Manage the expectations of clients and senior management and tactfully push back when they make unreasonable demands
- Allow employees to experiment with their work, take calculated risks, and innovate
- Defend the work of your employees and take accountability without assigning blame and pointing fingers when mistakes are made

---

54 "9 Warning Signs That Your Organization Is Low-Trust." Discover the Treasure You Seek. Accessed July 05, 2019. https://jkstalent.com/managerial-courage/#.XR84Oi0ZNQI

55 "Managerial Courage Is a Winning Skill," (2016, March 10). Retrieved from https://jkstalent.com/managerial-courage-winning-skill/#.XABOLacZNQI

- ◆ Admit your own mistakes and apologize when necessary
- ◆ Put your employees in the spotlight, negotiate for them to be at key meetings, support their learning, and allow them to shine

The following scenario, which is based on a true story, provides a good illustration of how the lack of managerial courage can lead to employee burnout, disengagement, and other negative consequences. The case explores the dynamic between a team of directors all working within the same government branch (the role of formal leader) and a group of managers reporting to them. The managers were trying hard to absorb all the stress to shield their employees from the negative impacts of the leadership gap that existed at the directorial level.

Burnout Recognized by the World Health Organization

In 2019, the World Health Organization (WHO) identified burnout as an important factor affecting health.

Burnout is a syndrome conceptualized as resulting from chronic workplace stress that has not been successfully managed. It is characterized by three dimensions:
- ◆ feelings of energy depletion or exhaustion;
- ◆ increased mental distance from one's job, or feelings of negativism or cynicism related to one's job; and
- ◆ reduced professional efficacy.[56]

As a result, the World Health Organization plans to develop evidence-based guidelines on mental well-being in the workplace.

---

56 "Burnout an 'Occupational Phenomenon': International Classification of Diseases," World Health Organization, posted May 28, 2019, https://www.who.int/mental_health/evidence/burnout/en/.

HOW A LACK OF COURAGE CAN LEAD TO MANAGER AND EMPLOYEE BURNOUT

"Courage is not the absence of fear but rather the judgment that something else is more important."
~ Ambrose Redmoon

Several years ago, my longtime colleague Jill and I were retained by a government organization composed of highly educated knowledge workers and scientists. Our goal was to gather information and make recommendations to shed light on low employee-engagement results. When we analyzed the data, we noticed that engagement results for the frontline employees were relatively high compared to other frontline employees in the government. However, engagement levels for frontline and middle managers were much lower, hovering around the 30% mark.

We theorized that the managers were acting as buffers and shielding their staff from the muck rolling down from high above. We confirmed this during focus groups with the managers involved, when they openly shared their feelings of overwork, lack of appreciation, and lack of respect regarding their work from their directors. Their efforts and hard work were not being recognized, and the directors blatantly disregarded the recommendations they had formulated as scientists.

Let's be clear: these managers weren't newbies or generalists—from the outside they were recognized as experts in their field and had greater technical expertise than the directors they reported to, who tended to be bureaucrats brought in from other government departments. The insecurity and lack of courage at the director level resulted in:

- The directors not pushing back when senior management made impossible demands, which led to managers and their teams working under tremendous pressure
- A ridiculous number of rewrites—for example, one manager mentioned how he was on draft 130 of a PowerPoint

presentation. When we reviewed the assessment results, it was clear that the reason for all the rewrites included that the directors:

◈ Had an inability to provide clear direction, as well as a lack of communication skills and courage to provide specific feedback. This left managers and their team to guess what was required, which was hit-and-miss. (They were scientists, not mind-readers.)

◈ Lacked courage and expertise to defend the recommendations developed by the managers when they presented to senior management for approval. This resulted in managers and their teams having to continually go back to the drawing board and revise the recommendations that had it the mark in the first place.

◈ Behaved in an insecure manner and did not invite their direct reports (managers) to meetings with the members of senior management. This resulted in the managers missing key learning opportunities that could have helped them position their work in a more suitable way for audiences consisting of members from senior management. There would have been a lot less time wasted in endless rounds of rework, and workflow would have been a lot more efficient.

In the end, the managers were turning themselves inside out trying to please and ultimately burning out. At the time we were conducting the assessment, the participants were sad and worried because one of their high-performing and hard-working colleagues had just gone on extended sick leave for a second time. That's when I realized that lack of managerial courage can lead to overwork and employee burnout.

Leap Toward Your Dreams

To become a great leader, you need to build your courage and confidence. Once you begin to take the appropriate steps toward this goal, such as intentionally stepping out of your comfort zone, you'll gain a greater insight about how to motivate your employees to grow their own courage and confidence. Together you can encourage and support one another to leap out of your comfort zones and toward your dreams or your vision.

So, what does it means to leap out of your comfort zone? It means connecting with your heart and soul to clarify what you want to create in your life, identifying what's blocking you from it, and then crossing that threshold.

But we often find that our heart's desires live in that sacred yet scary space beyond our comfort zone—a place we may not want to go because it's, well… uncomfortable!

So often, we trick ourselves into thinking that our comfort zone is safe, but ultimately it keeps us small, stunts our growth, and prevents us from living our dreams. All our dreams are patiently waiting for us just beyond our comfort zone—excited for us to bravely leap toward them.

If you think about what may be holding you back from making the leap, one word usually comes to mind: *fear*. It creeps up when you get excited about living life to the fullest; just when you're ready to move forward, your mind bombards you with "shoulds," "can'ts," and "don'ts" until your thoughts slowly eat away at your courage.

Your heart's desires won't disappear simply because you ignore them. You might repeatedly follow their call…only to turn back each time you bump up against the limits of your comfort zone, leaving you with a nagging frustration and lack of fulfillment. Follow this pattern often enough and you'll end up in an awful place: the land of regrets.

One way to avoid this all-too-common pitfall is to shift your thinking. Notice that fear presents an opportunity to demonstrate courage. For instance, I was so afraid of public speaking at the age of twenty-five that I couldn't give a speech at my own wedding!

Since then, I've shifted my thinking and realized that courage cannot exist in the absence of fear. Now, decades later, I look for opportunities to grow by speaking in front of increasingly larger audiences and actually make a living at it. You, too, can begin by taking it one step at a time…and create the life you desire.

Go ahead, venture beyond your comfort zone! Leap toward your heart's desires so that when you look back on your life, you will be grateful that "I wish I could have" was replaced by "I'm so glad I did"!

"Fearvana"

From the outside looking in, leaders who we look up to seem calm, cool, collected, and very confident. However, when you step into their shoes and advance your career, you'll have moments when you shake in your boots. Remember that if you feel fear as you advance your career, you're not alone.

Fear can manifest in many different forms and situations. As a manager, common instances where fear rears its head include making presentations to senior management or key clients, being promoted to the management table and having to deal with colleagues whom you still find intimidating, having difficult conversations with employees, or starting a brand-new project. Other common fears include making mistakes with potentially serious financial and other implications, fear of failure, and of leading a team that needs to be built from the ground up.

You see, the difference between someone who is looked up to as a leader and someone who isn't regarded as one is not about whether or not they feel fear. Virtually everyone feels fear. It's what we do with our fear and how we react to it that makes a difference in the way we live and in the way we lead.

Here is an account of my friend Akshay Nanavati. He is much more than a success coach. He is an expert in pushing human limits and in facing and leveraging fear to take his life to the next level while inspiring others to do the same.

FROM EMBRACING FEAR TO RUNNING AROUND THE WORLD FOR PEACE

A Glimpse into the Life of Akshay Nanavati, Author of *Fearvana*

While taking a course several years ago, I had the pleasure of meeting an inspiring thought leader named Akshay Nanavati. After overcoming drug addiction in high school, Akshay enlisted in the United States Marines, despite the doctors telling him that boot camp would kill him because of a blood disorder he was born with. When he returned from a tour in Iraq, he battled post-traumatic stress disorder (PTSD), depression, and alcoholism. After he overcame all three and fought his way back from the brink of suicide, he made a choice to dedicate himself to a path of self-mastery and service.

Today, Akshay embraces fear and leverages it to face life's challenges and to push human limits. In addition to being a US Marine veteran, he's an ultra-runner, explorer, speaker, entrepreneur, and author of the book *Fearvana: The Revolutionary Science of How to Turn Fear into Health, Wealth and Happiness*. Even the Dalai Lama endorsed his book, stating that "Fearvana inspires us to look beyond our own agonizing experiences and find the positive side of our lives."

Since we first met, Akshay has done INK talks (India's version of TED talks) and has been featured in many media outlets, such as CNN, *Inc.* magazine, *Forbes, Runners World, Bloomberg,* and *Fast Company,* as well as on major US television networks such as NBC, ABC, and CBS. Akshay has also begun to run around the world for peace. At the time of this writing, he had just completed the first leg in this journey, running 167 miles in a week across Liberia to raise money to build schools in one of the poorest countries in the world through the Fearvana Foundation.[57]

Akshay's motto is: "Every day, I continue to embrace fear and struggle so that I can live my life as fully as possible." Through Fearvana, he teaches us how to transform fear into courage. These lessons are important for any person who wants to grow, and even more important for leaders.

---

57   To learn more, please visit the Fearvana Foundation website: http://www.fearvanafoundation.org.

Here is a summary of a powerful exercise that Akshay developed, which is featured in his book *Fearvana*.[58] This exercise can help you and your employees to embrace your fear so that you can build enough courage to get out of your comfort zone.

1. Use your growing awareness to identify your limiting belief.
2. Choose a limiting belief to work on.
3. Recognize and accept that this belief is not a fact.
4. Identify and write down the subconscious and conscious forces that have you holding on to that belief.
5. Remember that there are two driving forces of all human behavior: pain and pleasure. Identify the pain and pleasure of letting go of your belief and reflect on it to identify the source of it.
6. Find the evidence that led to this limiting belief by looking back into your past to figure out what event led to its creation.
7. Reframe the evidence once you find the event that led to the belief. Choose a new meaning for that event.
8. Gather new evidence to fit the new belief from your own life, books, and other sources of inspiration.
9. Condition the new belief by taking action in support of it and continue to find evidence to support it.

When you confront your fears and push through them, you also help others.

Being a people leader isn't easy. You're likely to face fear, anxiety, and even panic on a regular basis—if not your own, then that of your employees. The path to leadership growth involves learning to manage fear in yourself and others. Given this reality, it's important to follow Akshay's example and, rather than run away from fear, run toward it.

Fear plays a big part of the leadership journey. When your employees, colleagues, and others see you transcend your fears, they'll be inspired to stretch and grow as well. There are steps you can take to help you and your

---

58   Akshay Nanavati, *Fearvana: The Revolutionary Science of How to Turn Fear into Health, Wealth and Happiness* (New York, NY: Morgan James Publishing, 2017), 106-107.

employees embrace your fears. As with Akshay's exercise, raising our awareness about our fears and limiting beliefs is the first step toward leaping out
of your comfort zone.

Leaders Nudge Others out of Their Comfort Zone and into Their Growth Zone

In an article published in *The Hub* magazine in 2018, renowned author and
leadership guru Patrick Lencioni says that

> The best managers and leaders care more about the long-term
> development of their employees than they do about protecting
> their own short-term reputations with those employees. That
> means they are willing to push those employees to do more than
> they think they can.

> This, of course, requires a measure of patience and good judgment,
> but more than that, it requires a leader to endure the temporary
> disdain of direct reports who generally prefer to be comfortable
> more than to grow. In the end, those employees will pledge their
> gratitude for pushing them beyond their comfort zones.[59]

While I agree with Patrick that "Leaders Are Pushers," when it comes
to getting people out of their comfort zone, I believe it is important that
the "pushing" be carried out in a compassionate way so that you're not par-
alyzing your employees with fear and that you have an understanding of
each individual employee's risk tolerance first. It's highly unlikely that all
employees will "pledge their gratitude," and it's possible that some may have
a strong negative reaction. It's important that you tune in and pay attention
to the individual needs of employees. That is, while strongly encouraging
your employees to stretch and grow, you need to blend that with an understanding of their motivations, passions, interests, and goals. This way your
efforts can be more about lighting a fire in their hearts and less about lighting
a fire under their rears.

---

59   Patrick Lencioni, "Leaders Are Pushers," *The Hub*, posted January 2018, https://www.tablegroup.com/
hub/post/leaders-are-pushers.

Often, it is better to nudge than to push. Create a safe space for your employees to learn to fly, then help them celebrate as, over time, the small steps add up to a big leap. Helping your employees feel like you'll be there to catch them if they fall will help them feel like they have a safety net and build the courage they need to make the leap. A skilled leader will learn to know when it is necessary to push and when it is better to nudge.

Chapter 12
FOSTERING INCLUSION:
YOU'VE GOT TO WALK THE TALK

"Belonging has always been a fundamental driver of humankind."
~ Brian Chesky

People tend to stretch and grow more if they feel like they belong and are included as part of the team. Despite this, support for Diversity, Equity, and Inclusion (DEI) remains a challenge for many institutions across industries. When I was diagnosed with fibromyalgia, the doctor directed my employers at the time to conduct an ergonomic assessment. The intent was to see if we could make changes to my workspace and equipment that could lessen the strain on my back and neck to help manage symptoms that made it painful for me to sit and work at my desk. Some of the fixes were simple, like adjusting the height of my computer.

On the other hand, ordering a new ergonomic chair for me would prove to be somewhat of an adventure for my manager. It took her three days of effort going back and forth and filling out forms and obtaining approvals to get me the darned chair, which was delivered to my office much later. As you can imagine, I felt terrible that my manager and director had to jump through all these hoops just so that I could work while managing my pain. I can tell you that I did not feel included by the organization—not because of my manager, as she was trying her best, but because of outdated accommodation policies and convoluted processes that made it difficult to get me the equipment I needed to be able to contribute my best at work.

In other instances, a barrier to inclusion is the fear and discomfort that managers may experience when it comes to implementing DEI strategies and having authentic conversations about accommodation.

In other instances, a barrier to inclusion is the fear and discomfort that managers may experience when it comes to implementing DEI strategies and having authentic conversations about accommodation. While I was updating the corporate accommodation policy for an organization, I also led the development and guided the implementation of certain recruitment-and-retention initiatives geared to diverse groups. As a result, managers at all levels would contact me for advice on how to address uncomfortable situations that arose during the implementation of DEI-related initiatives. In one instance, Harry,* a manager from a regional office, hired a highly educated specialist, Luke,* to conduct complex mathematical analyses. Two weeks later, Harry called me in a panic regarding his new analyst. "Lisa, Luke's not wearing his hearing aid! His cubicle is arranged so that his back is to the door. We have a work-related question to ask him, but we don't want to go into his cubicle, as we're afraid of startling him. I don't know what to do!"

We called a representative from the Ontario March of Dimes—an agency that helps people with disabilities find employment—who had helped us to recruit Luke. The representative advised Harry to have an authentic conversation with Luke about his needs for accommodation. She explained that sometimes hearing aids get hot or start to buzz, so the person wearing them might need to take them out in order to take a break. This information helped Harry better understand Luke's needs. Regaining his confidence and composure, Harry invited Luke into a conversation to explore ways for Luke to take breaks from wearing his hearing aid while remaining accessible to colleagues. This way, Luke's colleagues could be respectful of his needs, and everyone would feel included. The team met and together they devised a strategy where when Luke had to remove his hearing aid, he would put up a sign outside his cubicle indicating that he was taking a pause from wearing it so that he wouldn't be caught off guard. Luke also put up a rearview mirror in his cubicle so that he could see whether his colleagues needed his attention even when he was facing away from the cubicle door. Colleagues also agreed to send Luke a text or an email with questions in situations that could not wait until Luke was able to comfortably wear his hearing aid once again.

I really like this true story, as it illustrates a very common occurrence with a relatively simple solution: managers need to get informed about ways to respectfully ask employees about their need for accommodation. I've received similar phone calls about accommodations for religion, family status, and a wide variety of disabilities.

To increase their ability to accommodate and thus create a more inclusive work environment, managers can get advice from experts, become familiar with the corporate policy, build the courage to have respectful and genuine conversations with people with diverse needs, and engage team members, when appropriate and with consent of the individual who requires accommodation.

Regardless of the specific case, the underlying message remains the same: to help people from diverse backgrounds, you need to transcend the awkwardness you might feel and notice that you have a lot more in common than you think. Inclusion flourishes when all parties demonstrate a desire to gain mutual understanding, operate from a place of compassion, and make an effort to have authentic and respectful conversations and create mutually beneficial solutions. As a manager, you can create an atmosphere where people from all backgrounds have a say about how they're treated at work and feel comfortable voicing their needs. Ask them powerful questions and listen carefully to their responses and you'll have most of the answers you need to implement DEI in the most respectful and meaningful manner.

Diversity, Equity, and Inclusion Is 99.9% About Relationships

I met Jacqueline Lawrence when we worked for the same organization, where she was the Policy Advisor on diversity management. Her passion, knowledge, and expertise regarding DEI continues to inspire me to this day. She is now the Diversity and Equity Coordinator for the Ottawa-Carleton District School Board, where she is having a powerful and important impact on the lives of youth as well as staff and the community at large. Her background includes being a Parliamentary Assistant, Speech Writer, Executive Director of the National Women's Reference Group on Labor Market Issues, and Executive Director of the Multicultural Women's Association. She has also dedicated time to be a facilitator with the International Black Summit and serves as a co-host and producer of Black on Black, a community public affairs program that airs every Saturday morning on CHUO 89.1 FM.

As a published author, Jaqueline's work has been featured in the anthology *Jubilation: Poems Celebrating 50 Years of Jamaican Independence*, the international bestseller *Pebbles in the Pond (Wave Three): Transforming the World One Person at a Time,* and the anthology *Resilience and Triumph: Immigrant Women Tell Their Stories*, which captures the first-person stories of fifty-four racialized immigrant and refugee women across Canada.

Jacqueline invites you as a leader to build relationships from a space of authentic curiosity, which will help you get to know your clients, employees, and communities. As you hear people's stories, you'll get to know who they are, what's important to them, and what they bring to the table. This ultimately takes into consideration everyone's uniqueness, which benefits all and leads to a greater sense of openness to DEI.

THE WHY BENEATH THE WHY OF YOUR ORGANIZATION'S DIVERSITY, EQUITY, AND INCLUSION'S SYSTEMIC TRANSFORMATIONAL PROCESS

By Jacqueline Lawrence

"People will forget what you said, people will forget what you did, but people will never forget how you made them feel."
~ Maya Angelou

For over seventy years, organizations have launched or accelerated their focus on diversity, equity, and inclusion (DEI). Constantly changing demographics and social structures around the globe have resulted in a customer base and a workforce that is diverse in terms of age, culture, ethnicity, race, language, faith, gender identities, sexual orientation, abilities, and socio-economic dimensions. These and other changes contribute to DEI being a dynamic evolutionary process instead of a static one.

In my twenty-five years of doing this work, here are some of the things that I wished someone had shared with me before I stepped into DEI leadership roles in public, private, and not-for-profit organizations:

♦ *DEI's context is grounded in identifying and addressing systemic barriers.* DEI's context is grounded in the relationship between the legal foundation for your organization's existence and developing and implementing equitable and inclusive structures and systems to support your organization's success. Then comes the measurement to flag potential systemic barriers so that they may be addressed.

♦ *DEI is an evolutionary strategic process, not a program.* DEI is not a program but an inquiry-based evolutionary strategic process that identifies, addresses, and transforms systemic barriers that impact access and opportunity for all within your organization. It is linked to every area accountable for your organization's relevance and success.

♦ *DEI is not exclusively an HR accountability.* HR plays a pivotal role to ensure equitable recruitment and retention practices, including tapping into a diverse talent pool and laying the foundation for a respectful workplace culture. Once employees are assigned to their positions in various departments, every department is accountable. Therefore, each department needs to ensure that their management and operational systems are in alignment with DEI principles and practices.

♦ *DEI begins, lives, and dies in your organizational culture(s).* DEI invites you to listen closely in order to understand how your organizational culture(s) is experienced by clients, employees, and community members with one or more social identities in key areas such as safety, welcome, and inclusion. You will be able to listen for the concern behind the complaint of discrimination, harassment, or bullying that may alert you to new or ongoing systemic barriers in your organization. Listening will enable you to identify challenges and possible solutions.

♦ *DEI is 99.9% about relationships.* It could be said that nearly all of the DEI process is about building, nurturing, and repairing relationships with our clients, employees, and communities. Most often, the challenges and opportunities for these relationships are with the "Other." Biases develop due to the stereotypes of the "Other" that we see all around us: in books, on TV, on social media. These biases often impact how we treat each other and inform the decisions we make for and about our clients, employees, and communities.

♦ *Make the unconscious conscious.* Your most important strategy as a leader of DEI in your organization is to raise the consciousness of yourself and your team. This will allow you and your team to listen at a deeper level to help bring to light unconscious behaviors and practices that ultimately impact your strategies, objectives, and mission for inclusion.

♦ *Know the "why" behind your "why."* Many organizations have a mission, vision, or strategic objective or statement around diversity, equity, and inclusion. While these statements give direction, they often do not answer the questions *To what end?*, *What will shift?*, and *What will change or be transformed?* To this end, the person leading DEI and organizations must be clear about the "why'" behind their "why."

This gives you the fuel to keep going when you hit breakdowns and resistance and seek an answer to the question *Why did I say yes again?*

Jacqueline provides us with an overview of DEI and demonstrates how it is complex and multifaceted. She says that "As a leader, you are accountable for ensuring that the appropriate infrastructure is in place so that clients, employees, and the members of the community feel included whenever they interact with the people, structures, and processes of the organization. It is important to note that you will bump up against current and past practices. It is at this point that you remind yourself that your leadership capacity requires you to support the organization to move into a new space that includes all, rather than keeping outdated practices that do not serve current and future clients, employees and community members. Professor George Dei from the University of Toronto says it this way: 'Inclusion is not bringing people into what already exists; it is making a new space, a better space for everyone.'"

When it comes to the recruitment and onboarding process, organizations need to ensure that each step is accessible and that they and their employees continue the work of removing systemic barriers. For example:

- ◆ Review interview questions for bias to ensure a more equitable process.
- ◆ Make an effort to reach out to members of diverse groups to ensure that there is good representation in your talent pool.
- ◆ Welcome and initiate respectful, open, honest conversations about the need for accommodations and raise awareness about self-disclosure (where a person discloses their social identities).
- ◆ Ensure that employees help new colleagues from all diverse backgrounds feel welcome.

As highlighted by the Maya Angelou quote that Jacqueline chose, the basis of it all is that people want to feel respected and feel like they belong at work and in the community. Your job as a leader is to do everything in your power to create conditions at work that encourage employees to be their authentic selves and ensure that they are supported and there are opportunities to leverage and celebrate all their skills and knowledge to serve your clients effectively and efficiently.

Walking the Talk on Inclusion

The Sodexo Group—founded in 1966 by Pierre Bellon in Marseilles, France—is the worldwide leader in "Quality of Life Services." A philosophy of service to clients, employees, and the community permeates everything they do. Here is how Sylvia Metayer, CEO Corporate Services Worldwide, sums it up:

> Through all of our Quality of Life services, be they food services, landscaping, or facilities management, we actually touch the quality of people's lives. We can actually make organizations perform better. We can make schools teach better. We can make hospitals heal better. In my world, we can make companies have more engaged and productive employees. We also contribute, over the long term, to the communities in which we serve.

Today, Sodexo Group employs close to 430,000 employees representing a hundred professions in eighty countries, and serves over 75-100 million customers every day. To say that Sodexo is a large and successful multinational employer is an understatement. In fact, the Sodexo Group is the nineteenth largest employer in the world.

The company emphasizes that quality of life is central to the performance and growth of individuals and organizations. From what I have learned and observed, this quality-of-life philosophy begins with their employees and translates into quality-of-life services for clients. They are dedicated to improving the quality of life for individuals, organizations, clients and communities around the globe.

I met Anna-Karina Tabuñar (who is featured in chapter 4 of this book) several years ago when I was inspired by her work on inclusion. While running a business as a communications consultant, she gave a voice to people with disabilities through her award-winning *Canada in Perspective* TV show and her documentary *Talent Untapped*. I saw her make the switch from entrepreneur back to a corporate job as Director of Corporate Affairs at Sodexo Canada. If you are (or have ever been) an entrepreneur, you can imagine what a difficult choice that would be. However, thanks to Sodexo's inclusive and people-first culture, Anna-Karina transitioned successfully and is extremely happy about having joined the Sodexo Canada team.

Anna-Karina and I met for lunch on a hot summer day at a café in trendy Westboro village in Ottawa. When I asked her about making the switch, she told me what a wonderful employer Sodexo has been and that they "walk the talk" on inclusion. I was overjoyed to find that a large, long-standing corporate private sector organization was so focused on its people. I wanted to learn more, so I asked Anna-Karina if she could provide me with additional information. She introduced me to the newly appointed president of Sodexo Canada, Suzanne Bergeron, who also serves as vice president of Human Resources. Suzanne leads a workforce of 10,000 people across the nation, serving over 185 corporate clients at 220 locations and offering over 100 services to clients from a wide range of sectors, including corporate, universities healthcare, energy and resources, and engineering and construction.

Given that Sodexo is a top employer and renowned as a global leader on DEI, I asked Suzanne questions about how Sodexo Canada integrates DEI into all aspects of their business, that is, to describe how they walk the talk when it comes to inclusion. *(Note: Sodexo refers to DEI as Diversity & Inclusion or D&I.)*

HOW SODEXO "WALKS THE TALK" WHEN IT COMES TO INCLUSION
Suzanne Bergeron, President of Sodexo Canada[60]

What does inclusion look like at Sodexo?

In our view, D&I represents a frame of mind, a way of living and leading. To be able to be your whole self, to be accepted, and above all, to be recognized for your differences—these are the principles at the heart of our business. And for the last 50 years, our culture has been built on inclusion. Our data shows that we are ahead of most other Canadian organizations in employing people from minority groups, Indigenous communities, and people with disabilities. This representation allows us to better reflect and serve our clients and communities. We also have gender parity at all levels of the organization, and it is

---

60   Learn more about Sodexo: https://ca.sodexo.com/home/about-us/sodexo-group.html.

my privilege to be the first woman president of Sodexo Canada.

Why is it important to have gender-balanced teams?

In our recent global survey of 50,000 managers, we found that gender-balanced teams consistently deliver better results in terms of employee engagement and client performance as well as 23% greater profitability. D&I is the right thing to do, and it is also good for our bottom line.

Globally, on average, women account for less than a quarter (24%) of senior roles within organizations.[61] In contrast, Sodexo has set an ambitious global target to have 40% of our senior leaders comprising women by 2025.

We are working toward D&I as a priority with dedicated resources and a clear strategy, including:

♦ *Succession*—We're reviewing our succession plans to ensure a pipeline of qualified women who are ready to rise up the ranks.

♦ *Recruitment*—Our talent-acquisition team has a clear mandate to recruit for gender parity. We have a similar mandate and plan to recruit and develop more employees with disabilities.

♦ *Mentoring*—We have a global mentoring program for women leaders and high-potential women. Sodexo takes part in the national mentoring day with people with disabilities. This day provides learning for both mentor and mentee.

♦ *Employee Involvement*—We involve all employees at all levels to ensure that D&I is everyone's business. Everyone has an important role to play in this constantly evolving journey. Our volunteer employee business resource groups (EBRGs) play an important role in bringing together employees with interests in various aspects of diversity, including Women in Leadership (WiLL), All Disabled Employees Possess Talent (ADEPT), Cultural Diversity, Sharing Among Generations (SAGE), Pride for the LGBTQ community, and Native American and Aboriginal Council (NAAC).

What are concrete examples that Sodexo "walks the talk" for D&I?

♦ We have a global CEO of Diversity and Inclusion.

♦ Our work in D&I has become a key differentiator for us with our clients and prospective clients.

---

61 "International Business Report: Women in Business 2018," Grant Thornton, posted March 8, 2018, https://www.grantthornton.global/en/insights/articles/women-in-business-2018-report-page/.

- For all our leaders, 10% of salary bonuses is directly linked to achieving our D&I objectives.
- There is mandatory training on D&I for all salaried employees.
- As the saying goes, "What gets measured gets done." We have established a series of key performance indicators (KPIs) to track our progress in achieving our D&I goals.
- With our second global survey on gender-balanced teams at Sodexo, we have seven years of data on the positive impact on the bottom line.

What are the top pieces of advice you'd give to new and aspiring leaders regarding D&I?

- Involve all levels of the organization. D&I is not just an initiative reserved for the C-Suite. To have a real impact on culture and mindset, everyone must take responsibility. EBRGs are an effective, inexpensive way to get everyone engaged and activated.
- Set measurable goals. Without measurement, without KPIs, this path will be much longer, and the changes too small for the impacts to be seen and felt.
- Act with humility and transparency. It is important to challenge oneself, to review these strategies regularly, to question, to measure and above all to hold each and every one responsible and accountable for his or her defining role.
- Never, ever tolerate a behavior from anyone that does not promote your D&I culture.

I had the pleasure of spending time discussing various aspects of corporate culture and leadership with Suzanne, Anna-Karina, and Normand St. Gélais, Sodexo Canada's Director of Corporate Responsibility (Diversity, Inclusion, Sustainability & Stop Hunger Foundation).

Suzanne models for employees the importance of withholding judgment when people make mistakes, engaging them in open discussion to clarify the intent behind their actions. What I appreciate about what Suzanne does is that when someone makes a mistake and others take offense, she not only advises the person to make a sincere and genuine apology, she also speaks to those who felt offended to encourage them to be gracious and accept the sincere apology and to forgive the person and move on. This simple approach can go a long way toward creating an inclusive workplace culture where people seek greater understanding and help others feel like they belong and are valued, rather than a workplace where people continually feel judged for their past mistakes. This philosophy breeds greater civility and professionalism at work and supports a spirit of collegiality. It leads employees to become more comfortable and confident about putting themselves out there to innovate and stretch outside their comfort zone.

Another important takeaway from this meeting was to be able to strike a balance between people's individual quality-of-life needs and the need to produce results. For instance, Sodexo has adopted a flexible work schedule for employees who are part of virtual teams spread around the globe. Suzanne underlines the importance of balancing accountability and flexibility in the work schedule to ensure that employees and leaders are accessible during normal work hours and come to work at the office when needed.

Managing Inclusion from the Middle

Many organizations invest a great deal of time and effort to create an inclusive work environment. They have top-down initiatives to assess organizational maturity, communicate corporate values, and highlight senior-management commitment. They have bottom-up initiatives led by volunteer employee councils (also known as Employee Business Resource Groups [EBRGs]) to promote and celebrate the spirit of diversity. These efforts have a great deal of merit and are important elements of a sound inclusion strategy.

Managers are the gateway to the organization and major catalysts for DEI, given that their responsibilities involve hiring, onboarding new employees, communicating with teams as they lead them in day-to-day operations, managing performance, and ensuring that proper accommodations are in place for employees based on their diverse needs.

Then why is it that HR and senior management within these same organizations are left scratching their heads to figure out why they aren't achieving the desired DEI outcomes?

There is a need for greater focus on supporting middle managers, as while they are often overworked and under a great deal of pressure to achieve results, they are also the ones senior management, HR representatives, and employees rely on to implement the lion's share of DEI initiatives. Managers are the gateway to the organization and major catalysts for DEI, given that their responsibilities involve hiring, onboarding new employees, communicating with teams as they lead them in day-to-day operations, managing performance, and ensuring that proper accommodations are in place for employees based on their diverse needs. Managers do all this while dealing with competing priorities, fighting fires, and juggling numerous demands. To add to the complexity, times of fiscal restraint see many managers having to figure out how to engage and motivate employees during periods of significant downsizing.

At the end of the day, middle managers are the ones who have the greatest impact on the success of initiatives designed to effect cultural change. Many HR initiatives designed with the best intentions of senior management and HR experts unravel because they did not take into consideration the needs of middle managers. Over the years, I've worked with several hundreds of managers at all levels, from a range of organizations. The vast majority favor creating inclusive work environments and leveraging diversity to help the organization succeed. At the same time, many are still at a loss regarding how to accomplish all this while they meet pressing demands.

In order to successfully create inclusive work environments, organizations need to concentrate meaningful levels of effort and resources on supporting middle managers to integrate DEI. It's not enough to "sell" managers on the benefits of implementing inclusion initiatives for their organization—organizations need to support middle managers and help make it easier for them to create inclusive work environments. Managers not only need the proper skills and personal attributes but also to be better equipped to integrate DEI into their daily human-resources and business activities, as well as into their strategies.

Organizations can support middle managers by ensuring that they have the knowledge, tools, and strategies they need to create inclusive work environments. Progressive policies and senior-management commitment provide a solid foundation; however, by simplifying related processes (such as strategic recruitment and simplified accommodation processes), managers can more easily integrate key elements into their daily operations, which will lead to desired results.

Here are some of the common ways that your employer can support you if you are a middle manager working to create a more inclusive work environment:

- ♦ *Provide you with easily accessible and useful information* so that you may seek and keep abreast of excellent resources available in your community to help you connect with potential candidates, with the goal of developing a talent pipeline of qualified candidates from diverse backgrounds.

- ♦ *Ensure that you work with recruiters that engage in strategic recruitment in partnership with outreach organizations.* Work with your HR representatives to partner with outreach organizations and employment agencies dedicated to helping job seekers from diverse backgrounds to land work. Collaborate with recruiters and advertising agencies to simplify processes for posting job ads using media geared to qualified candidates from diverse backgrounds.

- ♦ *Raise your awareness about DEI and foster awareness among your employees.* Depending on the community you're in, you may be able to access free or budget-friendly cross-cultural training. In addition, seek available online training resources and videos and encourage participation in any training offered by your organization.

- ♦ *Equip you with a list of key contacts within your organization who can provide you with additional support.* For instance, ensure that you have access to internal advisors with the necessary skills to help you become better equipped and supported. Support your EBRG and DEI councils and encourage your employees to take part. Put forward ideas through EBRGs to create a more inclusive workplace and also ask members for advice regarding useful resources.

- ♦ *Ensure that you are equipped to navigate simplified accommodation processes.* Progressive employers review existing related processes and establish the necessary infrastructure for requesting accommodation, and continually look for ways to support and simplify accommodation processes.

♦ *Ensure that you and your team are well aware of accommodation processes and how to use them.* HR and facility-management representatives can help you interpret policies, access external expertise (e.g. ergonomic experts, occupational therapists, and contractors for office adaptations), and implement accommodations.

A quick search on your company intranet or a call to your HR representative or your EBRG can help you access company resources that will help you become better equipped to foster a more diverse and inclusive team and work environment. If you work for a smaller employer, search for outreach organizations and employment agencies for support and advice.

Fostering a Spirit of Inclusion in Your Team Will Help You Serve Your Clients Better

An added benefit to fostering inclusion among employees is that not only will you create a more respectful and productive work environment where people of all backgrounds can flourish, you will also lead your organization to serve your clients better thanks to gaining greater insights into their needs.

Claudio, the world-traveling, world-renowned engineer you met in an earlier chapter, shared the process he goes through to prepare his team for international work on teams consisting of engineers and laborers from around the globe and from the local labor pool, working together for foreign clients.

As a leader, you need to prepare yourself before communicating goals with the members of the team. You can start by becoming familiar with the cultural norms and protocol and raising the awareness of the people you brought with you from your home country. In addition, be sure to learn about the history, the religion(s), and the temperament of the country in which you will be operating, so as not to inadvertently offend your clients or the members of your team that you hired locally.

Always keep in mind that when you are dealing and negotiating on the world stage, you must know what you can say or not say: one false move or bad word can kill your chances of landing a contract. For instance, if you hand your business card to a client in most Asian countries with your left hand, or even worse, if you throw your card across the table, there is little chance that you will sign a contract with the clients that you have just insulted. Another example is that if you cross your legs and point your foot to your client's face, you will have grossly offended them.

A leader must ensure that his team is aware of these things, so as not to fall into the trap of making the wrong move. The important thing is that your team trusts your leadership and knows that you have their best interests in mind. It is obviously easier to be a leader in your own country then on the international stage.

The key lesson from Claudio's extensive international experience is that to properly integrate DEI into your work and foster a truly respectful and inclusive environment for all parties, you need to do research to raise your own awareness and that of your employees so that you are well equipped to succeed both nationally and internationally. The more aware and well versed your team, the more you will build trust among colleagues and with clients. When you create a corporate culture that is truly inclusive, it benefits everyone.

Chapter 13
ATTRACTING THE BEST AND HOW TO LEAD THEM

"This is a collaborative enterprise... You have to surround
yourself with good people and help them to do what they do
well, as opposed to micromanaging."
~ Robbie Myers

When I started working in the business world, in the 1990s, the process of bringing in new employees to work for you was simply referred to as "staffing and recruitment" (attracting and hiring workers, both from internal and external pools). The process for keeping and motivating employees so that they work to achieve results for your company was referred to as "retention" (building knowledge and skills through learning and growth, managing succession, remuneration through compensation and benefits, and any other program designed to encourage good employees to stay and continue to advance their career with the company). Nowadays you'll hear talk about "talent management" and "talent acquisition." Therefore, do your homework, learn about your organization's talent management framework and associated strategies, and get up to speed on the latest HR policies, practices, and trends. If you hold or are aspiring to become a formal leader within your organization, you need to learn about human resources management and talent management in order to become a great talent scout and build a top-notch team. You also need to know how to motivate your people to give their best and be engaged at work.

I won't dive too deep into talent acquisition at this point other than to highlight a few key points. In order to get the best talent for your team, you need to:

- Get clear on what your company offers its current and prospective employees and learn how to communicate your employer brand.
- Develop highly targeted recruitment/talent-acquisition strategies designed to communicate your employer brand and attract the audiences you're trying to recruit.
- Never settle. Someone you hire today may one day become your boss, so be sure you hire great workers with strong values, integrity, caring attitudes, and leadership skills so that they can be autonomous and good team players.
- Connect with members of diverse groups through partnerships, employment agencies, and other community organizations.
- Partner with professional associations and agencies to help you find the right talent—people who are aligned with your vision, goals, and objectives and who match your needs.
- Simplify processes by integrating D&I activities into your operations. For instance, if you're attending a trade show or a networking event, be sure to also act as an employer brand ambassador. Be on the lookout for talent and connect with potential candidates while undertaking your business-development activities.

Studies have shown that employees' lack of control over their own work causes a great deal of work stress.

Also, as a leader in charge of talent acquisition, you need to ask yourself: based on the way the work is structured, will new employees have the authority to make appropriate decisions for their level and feel a sense of autonomy once they are up and running in their roles? This doesn't mean they get to decide everything or do what they want. This is more about having a sense of ownership and feelings of accountability where they can be recognized for the value that they bring. Studies have shown that employees' lack of control over their own work causes a great deal of work stress.[62] The way I've seen it play out is that the better the high performer is at their work, the more autonomy they want, and they will resent you and resist if you don't let them take charge of their files.

The Irony of It All: Leading High Performers Can Lead to High Stress

"The best executive is the one who has sense enough to pick good men to do what he wants done, and self-restraint enough to keep from meddling with them while they do it."
~ *Theodore Roosevelt*

Every manager and executive expects to have to deal with non-performers at various points in their career. It's just the way it is when you work as a people leader long enough. However, non-performers are not the only source of stress for people leaders.

About fifteen years ago, an exasperated director came to me for advice because some of his employees were driving him to the brink. What took me aback was that these were not a group of disengaged non-performers; they were part of a team of top-performing, high-achieving managers and senior analysts with some of the best minds in the organization. That day, I came to the realization that leaders are often blindsided by something that few people talk about: high-potential and high-performing employees can be very high maintenance.

The truth is that there are different types of high performers, and there seem to be two extremes. At one end of the spectrum, you have dutiful followers who fall into place and put you on a pedestal. They do what they're told and turn themselves inside out to please you. At the other end are "wild-eyed" eccentrics who are passionate change-makers. These are the high performers who have the potential to drive you bananas if you haven't learned how to treat them properly.

---

62 "Stress at the Workplace," World Health Organization, accessed June 24, 2019, https://www.who.int/occupational_health/topics/stressatwp/en/.

Many of my clients with this type of high performer on their team have learned this lesson the hard way. For example, I've witnessed scenarios in which a manager worked hard to recruit the best and the brightest analyst they could find—an autonomous self-starter who took initiative. Then, the minute their employee orientation was over, the manager began to micromanage the brilliant self-starter. This is the worst thing you can do to a high performer.

This approach doesn't work because high performers accustomed to taking initiative and achieving results often respond negatively to micromanagement—quickly becoming frustrated, annoyed, and disengaged. They use their high degree of intelligence to challenge you, push back, or find another job and leave. Ones who are more conflict averse may stay, repress their emotions, burn out, and go on stress leave—or channel their anger and frustration to take you down one mind game at a time. These are the ones who know their value—and they know you know their value and that you depend on them for your team's success. They know they have a certain measure of clout due to their talents.

Remember that high performers, more than anyone, hate to be managed. Instead, they want to be led and also seek opportunities to lead others. They have very high expectations of you and may call you out on your B.S. and zero in on your weaknesses to push your buttons if there's even a hint of you trying to dominate them.

Keep in mind that high performers, more than anyone, hate to be managed. Instead, they want to be led and also seek opportunities to lead others. They have very high expectations of you and may call you out on your B.S. and zero in on your weaknesses to push your buttons if there's even a hint of you trying to dominate them. Misrepresent the truth to them and break their trust, and they will hold you accountable and not let it go. This is why, as a leader, you need to learn the art of motivating high performers. It's important that you avoid any interactions that may be perceived as undermining them or insulting their intelligence. Keep your own ego in check and allow them to have significant leeway in how they complete their work.

Value your high performers and treat them with respect—for example, by giving them the autonomy they need to achieve desired results and creating opportunities for them to share their ideas. The rewards that you and your team will reap will be well worth the effort.

High performers give a lot and expect to be recognized and compensated in return. If they pour their heart and soul into their work and you give them an average performance rating, look out! When it comes to their files and their projects, they want to co-lead (and in their mind, they are *the* leader). In fact, they may even be fantasizing that they have taken over your role and are doing a much better job than you. You have the choice to resent them for this or to embrace them and help them grow as a leader so that they could one day step into your position or another leadership role. They could be right in that it is very possible that they are smarter and more gifted than you. When it comes to being recognized, high performers don't like platitudes that carry little meaning. For example, exclaiming, "Great job!" and giving them a high-five works for some but is not always appreciated by certain high performers.

Rather, feedback needs to be specific, genuine, balanced, and truthful. For instance, if one of your employees conducted research for you and prepared a presentation that you successfully delivered to management, you may want to say something like, "Thank you, Amy, for all the research you did to help me deliver a solid presentation to management. Those stats you pulled for me really drove home the importance of the initiative. I could see that management really understood the problem once I shared your analysis. I know we got approval and funding for the initiative thanks in large part to your contribution. Thank you. I really appreciate your work."

In a similar vein, when providing constructive feedback, avoid being condescending or blaming, and get right to the point by asking questions such as: *What are your thoughts about the situation?*; *What do you feel did and didn't work well?*; and *What can we learn from this situation, and what will you do differently next time?* You'll find that high performers tend to be good at analyzing issues and will likely come up with the solution for making things work better next time. This gives them the opportunity to address the situation on their own and to learn from their mistakes. Do this respectfully and mindfully, and they'll take their work to the next level the next time around.

In addition, renowned leadership author Patrick Lencioni recommends that leaders not only thank employees for the work that they do and for being a good team player but also thank them for the positive impact they're having on your life as their manager.[63] For instance, "Ali, when you stayed an extra hour to help me close that difficult file for the vice president, it allowed me to get home in time to be with my children for supper. I would have had to stay until eight p.m. if I'd had to do this all on my own. This really means a lot to me, and I really appreciate it. Thank you."

Another characteristic of high performers is that they love to challenge the status quo. Typically, this desire comes from a good place of wanting to solve problems. However, because they're so focused on the task at hand or on analyzing problems, they may lack diplomacy and rub others the wrong way when they eagerly share their observations on how to improve things. And if you disagree with one of their brilliant ideas, then you have a new problem on your hands unless you become very skilled at explaining the rationale for your decision.

These tendencies make perfect sense if we stop to think about it. High performers are often the subject-matter experts or "go-to" people and didn't get that way by being weak of character. You need to coach and guide them, help them become aware of others' needs, and help them boost their interpersonal skills. Come up with a shared vision and ensure they have access to the proper resources and equipment, and then get out of their way.

My former director and one of my favorite bosses had leading high performers down to an art. Coincidentally, his name is Arthur Lacroix and he goes by "Art." His top-performing employees loved him. Many of those he mentored went on to become vice presidents, national directors, and business owners.

Although Art retired from his director role in 2008, I still keep in touch with him and consider him one of my longtime friends and mentors. His impact is still being felt by many of his former colleagues. When we talk about Art, we all agree that he's one of our favorite and wisest bosses. On a very personal level, Art was there for me when my father was diagnosed with lung cancer and subsequently passed away. I was thirty-six, and I was devasted. Art allowed me the time to grieve and then picked me up, dusted me off, and helped me to get

63   Patrick Lencioni, The Truth About Employee Engagement: A Fable About Addressing the Three Root Causes of Job Misery, (San Francisco, CA: Jossey-Bass & Pfeiffer, 2016).

back on track. Given that I'm writing about great leaders, I sat down for coffee with him one day and asked, "What's your recipe for motivating and engaging top performers?" His list was simple yet very effective—it served him and his employees well for thirty-five years.

ART'S FIVE STEP RECIPE FOR "LIGHTING A FIRE IN THEIR HEARTS"

1. Hire people who are smarter than you.
2. Be nice to them.
3. Give them a lot of rope (i.e., leeway) to try new things and grow.
4. If they get into trouble, then you step in and defend them publicly—even if they are wrong—then they will always have your back.
5. If they do well, give them the credit (congratulations). A bonus is that when you give credit for work well done, it also reflects well on you as their leader.

Art kept things real and was forthcoming when sharing his own faults and mistakes. One thing for sure, we knew Art believed in us and always had our backs. He truly cared and had compassion for his employees, and he also liked to have fun at work. On the day he retired, we threw Art one of the biggest and best retirements parties I've ever been to. People from offices across Canada came to show their gratitude and wish him all the best in his new adventure. When he left the parking lot, we surprised him at the garage entrance with handmade posters to let him know just how much he meant to us.

Chapter 14
DEALING WITH FEAR, JEERS, TEMPERS, AND TEARS (INCLUDING DURING PERIODS OF TRANSITION)

"Seventy-five percent of careers are derailed for reasons related to emotional competencies, including inability to handle interpersonal problems; unsatisfactory team leadership during times of difficulty or conflict; or inability to adapt to change or elicit trust."
- Center for Creative Leadership

I f you are more of a "thinker" than a "feeler," one of your biggest challenges as a leader may be to become more comfortable with being uncomfortable when it comes to dealing with your employees' and colleagues' emotions, as well as your own.

Having worked both in HR and as a coach for many years, I've become very attuned to the manner in which people express their emotions at work. When people are happy and engaged, they express joy through genuine smiles and laughter, as opposed to a fake corporate laugh or a sarcastic chuckle. When they are fearful or unhappy, they may jeer, their tempers may flare, and they may even shed tears. As a leader, you need to understand many emotional triggers for yourself and others. You need to appropriately manage your own emotions and facilitate difficult and awkward conversations when employees become emotional at work.

What would you do if you were a manager and you had to have a difficult conversation with an employee and they started to cry?

To illustrate, I'll share a conversation I had with one of my coaching clients. Leslie* is a top performer and a subject-matter expert in her field. She's at the point in her career where she's trying to decide whether formal leadership is for her. I asked her, "What would you do if you were a manager and you had to have a difficult conversation with an employee and they started to cry?" Her nonverbal cues said it all—while sitting on an office chair, she began shuffling her feet as she backed her chair up toward the door and a look of sheer terror came across her face. When I said, "People are human; they will bring their emotions to work. It's not easy for most people to separate that part of themselves, so as a leader, you'll need to deal with others becoming emotional." Leslie made a face and exclaimed, "Blech!" Amused, I asked, "Did I just hear you say 'Blech'?" We both burst out laughing, and she acknowledged that while she was an expert in her field, she still had a lot to learn before making the shift to leading other people.

What Leslie—like others who believe that people should leave their emotions at home— fails to comprehend is that most people are not able to neatly compartmentalize their personal and professional lives. They are intricately connected and intertwined. Indeed, during my lengthy career working to help people deal with their work situations, I have met only a handful of people who truly have this ability to separate what happens to them at the office from what happens at home.

Deep down inside, the reason why managers often hate providing constructive feedback or conducting performance-management conversations is that they're afraid of the reactions they may elicit. Many managers worry that their employees will become emotional, and they lack the confidence or feel ill-equipped to handle crying and other types of emotional outbursts.

In addition to difficult performance conversations, there are also other scenarios that tend to bring emotions to the forefront. For instance, emotions run high during periods of transition, when there is tension due to gossip, or when employees feel isolated and excluded from the rest of the team. When these scenarios are not handled properly—for instance, when gossip is not brought under control or emotions are not considered or validated—it leads to increased toxicity and lowered morale and engagement within the organization. Left unchecked or repressed, it can often lead to escalation of conflicts and/or employee relations issues.

You need to show leadership through the way you manage your own emotions and how you help others manage theirs. A good way to start is when an employee becomes upset, look for both the verbal and nonverbal cues. Take the time to listen attentively and validate what they're going through, which should not be confused with agreement. Whatever you do, do not minimize or dismiss their feelings, as this will either cause the employee's emotions to escalate or for the employee to shut down. Next, don't rush them through to a solution but be genuine; hold space for them and actively listen. Here's one good way to remember how to tune in and L.I.S.T.E.N. that I've found effective in my work as an HR representative and as a coach:

- ◆ L = Look at and Lean in
- ◆ I = Inquire
- ◆ S = Stay present
- ◆ T = Take note of the circumstances
- ◆ E = Empathize
- ◆ N = Notice Nonverbal cues

This is highly effective at the individual level. However, there are instances when you need to help manage the emotions of your team. Moreover, if you're a senior executive, you need to manage the sum of the emotions being felt and expressed by all employees in the organization—no easy feat but one that's crucial as you advance your leadership career.

Listening does not necessarily mean that you agree with what is being said. It's about being present, hearing, and taking someone's input into serious consideration rather than dismissing them. It's about demonstrating respect for employees and circling back to communicate decisions clearly.

Lewis Eisen is a policy-writing consultant, a speaker and trainer at Perfect Policies, a former public servant, and the author of *Respectful Policies and Directives: How to Write Rules that People Want to Follow* and *Unlocking the Golden Handcuffs: Leaving the Public Service for Work You Really Love*.[64] Lewis shared with me that he had a leader who was a good listener and was able to effectively communicate her decisions. Lewis said that he felt respected in all their interactions, even in situations where he and his manager needed to agree to disagree.

YOU CAN AGREE TO DISAGREE WITH EMPLOYEES...PROVIDED THAT YOU LISTEN, ARE RESPECTFUL, AND EXPLAIN WHY
By Lewis Eisen

A good leader is, for me, someone who treats me respectfully.

I remember one manager in particular. She was a subject matter expert who had moved up the ranks over the years. Although she wasn't a particularly strong visionary, what stands out in my mind about her was that I always felt listened to and respected.

Whenever there was disagreement regarding an issue, she would listen to all sides before making her decision. For instance, she would say, "I hear that you have this concern and that you would like us to do X. I've also heard from the other people, and considering all the circumstances, I'm making the decision to proceed with Y. I understand that you may not be happy with that; however, I think it's the right decision in this case." Although I often disagreed with her decisions, I always felt like I had been heard.

---

64   Perfect Policies, www.perfectpolicies.org

An important takeaway from Lewis's example is that listening and respectfully explaining decisions is an important skill for any leader. It's highly unlikely that you'll always agree with everybody you work with. Therefore, it's important to learn how to have open and honest conversations so all parties feel listened to and respected.

Employees who are not necessarily in agreement with a decision are more likely to do what's needed if their manager takes the time to explain the rationale behind their decisions.

Change Is the New Normal: Boosting Resilience During Periods of Transition

You've probably heard the expression that "change is the new normal." Organizational transition is triggered when a change is announced and people in the organization will have to shift the way they work, behave, and interact with one another. Examples include: reengineering the way the organization operates, redesigning work processes, bringing in new technology, changing the organization's structure, and undertaking a workforce adjustment such as during times of changing roles, massive growth, or downsizing (or "right-sizing," as some may say at their own risk). These issues can happen independently or as part of a large organizational change initiative that includes some or all of these aspects.

As a leader in your organization, be it as a manager or as CEO, you will need to lead your people through each phase of a transition. There are a number of highly effective models that can help in this area, such as ProSci's ADCAR (Awareness, Desire, Knowledge, Ability, and Reinforcement), Lewin's Change Management Model, and Kotter's 8 Step Change Management Model.[65] However, I am partial to an oldie-but-goodie model of transition developed by consultant William Bridges and published in his book *Managing Transitions* in 1991.[66] Bridges' model includes the Three Phases of Transition (Ending, Neutral Zone, and New Beginning) and the Four Ps of Change Management (Purpose, Picture, Plan, and Part).[67] Bridges distinguishes between *change* and *transition* as follows:

---

65   Nick Greene, "6 Essential Change Management Models to Help Innovate & Grow," *TallyFy*, accessed June 24, 2019, https://tallyfy.com/change-management-models/.

66   "Bridges' Transition Model: Guiding People Through Change," *Mind Tools*, accessed June 24, 2019, https://www.mindtools.com/pages/article/bridges-transition-model.htm.

67   Rory Cellucci, and Darlene Slaughter, "The 4 P's of Change and Transition," *Linkage*, posted April 2, 2014, http://blog.linkageinc.com/the-4-ps-of-change-and-transition/

> Change is situational; it is the external event that is taking place, a new strategy, a change in leadership, a merger or a new product. The organization focuses on the outcome that the change will produce, which is generally in response to external events. It can happen very quickly.

> Transition is the inner psychological process that people go through as they internalize and come to terms with the new situation that the change brings about. The starting point for dealing with transition is not the outcome but the endings that people have in leaving the old situation behind. Getting people through transition is essential if the change is actually to work as planned.[68]

What I appreciate most about Bridges' model is that it is simple, easy to understand, and focused on the human experience so that people moving through transition as a result of organizational change can easily relate to it. My clients report that Bridges' model helps them understand how change triggers internal reactions, which in turn helps them feel validated, increases their awareness, and empowers them to take action to successfully navigate the transition period.

In addition, I like to overlay Elizabeth Kübler-Ross's model of the five stages of grief—denial, anger, bargaining, depression, and acceptance—which is also very useful for explaining the cycle of emotions people go through when they experience loss in the workplace. These stages are fairly universal, but each person (and workplace) moves through them in their own way and at their own pace.

It's important to keep in mind that although these models can give a sense of what might occur in the broader sense, given that human beings are involved, individual reactions and outcomes may be unpredictable. While some of your more resilient employees may experience change as positive and exciting, more often than not, change can bring about a sense of loss, fear, and uncertainty as people grieve and eventually let go of the way things were in the past and get ready to transition to new beginnings.

---

68   "What Is William Bridges' Transition Model?" William Bridges Associates, accessed June 24, 2019, https://wmbridges.com/what-is-transition/.

The effects of a major transformation initiative can last for years. One public servant shared with me that "We are still picking up the pieces, and we are still recovering," six years after a change in organizational structure and business model.

So, how does change and transition play out in the workplace? I've supported many leaders through these cycles many times within organizations, both as an internal senior HR business partner and as an external consultant. Although my involvement in change and transition management has been a constant in my career, there are two periods that stand out the most. The first was when the Crown Corporation[69] I worked for was implementing a large workforce adjustment, where the organization was trying to get back on track after going from approximately 4,000 employees down to 2,000, in the space of a couple of years. The second was over a decade later, when I was running my own business as an HR consultant and offering services to the Canadian Federal Government. The Federal Public Service went through a major downsizing initiative, which resulted in major job cuts and deployments, affecting thousands of people, and impacting tens of thousands more who had survived the cuts and were left to pick up the pieces of this major upheaval. The effects of a large transformation initiative can last for years. One public servant shared with me that "We are still picking up the pieces, and we are still recovering," six years after a change in organizational structure and business model had taken place.

I worked to support employees and leaders through these painful times, both at the individual and organizational level. At the individual level, I was engaged to provide career transition services to close to 100 people who had lost their jobs. In addition, I collaborated with other highly skilled consultants, to either help collaborators with the implementation or to be the consulting lead, responsible for pulling together teams to deliver workshops. Together, we brought together teams of employees and their leaders who were suffering the pains of transition in order to teach them about the phases of transition so that they could see that they were not alone and that it was a normal part of the process to grieve, to create a safe space for them to vent their frustrations (which

---

69   A crown corporation is any corporation that is established and regulated by a country's state or government. Source: Will Kenton, "Crown Corporation," Investopedia, updated January 8, 2018, https://www.investopedia.com/terms/c/crowncorporation.asp.

is a manifestation of the fear and uncertainty), and to help them to begin to piece together a vision for the future so that they could start to move forward, toward their new beginnings. Here are some insights I gained during this period of massive transition:

- ◆ *Change is ongoing and inevitable*; therefore, as a modern-day worker and especially as a leader, it would be very beneficial for you to do the inner work (self-reflection, shift in mindset) to boost your resilience and also learn more about change and transition management.

- ◆ *It's important to understand that change brings emotions to the surface.* It isn't enough to say, "The past is the past, and now we need to move forward." You need to acknowledge the fear and the pain and recognize that not everyone will experience or react to it in the same way.

- ◆ *Resistance and feelings of fear and frustration is normal.* You need to create a safe space that will allow people to vent and "clear the air" without taking it personally—it helps them to process their own emotions, and this helps them move forward; otherwise, feelings will fester and boil over in a much less constructive manner.

- ◆ *Everyone moves through changes and adjustments at their own pace.* Trying to rush them or plough through without acknowledging what they're experiencing will only lead to greater resistance and long-term issues with engagement and productivity.

- ◆ *Those who survive need support too, and sometimes even more so.* Survivors of major organizational changes are traumatized. Oftentimes, while their workforce-adjusted colleagues have moved on with their lives, survivors are still struggling to pick up the pieces within an organization that has gone through the wringer. If leaders do not handle things properly, they'll end up with a resistant, tired, burned-out, and much less productive workforce, and this state can last for years.

In sum, it's very important as a leader to check in with yourself and manage your own emotions, practice and model self-care, and find ways to boost your resilience and help your employees boost theirs. If you're able to, this is a good time to engage external professionals to provide an objective perspective and to help you navigate the murky waters of the transition period.

As a leader, change and transition can be very difficult for you and your team. While leading your employees through transition, whether it is your team or the entire organization, you will encounter two major obstacles (among many) that you'll need to surmount. First, you'll need to work on yourself to raise your awareness about how the transition is affecting you as an individual and manage your own emotions, because you are human too. Second, you'll need to manage the resistance that normally shows up once the change is announced or launched. A skilled and emotionally intelligent leader will not take it personally and instead recognize that at the root of resistance lies fear.

Some of the questions that commonly arise for employees going through transition are:

- ♦ "How is all this going to affect me?"
- ♦ "What does it mean for my future?"
- ♦ "Am I going to lose my job or have to learn a new way of working?"
- ♦ "Will I be able to succeed, or will I fail in the new environment?"
- ♦ "How is it going to affect my team?"
- ♦ "What about the impact on my family?"

In addition, those who care deeply about their colleagues may fear for them. For instance, one of the complaints I heard during transition workshops and one-on-one coaching was that following massive organizational changes, individual employees felt isolated if their friends lost their jobs or were moved to a different team. I heard things like, "I just lost my lunch buddy" or "I hope my colleague is okay; she's a single mother, and now she has no job."

One of the most important things you can do after major organizational upheaval is to create a safe space for your employees to share their concerns and support one another. Encourage them to keep an eye on current, former, and new colleagues and to show compassion and patience with those struggling; mention that they can come to you or Employee Relations/HR if they're struggling or seeing others struggle. Larger employers may have an Employee Assistance Program (EAP) or a hotline that can connect employees to mental health and other professionals for added support. If this is the case in your organization, share the EAP number with them and become informed about other resources that can provide support during a time of crisis.

Applying the Four Ps of Change Management

One of my favorite things about collaborating with Jean-François Pinsonnault, a gifted facilitator featured in an earlier chapter, was to watch him take groups through Bridges' Four Ps of Change and Transition. These are my key learnings:

1. *Purpose*—Share the "Why" behind the change and what the leader and/or organization are aiming to accomplish so that people can gain greater insight into the reasons for the changes taking place.

2. *Picture*—Offer an explanation of the desired end state, including what's changing and what's staying the same. It's easier to contribute when we understand and have a clearer picture of the destination.

3. *Plan*—Share the plan to go from the current state to the future state, including major phases and milestone dates, and keep team members apprised of any course corrections. While the high-level, overarching organizational plan will likely have been developed by management, consultants, and task forces, involve employees as much and as early in the process as reasonably possible. For instance, gather front-line employee input into plans for implementing the solution in day-to-day operations. This will show that you acknowledge and value their expertise. It will help them take ownership and feel like they've retained at least some measure of power during this chaotic time. Plus, the implementation of the solution will run more smoothly as it will take into consideration their daily realities. Once the change is implemented, your employees will be more engaged in its success than they would have if they'd felt left out and like their opinions didn't matter to you.

4. *Part*—Employees want to know what part they'll play in the new organization/business model and understand how their roles and their work lives will be affected as a result of these changes. Whenever we asked employee focus groups about what was

hurting morale following transition, one of the three reasons most often cited was confusion about roles and responsibilities—that is, not knowing what their role and the roles of their colleagues were. Participants also cited unclear roles and responsibilities as a major source of conflict that affected not only team dynamics but also client service. For example, employees reported that when a client called with an issue, they would often be given the runaround because it wasn't clear who should address the inquiry and who had the authority to approve its resolution.

When you find yourself overwhelmed by change and transition at work, gaining perspective can go a long way. To get more grounded and to gain useful insights to get through the major changes, ask the following questions (and encourage your team to do the same):

- ♦ "Have I lived through change and transition in the past?"
- ♦ "What tools or resources (both internal and external) did I draw upon to get me through it?"
- ♦ "How did I grow from the experience?"
- ♦ "What lessons can I draw upon to ensure that I successfully manage the present-day transition (e.g., what will I do the same and what will I do differently)?"
- ♦ "What strengths can I build upon?"

As you become more skilled in transition management and managing emotions in the workplace, be sure to use and share models, tools, and strategies with your employees. For instance, when I introduced Bridges' Three Phases of Transition and Kübler-Ross's Five Stages of Grief during workshops, the vast majority of participants really appreciated knowing that what they were experiencing was normal and that although the road was bumpy, it would eventually bring them to new beginnings. Sharing models helps to normalize things for employees and helps them feel like they are not alone. Deepening their understanding about the effects of transition also helps them to build their resiliency as well as empathy for others in the workplace.

Chapter 15
BUSTING GOSSIP

"There's nothing more poisonous to a community than rumors and gossips. They taint the good character of those who effortlessly stand out. They provide mediocre individuals with a means to become relevant. They set in like gangrene and eat away at the sense of decency that differentiates humans from animals."
~ Wiss Auguste

One thing that can really turn team dynamics sour fast, give rise to strong negative emotions, get tempers flaring, and bring out the worst in people is office gossip.

When I did an internet search on "the origins of gossip," I was really surprised when Google offered the following results:

Late Old English godsibb "godfather, godmother, baptismal sponsor," literally "a person related to one in God," from god "God + sib" a relative (see *sib*). In Middle English the sense was "a close friend, a person with whom one gossips," hence "a person who gossips," later (early nineteenth century) "idle talk" (from the verb, which dates from the early seventeenth century).

In particular, I was surprised at the positive connotations and understood that the modern meaning is derived from the intent that gossip is idle talk between people who share a close bond—such as siblings or close friends—and feel comfortable enough with one another to shoot the breeze. As I continued my research into the origins of gossip, I found an article in *Scientific American*[70] that outlined reasons why people gossip, including:

- Friendship and common bond
- "Inner-circleness," collegiality, going along with the crowd
- Appearances—to look like are "in the know" (i.e., the "knowledge is power" mindset)
- A way to deal with stress (e.g., periods of uncertainty and transition)

Anthropological research has revealed that gossip has been around since human beings were able to speak. It was viewed as a way of staying informed about potential dangers and about dishonest people—it was an important means of survival. It is still being used as a way to discipline and make an example of those taking part in bad behavior. "One provocative view comes from anthropologist Robin Dunbar, who argues that gossip is the human analogue of social grooming, which is widely practiced by our primate cousins. Through gossip, we can create and maintain social bonds more efficiently, allowing us to form groups of larger size."[71] This type of gossip, considered good for creating healthy social bonds, is referred to as *prosocial gossip*.

It would be easier if the research on gossip would align. Instead, what you find is a hodgepodge of both convergent and divergent views. As a leader, you will need to use your common sense. Once gossip becomes mean, vexatious, and vengeful, then you can be sure it will have a negative effect on the workplace.

If the conversations in the office remained at the prosocial level, there wouldn't be so much strife. However, it seems that gossip has developed into a

---

70   Frank T. McAndrew, "The Science of Gossip: Why We Can't Stop Ourselves," *Scientific American Mind*, posted October 2008, https://www.scientificamerican.com/article/the-science-of-gossip/.

71   Tania Lambrozo, "Why Do We Gossip?" *NPR*, posted May 23, 2016, https://www.npr.org/sections/13.7/2016/05/23/479128912/the-origins-of-gossip.

sport in today's workplace. When gossip gets out of hand, you and your team members will suffer for it, and more than likely, so will morale, engagement levels, and productivity. It would be easier if the research on gossip would align. Instead, what you find is a hodgepodge of both convergent and divergent views. As a leader, you will need to use your common sense. Once gossip becomes mean, vexatious, and vengeful, then you can be sure it will have a negative effect on the workplace. I've seen this happen again and again.

For example, I was brought in to help at a call center of twenty employees. When I met with the director, he was not only concerned about gossip among the frontline, he was rightfully concerned about the managers also taking part in gossiping with one another and employees. If senior leaders notice that managers are gossiping with their direct reports, that's when they absolutely have to step in because a manager's job is to foster an inclusive environment rather than add to the toxicity. Gossip does not foster an atmosphere of respect and inclusion. The director retained me though he instructed me not to call this an anti-gossip workshop so as not to strike a negative chord with employees, as morale was already low. I was left to rack my brain regarding how I was going to lead a gossip-busting workshop without calling it that.

As I was mulling over how the heck I was going to make a silk purse out of a sow's ear, I asked myself, "What could be considered the opposite of 'gossip' as we know it?" Then, just like that, it came to me: "The opposite of gossip is appreciation!" I then offered the director to take the employees through a workshop called "Team-Building Through Appreciation," which also featured inclusion and clear communication as central themes. The topics for this workshop included:

- ♦ How you are more powerful than you think
- ♦ The importance of appreciating colleagues
- ♦ What's the opposite of appreciation?
- ♦ The Appreciation Game

Following a fun warm-up exercise, we launched into the meaning of the word *appreciation*, which the Oxford dictionary defines as "the recognition and enjoyment of the good qualities of someone or something." Synonyms of appreciation include *valuing, treasuring, admiration, respect, regard, esteem* and *high opinion.*[72]

---

72   "Appreciation," Lexico, accessed June 24, 2019, https://www.lexico.com/en/definition/appreciation.

Next, I asked the participants to reflect on the question, "Who do you appreciate in life and why?" and asked them to discuss their answers in small groups.

Really understanding and integrating discussions about what appreciation means is a good point of departure to deepen insights regarding how it contrasts with gossip. Once participants got a good sense of what appreciation meant (in general and to them specifically), we launched into how to apply it at work. The participants also identified the key benefits of appreciation in the workplace: "People who work in a team and appreciate one another get along and are happier at work." This was shortly followed by the question, "What is the opposite of appreciation?" As expected, "gossip," was the group's most popular answer.

Then, I took them through the differences between "malevolent gossip" and "idle chatter." Idle chatter doesn't hurt, is about sharing information of a general and non-threatening nature, and can be considered a healthy part of creating healthy social bonds and information sharing.

Idle Chatter

Here are several fictitious examples of idle chatter. Two friends are having lunch, and one might say, "Did you hear about Dierdre? She was transferred to another group. I hope she likes it there," or "Did you hear that Frank and Suzie had a baby? I'm so excited for them! I know they really love each other and will make great parents." Another example is genuine concern: "Did you hear that Toni is back in the hospital? I'm really worried about her, as she hasn't been herself lately. Being a manager is really hard work, and I'm sure it took a toll on her. How about we get her a get-well-soon card and collect money for a gift to show her we're thinking about her."

This is talking about people in a way that is genuine, sharing information and showing joy (as in the case of Frank and Suzie) or concern (in the case of Toni). Some refer to this type of interaction as *benevolent gossip* or *social gossip*, or as mentioned earlier, *prosocial gossip*.

Malevolent Gossip

Now, contrast this with talking behind someone's back about the same stories but this time with vicious intent to devalue and degrade the people in question: "Did you hear about Dierdre? She was transferred to another group. I think it was a good move because most of us just couldn't stand her anymore. She was so freakin' annoying and always trying to suck up to the manager. If I hear her nasally voice one more time, I'm going to pop a vein. Did you see what the short skirt she was wearing the other day? Argh!" or "Did you hear that Frank is a new dad. Let me catch you up: Frank got it on with Suzie from the finance department in the board room. A few months later she announced to him that she was knocked up. They had a shotgun wedding because, well, her family is really traditional, and they threatened to disown her if she and Frank didn't get married. Anyhow, I hope his kid smells better than he does....talk about B.O.!" Finally: "Did you hear that the manager, Toni, is back in the hospital? Rumor has it that she was admitted to the mental ward. I wouldn't be surprised, as she's been acting really strange lately. Maybe she had a mental breakdown because she couldn't get along with any other manager in the division. Remember what a witch she was when I followed up with her about that report? Well, I kinda hope she gets better, but to be honest, I'm in no rush to see her back at work."

This is talking about people in a way that is mean, cruel, vexatious, and shameful. This is malevolent and hurtful gossip, which can be defined as "an exchange of negative information between two or more people about someone who isn't present… Pretty simple: if it is intended to be hurtful or ruin someone's reputation, it is malevolent gossip," say Sam Chapman and Bridget Sharkey, authors of *The No-Gossip Zone*.[73] In other words, conversations are not "idle chatter" if they are negative and would be considered hurtful or embarrassing by the person who is absent and the subject of the discussion. (There is a caveat: if the information is being shared alleges a potential threat, harassment, or abuse, then as a manager, you will need to pay close attention and take appropriate measures such as involving your HR or employee-relations representative.)

Despite the obvious negative repercussions, some researchers still claim that gossip can be good for business and for office morale. After working to make workplaces better for over twenty-five years, I say, "Hogwash!" It leads to a lot of drama and hurt.

As the "Team-Building Through Appreciation" workshop continued, I presented the group with research regarding the impact of gossip in the workplace. For instance, in The No-Gossip Zone, the authors cite a study

---

73   Sam Chapman and Bridget Sharkey, The No-gossip Zone: A No-nonsense Guide to a Healthy, High-performing Work Environment (Naperville, IL: Sourcebooks, 2009).

conducted by the Randstat Corporation showing that employees reported that gossip in their workplace was their number-one annoyance. Chapman and Sharkey also state that, according to a study conducted by Equisys, office gossip wastes up to sixty-five hours per employee each year. And this doesn't count the loss of productivity as a result of overall toxicity and lowered morale and engagement. That amount of lost productivity surely has an impact on the bottom line.

Still, in order to put forward a balanced argument, I could not ignore the perspective that gossip is beneficial because it:

♦ Identifies conditions you should change
♦ Helps protect society
♦ Relieves stress
♦ Helps with self-improvement
♦ Helps to establish cooperation and trust

This counterintuitive perspective is advocated by many experts (including Fast Company's Stephanie Vozza)[74] and reinforced by research conducted at renowned universities such as Berkeley and Stanford. However, after having worked to resolve countless workplace conflicts and supporting people as they dealt with the pain and serious consequences, I continue to stand firm and strongly believe that the costs of malevolent gossip to the organization far outweigh its benefits—a belief that is backed by research, as well as years of my own firsthand experience.

I realize, however, that when you speak of changing behavior, statistics and logic only go so far. That's why it is important to reach people at an emotional level, which is what I strived to do with the workshop participants. None of them could argue against my claim that "gossip poisons teams and the work environment," but I wanted to help them see that there's a better way. So I used a tried-and-true approach to help them reflect on the impact of their actions—a favorite self-leadership method to raise awareness and effect transformation: I asked the participants to delve deeper into why they gossip and what's in it for them.

To get everyone involved, I asked them to answer the following questions using sticky notes and to place them on the corresponding flip chart:

---

74   "Five Hidden Benefits of Gossip," *Fast Company*, posted March 5, 2015, https://www.fastcompany.com/3043161/five-hidden-benefits-of-gossip.

♦ Flip Chart 1: Why do I gossip? What's in it for me/what are the benefits?

♦ Flip Chart 2: How is it not benefiting me/my team?

♦ Flip Chart 3: What does it feel like when others gossip about me?

Then, I asked for volunteers to come up and read the contents of each flip chart. The first volunteer went to the front and began reading the benefits of gossip that were listed on flip chart #1. Responses ranged from "It's fun" to "It helps me feel part of the team." We had a few laughs and the energy in the room remained high. Then the volunteer for flip chart #2 read the expected negative impacts of gossip on the team, such as, "It's bad for morale" and "It can hurt the team dynamics." There was a lot of nodding and agreement and clear recognition that gossip could have negative implications for a team. The participants became a little less jovial and a lot more thoughtful.

The energy in the room suddenly shifted and became very quiet and still. There was a sense of sadness that sucked the air right out of the room—you could literally hear a pin drop as the volunteer read out note after note: "I feel isolated," "I feel alone," "I feel unloved," "I feel like no one cares about me," and "It hurts."

What happened next has stuck with me to this day. When the volunteer began reading out the sticky notes for flip chart #3 ("What does it feel like when others gossip about me?"), the energy in the room suddenly shifted and became very quiet and still. There was a sense of sadness that sucked the air right out of the room—you could literally hear a pin drop as the volunteer read note after note: "I feel isolated," "I feel alone," "I feel unloved," "I feel like no one cares about me," and "It hurts." People bowed their heads with knitted brows, and the collective pain was tangible as the volunteer read the answers regarding the negative effects of gossip on an individual.

Suddenly, things felt very heavy, which presented an opportunity for me to drive the point home by asking tough questions: "Did you realize that you had this much power to negatively impact another person's life? Is this how you want to make people feel when they find out that you're talking behind their backs?" There was a powerful shift that happened thanks to this simple and honest self-reflection exercise. We concluded the exercise by looking at Maslow's hierarchy of needs, which shows that "Belonging" and feeling included is a human need.

From there, I slowly brought the team back to talking about strategies to curtail gossip. For instance, managers need to work to establish ground rules founded on respect, and each employee is accountable for the energy they contribute to the group, be it positive or negative. We also talked about encouraging others to speak up about gossip if they had a conflict rather than getting sucked into the vortex. Lastly, I demonstrated to participants how they could find their power in the situation and strategically change the subject whenever someone tried to engage them in badmouthing other colleagues.

We concluded the session with a brainstorm of ways to appreciate one another and to show gratitude for kindness extended to us. We also talked about using compassion when a colleague seems "off" and to support those struggling by respectfully asking them if they need help. These types of behaviors go a long way to enhance team dynamics.

The moral of the story is that, as a manager, you set the tone. Resist the temptation to gossip in general, and never, ever, take part in malevolent gossip about one of your direct reports with the others on the team. You are the role model and set the standard. It's your job to foster a positive work environment where all team members feel like they belong. Communicate crystal-clear expectations, and if you notice that members of your team are gossiping (beyond idle chatter), nip it in the bud before the toxicity takes hold.

The bottom line is: Do not tolerate malevolent gossip. If some employees continue to disparage, bully, ostracize others, and make their lives miserable, then you may be left with no choice but to sever the ties, say goodbye, and send them on their way. Not dealing with these types could lead to all your good employees becoming disengaged, getting sick, or finding someplace else to call home. Meanwhile, you'll be left with a handful of bad apples who will torture you and any new employee you bring on board.

Chapter 16
SAYING GOODBYE AND DELIVERING BAD NEWS TO EMPLOYEES IS HARD TO DO

"The decision to fire someone often comes with substantial anxiety and consideration."
~ Suzanne Lucas

Employees come, and employees go. Their departure can be either voluntary or involuntary. A voluntary departure is where people resign from their job to go to a better opportunity or to leave their boss or the organization. An involuntary departure is where you need to terminate an employee either as a result of a workforce adjustment (i.e., a lay-off), due to poor performance (e.g., they are not meeting objectives or aren't a good fit/aligned with the organization's objectives), or for just cause (e.g., a serious offense or lapse of judgment with serious consequences that justifies severing the employment contract immediately, oftentimes without notice or severance).

When people leave of their own volition, you may feel betrayed, stabbed in the back, or really sad, especially if the employee was a high performer who you invested time, energy, or money in, or simply someone you enjoyed having on your team. Once you've gotten through the grieving period, do an honest self-evaluation regarding their departure: Was it something you did or didn't do, was it the company, or was it just that the person wanted to advance their career? Whatever the reason, be sure to take with you some lessons learned.

If the departure was involuntary, you may feel guilty as you think about the impact it will have on the person's life and the lives of those depending on the person to earn an income. You may also fear strong emotional reactions in the aftermath and feel angry or sad that it had to come to this. Again, once your grieving period is over, assess lessons learned.

The best way to avoid this scenario is to ensure that your selection practices are solid so that your workforce consists of talented, honest, and productive employees who are fun and interesting to work with. My advice to managers is always this: "Never settle during the recruitment and selection process. Every person you let through the gates of the organization has a potential to influence how well your team functions. The sum of your hires will greatly influence the workplace culture. Plus, you never know if the person you hire will end up being your boss or your even your president."

In the event that you do hire someone who ends up not being a good fit or who behaves in a manner that's inconsistent with corporate values, then you need to deal with them swiftly. First, check to make sure you're doing all you can to onboard them properly: welcome them, introduce them to their colleagues, train them, provide feedback on their work, and set them up for success. If you and your team are making every effort and the bad performance or bad behaviors persist, you need to deal with it. Pay attention to red flags and follow progressive discipline.

When the time comes to do the deed, be sure to follow due process and at the same time remain compassionate and do what you can to help the person maintain their dignity.

Whatever the reason for departure, you can pretty much guarantee that saying goodbye to employees is something that keeps most managers awake at night. Yet, if you are going to be a leader at any level for an extended period of time, it's highly likely that you'll have to go through this process. If you're ever in this situation, be sure to involve your HR representative and seek legal advice, as laws and legislation governing these matters vary from jurisdiction to jurisdiction. When the time comes to do the deed, be sure to follow due process and at the same time remain compassionate and do what you can to help the person maintain their dignity.

Karen Baker-Anderson, past Executive Director of Inuuqatigiit (formerly the Ottawa Inuit Children's Centre), shares this sound advice for managers who need to have difficult interactions with employees:

> If someone is not a good match for your organization, then some-
> times they are not successful for other reasons, such as they are
> in way over their head in their jobs, or they are really unhappy. I
> am proud that I've only had to fire two people in eight years, and
> neither case was a wrongful dismissal. Treat people fairly, do the
> proper documentation, have honest conversations with people.
> One person I let go of, I helped to find a different place where
> there was a better fit.

Many leaders I've worked with have shared with me that one of their worst nightmares is to be put in a position where they need to deliver bad news to employees. However, sometimes it's necessary to do so, such as in cases of retrenchment[75] or chronic poor performance.

Delivering news about terminations or challenging performance conversations (e.g., telling someone that they just got a "needs improvement" rating) can be awkward, scary, and uncomfortable, yet absolutely necessary. Another touchy subject is informing employees regarding your decision (or a corporate decision) to not give them a raise. Karen addressed this very topic during our conversation:

> There are other types of tough decisions that need to be made
> when it comes to leading employees and managing their expec-
> tations. For instance, when groups of employees want raises, it is

---

75   Forced lay-off of employees by a firm, usually to cut down its payroll. Read more: "Retrenchment," Business Dictionary, accessed June 24, 2019, http://www.businessdictionary.com/definition/retrenchment.html.

not always possible to say yes just to please them. What is important is that you do the research, provide rationale, and come from a place of principle. As a leader you need to be informed, look at what the market is paying, and be able to explain why you are or aren't giving raises. For example, you can show how your research demonstrates that employees are already being paid fairly and find other ways to help them feel they are valued.

It's highly likely that at one point in your career as a people leader, you'll be put in the awkward position of having to publicly support the corporate direction or senior-management decision when, inside, your stomach is turning because you don't agree with the corporate line you are toeing. To make matters worse, you may even have to defend top-down organizational transformation initiatives that you don't buy into that can lead to lay-offs and which may even result in your own job loss.

However, even during lay-offs and terminations, it's important to remain compassionate to the people being let go, continue to see them as human beings, and try to support them and lessen the blow by ensuring they get a fair severance and access to career-transition services and an employment-assistance program. In the case of a good performer with good intentions who was in a job that wasn't a good fit, you may want to help them connect with others who might find their talents a better fit.

When you have supported employees in every way possible, it has become clear that they are not a good fit and never will be, or they are past the point of no return when it comes to performance and engagement, in the long-run, it is better to release them so that they can flourish elsewhere.

Chapter 17
HEALTHY BOUNDARIES AND THE ART OF SELF-CARE

"The art of leadership is saying no, not saying
yes. It is very easy to say yes."
- Tony Blair

I f you don't learn to set healthy boundaries or take good care of yourself, it can be the biggest career-limiting move you'll ever make. Believe it or not, if you decide to take on leadership responsibilities, your biggest challenge will be to take good care of yourself.

Through my coaching practice, I've seen the consequences for leaders who fail to practice self-care. I've also learned this lesson firsthand through my own my inability to set boundaries as a new leader in my early thirties. This led me to develop fibromyalgia, a lifelong chronic condition with an array of symptoms, including chronic pain and fatigue. After reading my story, you'll understand why I believe that self-care needs to be a top priority for your leadership development.

My Journey Back to Health by Learning to Say No with Grace and Confidence

At the age of thirty-three, I was Acting Director of Organizational Effectiveness (Talent Management and HR Policy in today's lingo). There was consensus that for a range of reasons, I was doing the work of three people. I was gaining weight while I skipped lunch, and I often sat at my desk for ten to twelve hours straight, pumping out documents to "feed the beast." The only time I looked up was to answer questions and deal with employee issues, as I was also responsible for leading twenty-two people who'd had no direction for years.

At home, I had a toddler and a husband who barely got to see me when I came home exhausted after eight or nine o'clock every night, including working weekends. One week, I worked 100 hours! When I finally took a week off to vacation with my husband and son, the vice president called me back to the office after three days. Dutiful and too tired to put up a fight, I did as I was told. Unknowingly, I was becoming a good candidate for *karoshi* (the Japanese word for death by work).

It's no wonder that a few months later, I was diagnosed with fibromyalgia. I could barely keep up with my septuagenarian mall-walking parents—I really felt I'd hit rock bottom when their eighty-one-year-old friend lapped me using her walker while we were walking at the mall!

I was racked with pain, guilt, and fatigue. Talk about a life- and career-limiting move: I had to take two months off work to understand my condition and reinvent myself so that I could function.

Shortly after I returned to the office, the newly appointed vice president of the HR Sector thought that I would benefit from seeing a coach so that I could learn to "better manage my stress and my time" (translation: so that I could get back to being able to handle a ridiculous workload).

It didn't take long for my coach to knock some sense into me and help me realize that I wasn't the problem: During my first session, Coach André asked me what I was working on. When I got through explaining the twenty project files on my desk, he said to me, "Lisa, you don't have issues with time management. The only problem you have is that you're taking on way too much work for one person, and you don't know how to say no."

That realization hit me like a ton of bricks. Up until that point, the thought of saying no to whom I was reporting and to colleagues, much less the VPHR, had never even crossed my mind. In that moment, one of my new personal and professional growth objectives was born. I became determined to set healthy boundaries and say no in a professional manner—my health depended on it. André had warned me that it would feel awkward at first and that I might come across as a little abrupt, but that with trial and error, practice, and focused efforts to build my courage and confidence, I would become much more finessed over time.

The moment I started to say no with grace and confidence is the moment my true healing journey began.

Learning to manage my approval-seeking tendencies and set healthy boundaries was worth it—it was the only way to get me back on the road to health. The moment I started to say no with grace and confidence is the moment my true healing journey began. This experience really drove home for me the connection between overwork, work stress, and the need to set boundaries in order to stay healthy at work. Over a decade later, I'm still setting healthy boundaries and practicing expectation management.

A Doctor's Burnout

Another person who experienced burnout is Dr. Marcelle Forget. She's been a chiropractor for over twenty-five years and is also a Health and Success Coach. Based on her own experiences and those of her patients, Dr. Forget shared that "Burnout can feel like the 'burning up of the soul,' and it sucks the passion out of the person. I was forever pushing myself even when my energy was low." As she suffered from burnout as well as chronic fatigue, she tried different things to try to boost her energy, but to no avail. Eventually, she realized that she needed to work on healing at the emotional level, given that the effects of negative thoughts can be more toxic to the body than harsh chemicals.

In order to spot potential burnout, fatigue, or depression, Dr. Forget suggests that leaders and workers pay attention to changes in themselves and in others. A good indicator is to notice if there is a sudden decrease in smiling or if you get the feeling that someone's smiles look forced.

Further, Dr. Forget states, "Leadership is all about energy and your ability to empower employees to work toward a clear vision. When you don't communicate clearly with employees and they don't understand what you are doing, it creates bad energy, tension, and toxicity within the team. Therefore, as a leader, you need to develop your awareness and intuition so that you can sense when energy levels among team members drop. Then, you need to be able to reenergize the group and reignite engagement. For example, you can celebrate wins and practice appreciation."

Dr. Forget invites us to be mindful of the body-mind-spirit connection and to realize that how we treat ourselves, and how we treat employees, can have a real and direct impact on health.

Self-Care for Leaders

Dr. Karin Lubin, the co-founder of Quantum Leap Coaching and Consulting and a thought leader for WOW Leadership and WOW TEAMS, is doing her part to contribute to what she calls the "Self-Care Revolution." She encourages leaders to practice self-care so that they can be their very best for employees.

During her interview with me, Dr. Lubin discussed how a lack of self-care among leaders can lead to disengagement and burnout (for the leaders as well as their employees) and keep workers and teams from fulfilling their potential. To light a fire in the hearts of employees, leaders need to feel healthy and energized at work, which requires self-care. When they do practice self-care, they're far more likely to display passion and enthusiasm—ingredients that are contagious and necessary in order to engage employees and get the best out of the workforce. Read on to learn more about Dr. Lubin's model.

WOW LEADERSHIP AND
THE NEED FOR SELF-CARE
An Interview with Dr. Karin Lubin

Dr. Karin Lubin speaks, writes, and teaches on topics related to her approach called WOW Leadership. During her interview, she discussed the fact that many leaders are burning out. She maintains that there are three key issues pointing back to the need for self-care as a leader:

- If you don't practice proper self-care, you risk burnout, which impacts your sustainability and long-term performance.
- It's more challenging to connect with employees if you're feeling depleted and resentful.
- If you don't practice self-care as a leader, you may not realize the impact on yourself, your employees, and the entire business.

Dr. Lubin uses the expression "being leaderful" when it comes to tapping into strengths and talents. Once a person gains greater clarity and identifies themselves as being a leader, they bring out others' strengths and help develop a culture of trust. She also stresses the importance of focusing on health and sustainability to ensure that you and your employees practice self-care so that you can perform and produce over the long term.

According to Dr. Lubin's model, the five actions a leader needs to undertake to establish and maintain a WOW TEAM are:

- *Integrate consciousness-based tools.* Raise awareness on all levels: mental, emotional, physical, and spiritual. Nurture self-care, authenticity, and a higher level of communication. Share information and have conversations with employees about how every employee can create leadership from within and achieve their fullest potential.
- *Intentionally create collaborative synergy.* Align team members' complementary passions, strengths, and experience with the team's collective purpose and vision.
- *Build intuitive leadership and self-leadership into the team.* Empower team members and validate their strengths to make the

team vibrate with renewed energy.

♦ *Build connection.* Connect team members through ongoing traditions that encourage celebration, appreciation, and love. Creating a sense of connection—among team members, with other people in the organization, and with the organization's purpose—leads to a greater sense of meaning and purpose. Remember to like, acknowledge, and collaborate with members of your team. Admire and be inspired by the people you lead.

♦ *Heal and transform team members.* This can be accomplished through personal self-care, awareness, and a willingness to use their past wounding as gifts that reveal their wholeness and help them find greater peace for themselves, their team, and the people they impact.

In addition, Dr. Lubin stresses the importance of talking about self-care with your team members. Engage them in a discussion about whether self-care is important to the group. If you see one of your employees struggling, meet them in private and ask open-ended questions such as:

♦ Are you happy?

♦ How are you feeling?

♦ What's going on?

♦ I would really like to hear—could you tell me more?

Both Dr. Lubin and Dr. Forget strongly recommend that leaders practice self-care—for their own benefit and also to model it for their employees. For example, I met a leader who models and promotes self-care by shifting lunchtime behaviors. Karen Bennet, a Marketing and Public Relations professional, noticed that many people on her team had gotten into the unhealthy habit of eating lunch at their desk. In extreme cases, stressed-out workers scarfed down food with one hand while continuing to type with the other.

Bennet set an example within this fast-paced environment by strongly encouraging employees to step away from their desk at lunchtime and spend half an hour together eating and chatting about non-work-related topics. She also let them manage their own time and take an active role in setting their work plans. Karen doesn't "clock-watch" and gives employees the flexibility they need to manage and balance their life while achieving results.

Learning to Say No with Grace and Confidence

Unless you're the CEO of the company, you likely have someone who is assigning you work and whose job it is to keep your plate full. Even as a manager or an executive, one of the challenges you'll experience is having to set healthy boundaries with senior management, colleagues, and employees. If you want to build and maintain solid working relationships, the key is to set boundaries in a manner that's not off-putting. You want to avoid coming across as a complainer or like you're out of control.

Being able to say no with grace and confidence is important, as it impacts your own well-being and that of your employees. Setting healthy boundaries helps you to create harmony between work and life and to create space for what is most important to you. When you do this, you model leadership behaviors; give your employees the best, happiest, most engaged and lit-up version of you; and benefit the company by nurturing a healthier, happier, and more engaged work force.

Why do so many of us struggle with setting boundaries? Why do aspiring leaders have trouble saying no, even when it's the most reasonable thing to do? Based on my own struggles and those of people I've worked with or coached, here are common reasons why you may have trouble setting boundaries:

♦ It takes a great deal of courage, especially if you've been brought up to be kind and helpful to others and to have a strong work ethic.

♦ You may worry about how you'll be perceived and fear that your setting boundaries will damage your reputation, limit your career, and lead to your being passed over for advancement opportunities.

♦ You may be so unaccustomed to setting boundaries that you don't know how to say no in a professional manner.

♦ You may worry about sounding abrupt, awkward, unconvincing, or overly direct.

♦ You may feel uncomfortable saying no when someone comes at you with a request, mostly because of guilty feelings that creep up when you look someone in the eyes and deny them assistance.

- You may have a strong sense of duty and responsibility that you feel you need to step up.
- Lacking trust in others' ability to deliver results, you may feel concerned that things won't get done properly and will fall through the cracks if you don't do them yourself.
- If you look for constant recognition and validation from others, you may be tempted to take on way more than your fair share. (Approval Seekers Anonymous anyone?)
- Delivering on tight deadlines can create quite an adrenaline rush and become addictive.
- You may see heavy workloads as a personal challenge and would feel like a quitter if you admit to being overworked or if you ask for help.
- You may not know how to delegate and ask others to take on some of the work, perhaps because you anticipate a negative reaction or would rather not inconvenience them.
- You may feel intimidated by certain people, especially if they're pushy; you may feel vulnerable and just can't seem to find the strength to say no to them.
- You may defer or submit to those who have authority over you, whether real (as in case of a manager who reviews our performance and can promote or terminate us) or perceived (as in the case of a colleague who name drops the VP or president every chance they get).
- You may not have learned the appropriate skills or language to manage expectations in a professional manner.
- You may lack of confidence in your ability to communicate your feelings and your needs.

You will also gain greater respect, and other leaders will think twice about trying to take advantage of you and push you around.

If you learn to set boundaries using tact, diplomacy, and grace, you may find that not only will you be able to help your highly engaged team to focus on priorities and achieve goals, you will stay healthier and be able to show up at work full of energy and creativity. You will also gain greater respect, and other leaders will think twice about trying to take advantage of you and push you around.

Beware of Boundary Pushers

There are people at work (both leaders and non-leaders) who have a talent for getting others to work way more than is reasonable or healthy. I call these "Boundary-Pushing Archetypes." They employ many different tactics and approaches to manipulate you into working to meet unreasonable deadlines. You can visit www.lightafireintheirhearts.com and download the Guide to Setting Healthy Boundaries for a tongue-in-cheek look, along with accompanying worksheets. There you will learn more about "The Sugar-Sweet Complimenter,' "The Buddy," "The Chicken," "The Victim," and "The Bossy-Boss," who are among the cast of Boundary-Pushing Archetypes that can make your life as a manager miserable at work. By the same token, ask yourself whether you are behaving like any of these with your colleagues and employees.

Practicing the Dos and Don'ts of Setting Boundaries and Managing Expectations

Chances are that at some point during your career, someone will attempt to push your boundaries so that you work beyond what is healthy for you. Here are some dos and don'ts of boundary setting to help you manage expectations and avoid becoming the "Office Martyr."

The Don'ts to Avoid Being Overworked

♦ *Don't automatically jump up when someone at the office yells "Urgent!"* If it's not life or death, you don't need to jump whenever someone says that something is "urgent." Check to see why they think it's urgent, and don't own it or take on the burden if it's not your problem. If colleagues aren't pulling their weight, the best way to get them to realize this, is to not cover for them. In other words, don't cover for them if they've shirked their responsibilities, haven't completed their tasks on time, or put pressure on others by involving them at the last minute. Don't take it upon yourself to make up for *their* lost time. Talk to your manager to determine the degree of urgency and make suggestions about who else could pitch in if it is indeed a true urgency. Try to deflect other people's stress and leave it with them. Be helpful, but if someone else's negligence caused the urgency, you shouldn't have to pay the price for it.

♦ *Don't become the "meat" in the sandwich.* If there are too many people or multiple managers putting in requests at the same time (especially tricky in a matrix organization), ask them to negotiate priorities and timelines with one another. You could also act as a catalyst and call a meeting with all the parties requesting work from you. You could discuss strategies with your manager to ensure that requests from all directions go through them first— this also allows your manager to realize all that's on your plate and at the same time intercept requests that shouldn't have come to you in the first place.

♦ *Don't become the office spackle.* Does everyone come to you to plug all the holes and fix all the problems? Don't let them convince you that the walls are going to cave in just because you won't work all weekend.

♦ *Don't create more work when your plate is already full.* If you have a wealth of ideas, make sure that you're measured and strategic about how and when you present them. You can develop a plan that spreads the projects out over the short, medium, and long term. You can suggest that others be given the lead, and even link into ongoing corporate initiatives. You can volunteer as an advisor rather than the lead developer. You shouldn't be rewarded with overwork and burnout for being innovative. In other words, just because you came up with an idea doesn't mean that you automatically should be the one to implement it.

♦ *Don't try to be the company hero.* (This one is a favorite of approval seekers; variations include The Office Mother, The Listener, The Best Friend.) Don't take on other people's work as your own. Of course, be a team player and help where you can, but don't take over other people's projects along with all the stress and responsibilities that go with them. Company Heroes say, "I'll help," and before you know it, they're running the show. Don't automatically "take one for the team." If your gut is telling you to run for the hills, listen to it. If you're tempted to throw on your cape, remind yourself that fame and fortune can be short lived. The glory disappears when you can't deliver on your own responsibilities or end up sick because of overwork.

The Dos to Manage Expectations and Set Boundaries

Now that you're a bit clearer on what to avoid, here are the dos of setting healthy boundaries with grace and confidence to help you better manage your workload.

+ *Do be proactive and propose realistic timeframes.* Don't commit on the spot. Say that to do an excellent job you need to look at what's needed to complete the work more closely and then you'll propose a timeframe. Tell them, "This is what I can realistically do. If I had more time, I could do this and this, and do more in-depth research." Always under-promise and over-deliver. For example, if you think that realistically you could do the task in two days, suggest that it will take you four days so that you build in a cushion for ad-hoc requests or other unforeseen delays.

+ *Do set priorities with the manager.* Say something like, "I'm working on X, Y, Z, and four other files. What could be shifted off my plate or be put on hold while I complete this urgent request?" Even better, propose what could be put on hold and ask for concurrence. (Follow up by email if possible). Ask or propose how another colleague could help. If you get ad-hoc requests, discuss their order of priority. What can wait until later, and what could be done by someone else? Understand and focus on the real needs to avoid unnecessary work.

+ *Do keep the manager informed with regular status reports.* Let your manager know of all the requests you have on your plate and keep them informed regarding potential delays. Propose what can be done. If someone is holding up your work, ask your manager if they could use their influence to help you get the responses you need (and escalate up the ranks if needed).

♦ *Do flag requests that fall outside the scope of your work.* Rather than cross your arms and say, "This isn't in my job description," you could say something like, "I wanted to discuss this request before I take action on it, as it may fall beyond the scope of my regular work. If you consider it a priority, I'd be happy to address it and could recommend how to shift the work on my plate to accommodate it."

♦ *Do be a solution finder.* Rather than whine about being overworked, tell your manager that you have too many competing priorities. Analyze what's on your plate and recommend a plan for how to achieve the top priorities. Then suggest how to address the outstanding issues and recommend which tasks could be simplified, put on hold, reassigned, outsourced, or ended. For example, if you're running legacy reports or offering a service that's becoming obsolete (and/or one that clients and colleagues are no longer using), you may suggest that these reports or services are no longer relevant to the organization and could therefore be dropped altogether to save time, effort, money, and other resources.

♦ *Do propose reasonable timeframes.* Here's a simple process that you can follow to propose reasonable timeframes:

  ✧ Broach the subject by saying something like, "I've analyzed what's on my plate. These are some ways we could deliver on top priorities and deliver the rest of the files within adjusted yet still reasonable timeframes."

  ✧ Offer to contact the various stakeholders to negotiate new timeframes if possible (especially effective for internal clients). For instance, you could say, "I just received an urgent request from senior management and it's a corporate priority. I'm calling to see if I can send you the deliverable due tomorrow by _____ (insert date) instead. I apologize for the inconvenience. Rest assured that if there's any way to speed this up, I will send it to you earlier."

♦ *Do keep your ego in check.* Things will not fall apart without you; avoid hoarding information and do transfer your knowledge to colleagues and your employees so that they can step in to help during peak periods. None of us is truly indispensable, and the company will not implode if you take a break. You will never please everybody even if you try to turn yourself inside out, so forget about trying to accomplish that and look after yourself.

♦ *Do let go of perfectionism.* Sometimes good enough will get the job done and help you get through periods when you're swamped. Look at your files. Yes, the report that will be available for client consumption and the briefing note to the CEO may need to be of the highest quality. However, the memo announcing the new members of the social committee or the internal "scent-free" policy and accompanying posters need not be written like academic papers.

♦ *Do boost your confidence.* People feel your confidence, and this engenders feelings of respect toward you where people will think twice before crossing your boundaries. Build your reputation: factually state all the things you've accomplished and market your brand within and outside the organization. Building your credibility will increase your clout making it easier for you to assert yourself. Also, use the following confidence-building techniques:

  ✧ Practice setting boundaries. Start small and build up your confidence.

  ✧ Use power poses (see Amy Cuddy's TED Talk[76]) to get comfortable in your space and boost chemicals in your body and brain that increase confidence and decrease stress-related hormones such as cortisol.

  ✧ Use relaxation techniques, such as breathing exercises to help you get grounded, stay present, and feel more confident.

  ✧ Remind yourself that you're not really "stuck" in your job. Every day, you decide whether to stay or go. Always be ready

76   Amy Cuddy, "Some Examples of How Power Posing Can Actually Boost Your Confidence," *TED Blog*, October 23, 2017. Accessed June30, 2019. https://blog.ted.com/10-examples-of-how-power-posing-can-work-to-boost-your-confidence/.

to make a break. Build your networks and keep your resume up to date. When you feel you have options, you may find it easier to set your limits.

♦ *Do network both inside and outside the company.* Get easier access to collaboration and information when you need it. Share best practices and ideas with peers from other organizations and supply-chain partners and ask for samples or templates when appropriate.

♦ *Do propose process improvements and identify tools to simplify your work.* Identify the irritants and bottlenecks that are causing process delays and work pileups. Propose solutions to your manager to get their buy-in. Use and adapt existing templates or develop new ones for repetitive tasks so that you're not reinventing the wheel every time.

♦ *Do sit on your hands.* Don't volunteer for every single project, even if someone stares at you or you feel like you're being 'volun-told.' As my boss Art used to say, "Lisa, stop putting your hand up every time they ask for volunteers at a meeting. You've got to sit on your hands!" Avert eye contact, sit on your hands, and get comfortable with awkward pauses. Only volunteer on extra projects if they're closely aligned with your work and your plate isn't already overflowing.

♦ *Do create space in your agenda.* Whether you or one of your employees schedule your meetings, be sure to build in cushions between meetings. Plan periods for thinking. Integrate practices for effective and efficient structured meetings so that you allow participants to connect for a few minutes before you launch into status reports. Once the meeting gets underway, use structured brainstorming so that decisions can be made as efficiently and effectively as possible and so that there's no time wasted with waffling and circular conversations. The idea is that you want to maximize meaningful, fun, and efficient interactions that will move files forward. Do not meet just for the sake of meeting without aiming to arrive at a decision or move files forward to achieve results. Adopt visual-management techniques to save you time during meetings so that you can have more space in your agenda to lead and engage employees, clients, and stakeholders.

♦ *Do let "the balls drop" and things "fall between the cracks"*
Sometimes, to get the message across, rather than jump in to save the day, you need to stop enabling others who constantly don't pull their weight and let the balls drop and things fall between the cracks. Often the consequences and accompanying embarrassment are sufficient for the person to take greater accountability the next time around.

Factoring In Long-Term Sustainability

When you first try these strategies, you may feel awkward and uncomfortable. That is perfectly normal. Setting healthy boundaries is a learning process, and just like when you acquire other skills, you can expect a learning curve. Learning to say no with grace can be challenging at first. As my Coach André taught me, "Initially, you're going to sound a lot like a toddler, saying 'no' to everything. People who are used to you saying yes to everything will be taken aback at first and then try to push the envelope. They may make comments like 'Are you okay?' or 'What's gotten into you?' Others might try to bully you and even undermine your efforts by trying to instill fear in you."

If you feel torn, remind yourself that chronically overworked and stressed-out workers pay a high price with their health, their relationships, their long-term career, and even their life.

Once you become more comfortable with setting boundaries, you'll notice that others begin to respect you and your time more; it'll become second nature and you'll have a greater sense of harmony and may begin to experience better health. Having said that, if you work in a highly toxic environment like I did many moons ago, setting boundaries could land you into trouble with the Boundary Pushers. If this takes place, you may need to ask yourself whether you need to change departments or find a job with a new employer. If you feel torn, remind yourself that chronically overworked and stressed-out workers pay a high price with their health, their relationships, their long-term career, and even their life.

When it comes to your job, my motto is, "Learn to love it or plan to leave it!" because staying and hating it and burning out will have a negative impact on all aspects of your life. This doesn't mean you should drop everything and quit your job; it means start gaining greater clarity on your ideal job and role as a leader, and then prepare to make your next career move. Once you make your move, set clear and healthy boundaries early, as it is easier than having to play catch-up later on.

If you experience a few weeks or months of successful boundary-setting, congratulate yourself! It isn't easy to shift in this manner, and it takes a lot of courage. However, be mindful and take notice if you happen to fall back into old habits. If maintaining your newly set boundaries seems difficult, remind yourself of the prize: more harmony and balance in your life, higher quality work, and a boost in productivity overall—and happier times for you, your staff, and loved ones.

Strategies to help you develop the proper mindset to support healthy boundaries include:

- *Make room for what is most important to you.* Reflect on what is truly most important to you and set boundaries to ensure there's enough time in your schedule to do to activities you love so that you can experience greater joy and meaning in your life. For example, spend time with your loved ones or pursue your passions and interests.

- *Set the boundaries with tact and diplomacy.* Observing what goes on inside and around you is very important. Keep track of the different reactions you get when you manage priorities and set boundaries. Remember that delivery is very important, so watch your tone and degree of intensity as others will mirror whatever energy you put out there. Keep it light and emphasize the benefits to organization and the team. Help management feel safe that you have the best interest of the file or organization at heart and communicate with confidence and conviction that your recommended approach will be win-win. Remember to start small and take baby steps. If you mess up, chalk it up to lessons learned and adapt your approach. Most important, remind yourself of all the benefits that you and your employees will reap from living a healthier and more harmonious life.

♦ *Work through the guilt you may feel after setting boundaries, and practice self-reflection to deal with the aftermath.* Check in with yourself or with a professional and examine the reasons behind why you may be feeling guilty. Journaling can serve as a helpful part of this process. The root of your challenges with setting boundaries can stem from your upbringing, your culture, fear, or even your early work experiences. Regardless of the reason, it is worth working to remove these blocks so that you can be happier and healthier, and serve as a positive role model.

♦ *Do it for others.* If your guilty conscience or sense of modesty is blocking you from setting boundaries to keep yourself healthy, then do it for those who depend on you to be there for them: your family, friends, and employees. Also, remember that when you set boundaries and model proper priority setting, your team benefits. I've often seen managers and directors burn out their teams because they say yes to all the demands made by those higher up the corporate ladder. Weak leaders don't know how to manage expectations of senior management or of the board, and the people reporting to them end up paying a high price, scurrying behind the scenes to deliver on all the promises within unreasonably tight time frames.

Remembering to Set Boundaries with Your Employees Too

When you're in a leadership role, you need to set boundaries with employees, as some may attempt to push the envelope and try their hand at upward delegation, particularly if they sense that you're a conflict-averse type who's concerned about hurting someone's feelings.

Further, certain employees are less autonomous than others and will want all your attention. They will knock on closed doors, text you their problems at all hours, and jump you before you've even had the chance to take your coat off or finish eating your lunch. Picture this: You're hunched over in an awkward position, trying to take off your boots and put on your office shoes. Before you know it, one of your employees invades your personal space and hovers around you like a drone. They try to make eye contact and ask you questions such as "Did you get my email about the file?" or "Can I take Friday off?" or "Can you fix the printer?" or "Can I get your signature?" or other questions that you're not able to consider clearly as you're just trying to get settled in for the day.

What happens if you don't address this type of behavior early on is that habits form, employees keep crowding you. You may slowly begin to feel claustrophobic and start to resent them. This eventually can lead to seething and even an angry outburst. It's best to begin addressing these behaviors early on. You can say something like, "Dina, thank you for bringing these issues to my attention. I just need a moment to settle in, so let's meet in fifteen minutes. If you have a question that requires deeper discussion, then please set up a meeting. By the same token, allow your employees time to settle in before you bombard them with questions. Remember that you're the model for their behavior. You can also announce during a team meeting, "I generally have an open-door policy, but I also need some quiet time to review files and prepare management briefings. So, when you see that my door is closed, I need you to respect that because I need to concentrate on moving our team's files forward. Therefore, unless it's a real emergency, please send me a meeting invite or wait until I open the door back up."

In addition, if you need quiet time or need time to think, you may want to be sure you take your lunches away from your desk and go for a walk or book a room elsewhere. For instance, whenever I coach, I strongly encourage leaders to meet with me in a meeting room or some other space away from their office, where we won't be interrupted.

Setting boundaries with employees is just as important as setting boundaries with your boss or clients.

Likely, you'll need to set boundaries about communications, requests for vacation, and how much time you need to review a file so that they're not dumping files on you at the last minute, the night before you present them to management for approval. You need to manage expectations and the approvals process to avoid backlogs; set clear milestones and include a cushion for each stage, while factoring-in extra time for potential delays. Follow-up to hold others accountable for respecting agreed-upon milestones, and to escalate if need be.

Setting boundaries with employees is just as important as setting boundaries with your boss or clients. When you do this up front and early, it's best for everyone involved. As a leader, part of your role is to help employees learn how to produce in a way that's healthy and sustainable.

Summary of Part III

Part III is all about the challenges that you are likely to face as a people leader. These are topics that are typically not taught in school. Therefore, it is not surprising that team leaders, managers, and directors who may be sent for leadership training may still feel at a loss when confronted with everyday challenges. I have noticed that most of the current leadership programs are based on logical, rational management models. They focus on sound management principles. These are extremely important. However, there is a missing component, which is the heart layer.

No matter what initiative, approach, or methodology you might want to apply, if your leadership style does not involve connecting with employees as human beings rather than as logical models, or if you are not able to understand their emotional needs in order to motivate them at the heart level, it will be much more difficult, if not impossible, to achieve the results you want. In Part IV, you will learn how to use the Light Your Leadership© Approach, the keystone of the strategies to light a fire in the hearts of employees.

PART IV

Becoming A Great People Leader: Strategies to Light a Fire in Their Hearts

"We need an education of the heart."

~ Dalai Lama

Chapter 18
INTEGRATING THE LIGHT YOUR LEADERSHIP© APPROACH

"The challenge of leadership is to be strong, but not rude; be kind, but not weak; be bold, but not bully; be thoughtful, but not lazy; be humble, but not timid; be proud, but not arrogant; have humor, but without folly."
~ Jim Rohn

So, how does one become a great leader? Besides learning from the greats, new and aspiring leaders need to study the art and science of making human connections. While some people are born with a natural talent, others need to do work and self-reflection, grow their emotional intelligence, and transform into inspiring and engaging leaders who embody a PEOPLE© mindset:

- *People-oriented*—Put people before profits and performance measures.
- *Enlightening*—Work toward becoming more self-aware and help others do the same.
- *Others*—Take others' perspectives into consideration in all actions and decisions and help them feel like they belong.

- ♦ *Purpose*—Make it your life mission to get clear on and execute your purpose and help others do the same; seek out and collaborate with others who share your "Why" or your calling.
- ♦ *Love*—Genuinely love people and draw courage from a deep sense of compassion to do whatever you can to help improve the human condition in both big and small ways.
- ♦ *Energy*—Realize that "Fun is Fuel!" and know how to create positive, healthy workplaces where people feel energized and look forward to coming to work.

This model is a particularly useful reminder that your most important assets are your people. You can use the PEOPLE mindset to keep you focused on what's most important in your work as a formal people leader.

Advice from One of the Greatest Leaders of Our Time

What's the recipe for engaging employees and managers at all levels? It really isn't that complicated. The best advice I can think of comes from one of my living heroes, Sir Richard Branson, CEO and founder of Virgin Enterprises, and a billionaire businessman and philanthropist with a huge heart. In my view, Sir Richard embodies what it means to have a PEOPLE mindset.

For those of you who are sports fans, one way I can describe it is that, to me, Branson is like the Wayne Gretzky, the Joe Montana, or the Pelé of business leaders—the best of all time. Here is the story of my brief and very meaningful encounter with Sir Richard Branson.

THE STORY OF HOW I MET MY HERO, SIR RICHARD BRANSON

Linda and I met at work and became fast friends in 2000. She knows that just like many people are huge fans of sports stars, musicians, or actors, I feel the same about great leaders who are making a significant positive impact on people and this planet. She also knows that Sir Richard Branson is at the top of my list. She knew what a big deal it was when she pulled me aside one day (just a few months before the writing of this chapter) and nonchalantly asked, "Hey Lis, how would you like to meet Richard Branson?"

I literally stopped in my tracks and said loud enough everyone in the room to hear, "Are you freakin' kidding me?!" I'm almost embarrassed to admit that I went all fangirl on her. "Of course I want to meet Richard Branson! He is like the best leader, and he is awesome and does so much to help others, and his employees love him, and look at all the innovation, and did you know that he's putting people and satellites into space, and…and…and…" and, well, you get the picture.

Ruma Bose, Linda's sister-in-law and author of *Mother Teresa, CEO: Unexpected Principles for Practical Leadership*, not only knew Richard Branson, she was going to interview him right here in Ottawa at the Canada 2020 Conference. Linda, her husband Jit, and I got to meet Sir Richard. We got to shake his hand backstage in between events, and then we followed him to a second event, in which Ruma led a panel, which was hosted by Tobias Lütke (CEO of Shopify), and which featured Michele Romanow (of *Dragon's Den*, the Canadian equivalent of *Shark Tank*), Government House Leader Bardish Chagger, and Branson.

Working up my nerve, I jumped at the opportunity to ask a burning question that I'd had for a long time:

Me (trying to keep it together): "Sir Richard, I'm writing a book on leadership and would really like to get some advice from you. What would be one top piece of advice to keep passion ignited in our employees? Thank you."

Sir Richard: "A good leader is a great listener. So, I think there is nothing more important than a leader being a good listener. We all know what we're thinking; we don't need to hear ourselves speak all the time. We've got to just be listening—listening, listening, listening—and then acting on it. A good leader is somebody that generally loves people, is a fantastic motivator of people, and is always looking for the best in people, and makes people love coming into work in the morning, love their job and be really proud of what they are doing, and I could carry on so you would have to read my book if you want to find out more." And so I did. In fact, I highly recommend Branson's books, including *The Virgin Way: Everything I Know About Leadership* and *Finding My Virginity: The New Autobiography*.

The highlight of the whole experience for me is that a billionaire business mogul known the world over answered so spontaneously and without a second's hesitation, speaking from the heart with such humanity and humility. He mentioned the words "listening" and "people" four times each. Sir Richard's recipe for great leadership and success is very simple: we need to listen, love people, see the best in others, and make sure they have fun and take pride in their work. That's it! No big bells and whistles. After all, your employees *are* your company. Without people working for you, you may as well be a company of one.

I felt vindicated by Sir Richard's advice because I often get challenged by people of the mindset that the CEO and other leaders in the company need to serve the client, the stakeholder, or even the Minister (in the case of government). To me, great leaders have it figured out just as Sir Richard Branson has: love and serve your people, create a fun and inclusive workplace, and help employees stay healthy and enjoy coming in to work every day. They, in turn, will take the best care and give it all they've got to make sure your shareholders and clients stay happy and well served, which translates to increased productivity, profits, and sustainability for your entire organization. When you hire the right people with the right skills and attitude and help them light the fire in their hearts, your company will succeed.

Just as interesting as what Sir Richard said is what he *didn't* say. As with all the great leaders I've interviewed, there was no mention of HR dashboards, HR analytics, or ROI. He didn't dehumanize employees, as many consulting firms have, by referring to them as "capital," "talent," or "assets" that need to be acquired like possessions and then managed; he referred to them as "people"— human beings who need to be inspired, supported and listened to.

Although measuring performance is necessary to help identify strengths, flag issues, and provide benchmarks, it should not be leaders' primary focus. HR dashboards and HR analytics are merely tools, but thanks to savvy branding by companies selling HR software solutions, they have become an obsession. As a result, resources that could be put toward learning, leadership development, and hiring help for burned-out employees are being diverted to measuring and reporting on performance rather than to what really helps your people perform their best to achieve the desired results.

My takeaway is that great leaders can inspire their employees by helping them tap into the intersection of what's most important in all aspects of their lives so they can find happiness and joy in their work.

In contrast, the focus of great leaders is to elevate employees so that they can connect with their passions and purpose and make great things happen. This ideal is expressed by the Japanese concept of *ikigai*, popularized in a 1966 book by psychiatrist Mieko Kamiya, *Ikigai-ni-tsuite*. As BBC journalist Yukari Mitsuhashi explains, "With no direct English translation, it's a term that embodies the idea of happiness in living." My takeaway is that great leaders can inspire their employees by helping them tap into the intersection of what's most important in all aspects of their lives so they can find happiness and joy in their work. As a leader, your job is to help create an environment where people can experience their *ikigai* so they can get paid for doing what they love while they serve others based on what is most important to them.[77]

In addition to listening, promoting *ikigai*, and having a PEOPLE mindset, another quality that sets great leaders apart is their ability to connect with others at the human level. This can be accomplished through "The 3 C's of Connection" and "The 8 P's of Ignition," which we'll explore in the next two chapters.

One leader who's demonstrated these values is Rene Bibaud, winner of the prestigious Canada's Outstanding Principals Award in 2014. Bibaud has been recognized for his leadership and vision, for making positive changes in the lives his students at Adult High School, and for inspiring employees and students alike.

"There is no reason to reach for the stars; they are already inside you."

---

77   Yukari Mitsuhashi, "Ikigai: A Japanese Concept to Improve Work and Life," *BBC*, posted August 7, 2017,   http://www.bbc.com/capital/story/20170807-ikigai-a-japanese-concept-to-improve-work-and-life.

Rene comes across as very compassionate, competent, and also very courageous, having fought cancer two times in his life, as well as surviving a heart attack and heart surgery.

Jennifer Adams, Director of Education at the Ottawa Carleton District School Board, said, "Rene is a man of great character and an inspiring instructional leader. He has tremendous impact as a principal and as a coach, mentor, and role model to staff and students."[78]

AWARD-WINNING HIGH SCHOOL PRINCIPAL
An Interview with Rene Bibaud

I met Rene in a bagel shop in trendy Westboro in Ottawa, Canada, shortly after he retired from a long career with the public school board. Following a little small talk about the weather (a favorite Canadian pastime), Rene began sharing his thoughts about self-leadership: "I have been a mentor my whole career. Everybody needs a mentor and 'go-to' people that can instill and pass along their knowledge."

Rene shared that his philosophy is "Greatness In, Greatness Out." Leadership is about being creative, collaborative, and courageous and having great energy and attitude. It's important to appreciate and tap into the diversity of the network available and also to remind people that there is no reason to reach for the stars; they are already inside you."

We discussed the shift in mindset that's important for leaders to make. Rene said that when you transition into leadership, "You need to be courageous enough to give up your past ways of thinking and look at things differently." He continued to share his wisdom by offering the following advice to new and aspiring leaders:

---

78   "Two Ottawa Recipients Among Canada's 'Outstanding Principals,'" *Ottawa Citizen*, posted May 20, 2014, https://ottawacitizen.com/news/local-news/two-ottawa-recipients-among-canadas-outstanding-principals.

In order to be in a leadership position, you have to commit a tremendous amount of energy—every day of every week of every month. You need to fuse together commitment, vision, action, and passion. It requires thinking and planning and knowing how to do this effectively. You need to be a good steward of the organization and believe that your best days are still ahead of you.

You set the direction, the current vision, and the strategy. Then you let others run with it, work on it together, and figure out the logistics. You need to empower people and be a cheerleader. People want to be led—not abused and offended. Help them feel that you want their success and that they know you are someone who will help them to succeed. Be sincere and compassionate and care about the plan.

Listen to everyone carefully and remember your conversations. Be very visible and deliver speeches that give them the sense that we're all here together and have an equal part to make this place special.

The most important lessons I took from my interview with Rene is that the ability to inspire others is essential to becoming a great people leader. If people depend on you to lead them to success, you need to learn how to inspire. This is not accomplished through a magic formula—it takes energy and the proper mindset. The ability to inspire is accessed by being present with people and connecting at the human level by helping them tap into their passions and personal power, recognizing their talents, and getting them excited about accomplishing great things together.

Connection Is at the Heart of Great Leadership

*"I define connection as the energy that exists between people when they feel
seen, heard, and valued; when they can give and receive without judgment;
and when they derive sustenance and strength from the relationship."*
~ Brené Brown

We've entered the Passion Age, where work and purpose are beginning to
converge once again—just like when artists became apprentices and artisans
became journeymen during the Renaissance, before the Industrial Age came
along and took the fun and passion out of work. During the Industrial Age,
when throngs of people left their agrarian lives to work in the city manufacturing plants, their expectations of employers were quite low. In eighteenth
and nineteenth centuries, people working in factories accepted that their new
lives consisted of going to work at the crack of dawn and performing routine
tasks all day (such as using machines powered by coal or steam engines while
working on an assembly line). Because they'd left their agricultural communities and could no longer grow their own food, they needed to earn money
to be able to afford to eat, so they worked long hours in dire and dank conditions in exchange for much-needed pay. The agents or managers representing
the employer in these establishments would lord over the workers and bark
orders to get them to work faster and produce more. Creating positive and
long-lasting relationships with employees was not at the top of the list for
formal leaders of this era.

*New leadership practices are needed to ignite
engagement of the modern worker through the
integration of servant leadership and progressive
values that foster healthy connections at work.*

The prevalence of outdated Industrial Age management practices continues
to have an adverse impact on society. New leadership practices are needed to
ignite engagement of the modern worker through the integration of servant
leadership and progressive values that foster healthy connections at work.

To illustrate the importance of creating meaningful connections and mutually respectful relationships at work, the following case study is based on an interview with Mario Vissa, president of Mario Vissa Inc., a high-end international interior design firm. He is my uncle and the younger brother of Claudio, who you met in an earlier chapter.

Mario is a brilliant designer and a real class act in every sense of the word. His work and his artistry have been recognized and appreciated around the globe, and his projects are often featured in design magazines and other media. His professional presence, elegance, etiquette, and hospitality are beyond compare. Mario is greatly admired by many and has become the go-to designer for many well-heeled clients in New York City and the surrounding areas. His firm has completed many projects from Halifax to San Francisco and Florida and many places in between. In fact, he counts among his clients important names from both the fashion and financial industries, among others. He also happens to have a generous, philanthropic heart.

Vissa built his prestigious company from the ground up based on his genius for creating beautiful and comfortable environments, combined with his leadership abilities. After forty years in business with his wife, Donna, Mario shares some of his keys to success: the importance of strengthening all relationships while cultivating people's pride in their work.

BUILD RELATIONSHIPS AND HELP PEOPLE FEEL PROUD OF THEIR WORK
A Case Study: Mario Vissa, President of Mario Vissa Inc.

When I asked Mario about his greatest accomplishments in his career, he answered, "My entire career is one big accomplishment: a string of projects that make up my professional life."

His journey began in the late 1960s, when he worked as a draftsman for the Montreal architectural firm Max Louis Architects. Mario was eventually put in charge of design and stayed with Max Louis until the early 1970s, with various parentheses as a consultant to engineering firms. Together with Max, as full partners, they founded a highly successful architectural and design company called Dimensions. This firm was rebranded as Mario Vissa Inc. when Mr. Louis retired. They had built a core team of five people. They also engaged engineers, other professionals, and various contractors to carry out the different aspects of each project.

Mario attributes his success to the power of connecting with employees, suppliers, and clients through warm relationships and mutual respect. Mario and his team wowed elite clients and established decades-long connections with them. As Mario Vissa Inc.'s brand continued to grow, the company began to land contracts throughout Europe, the US, and Canada.

After nearly forty years in business, Mario continues to design homes and institutions for senior citizens. When I asked him about the secret to his success, he replied, "Connecting with people honestly in order to establish solid and friendly relationships." In addition, he shared these tips for leaders:

- Treat *all* people with respect.
- Always hire and surround yourself with the best people available.
- Show everyone you care by being a great listener. Engage in conversations regarding their interests; ask open-ended questions about what is important to them. Invite them to share stories of their children and/or families and tell them a little about yours.
- Consult with employees and contractors to find solutions to questions and problems that arise daily on a job site. This will build trust and to motivate them to do their best.
- Model what it means to take responsibility. When necessary, be accountable to employees and contractors—for example, in cases where perhaps mistakes were made because you hadn't communicated your ideas clearly in the first place. This will also equip you to hold them accountable if needed.
- Be patient with employees and contractors. Model how work is done and notice if they need help; stay with them until they've got it.
- Learn to read the group of people that you work with. Be sure to engage with both the formal and the informal leaders. Say

good morning and goodbye to everyone, from the big boss who signs your paycheck, to the person who sweeps the floors or carries the bricks.

♦ Reward everyone involved in the project by making sure to recognize even the smallest effort; a heartfelt handshake and a bottle of wine, a holiday gift, or a Christmas present can go a long way to cement any working relationship.

♦ If one of your employees or contractors insists that their way is the best way, allow them room to experiment and be prepared to demonstrate the tasks for them. Be sure to reinforce and help them feel proud of what they have accomplished and do not scorn them if their method or idea does not work out; rather, recognize their talents while you gently guide them to the desired solution.

For example, Mario explains how he collaborates with contractors who are craftspeople and who are very passionate about their work. In his experience, these experts are not always open to suggestions on how to complete a task and he is often met with resistance (even though he is also an expert and has a keen sense for what needs to be done on jobs).

However, Mario has figured out that sometimes the best way to engage craftspeople who are being resistant to his feedback is to recognize their talents and expertise, and to model what needs to be done to achieve their vision for the project. He mentioned the need to take charge, gain credibility, and earn respect. He also underlined the importance of using humor, and to not take oneself too seriously in situations such as these. To this end, Mario has been known to climb up on to ladders on job sites in his fancy designer suit, with hammer or saw in hand, to demonstrate how work is to be done.

By using his keen emotional intelligence, helping his employees and contractors feel proud of their work, and thanking them for a job well done, Mario tapped into the wisdom of what motivates modern employees at work: the ability to connect at the human level and to build warm, long-lasting relationships with all. As a result of his approach, Mario built a thriving long-term business.

The following chapters provide ways that you can establish connections and ignite engagement. They map out an approach that you can use to inspire employees to be motivated, engaged, and productive in a sustainable and healthy manner.

Chapter 19
INSPIRE WITH THE 3 C'S OF CONNECTION

"To become truly great, one has to stand with people, not above them."
~ Charles de Montesquieu

In order to be considered a great people leader, it's crucial to connect with your employees at the human level. When employees experience a lack of connection at work, it can lead to feelings of isolation, disengaged teams, a general lack of motivation, and unhealthy work environments. During employees' focus-group sessions, I've heard time and again about how these feelings can erode trust, lower morale, and negatively impact engagement, workplace health, and productivity. On the other hand, I've also seen how teamwork can be heightened when leaders connect with their employees and encourage team members to see work situations from others' perspectives.

Leaders' actions set the tone for those who report to them, and their actions send the message of what is considered acceptable behavior. If their employees are going to feel connected with their fellow team members, that connection must begin with the leaders.

The 3 C's of Connection©

Through the years, I've noticed that great leaders embody three underlying values that I call "The 3 C's of Connection." They know how to connect with and inspire others by integrating the values of *compassion, courage,* and *competence* into everything they do.

The 3 C's of Connection Are at the Heart of Great Leadership

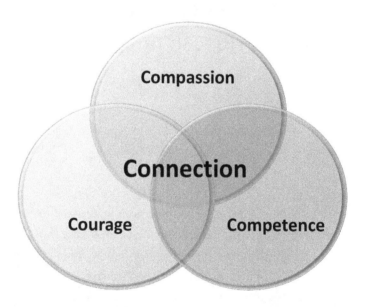

When these three values intersect, it leads to a deeper sense of connection and feelings of belonging to the team, the company, and the community. Further, leadership is like a dance where you go back and forth between doing things to help yourself become the best possible version of yourself, and then step outside yourself to help others grow and be the best they can be in life and at work.

Rally the Troops with Compassion

"It costs $0.00 dollars to be a decent human being."
~ Spirit Science

Merriam-Webster defines "compassion" as the "sympathetic consciousness of others' distress together with a desire to alleviate it." In my view, compassion is love in action. Compassion is central to connecting with employees and being able to see their struggles and their humanity, to understand their work experiences, and to "walk a mile in their shoes." It is also about the willingness and ability to actively listen to employees' and managers' concerns, take them seriously, assess the situation, communicate clearly, and then take action together.

Certainly, it's important for a leader to provide advice, guidance, and direction to their team members. In addition, an effective leader appreciates their employees, asks them questions, and listens attentively to gain a better understanding of their perspectives, what's happening on the frontline, the challenges they face, and their ideas about how to resolve them.

Compassion is also about recognizing people's innate need to feel like they belong. The evolutionary impulse to seek love and belongingness is so important that it's smack dab in the middle of Maslow's Hierarchy of Needs.[79] For this reason, in addition to building relationships and connecting with people at all levels, a great leader encourages and creates opportunities for their employees to connect with one another and with colleagues from across the organization.

Skilled leaders forge positive interpersonal relationships not only with their employees but also with senior management, colleagues, key stakeholders, and clients.

To lead from a place of compassion, you need to create environments where vertical and horizontal collaboration and collegiality (regardless of "level") is emphasized and takes precedence over hierarchy and assigned roles. Skilled leaders forge positive interpersonal relationships not only with their employees but also with senior management, colleagues, key stakeholders, and clients. This ability gives leaders greater influence and more leverage to manage expectations and negotiate reasonable timelines (so as not to burn out staff) and have decision-makers rally in favor of ideas brought forward by managers and experts from their departments.

Furthermore, individual contributors and their managers feel more engaged and motivated, as they can see how their work is meaningful and contributes to something greater than themselves. Those who work in compassionate organizations tend to connect with one another and break down the silos. As your

79   Saul McLeod, "Maslow's Hierarchy of Needs," *Simply Psychology*, accessed June 24, 2019, https://www.simplypsychology.org/maslow.html.

employees practice connecting through compassion at work, they'll also be more likely to extend these positive behaviors to their dealings with external clients and community stakeholders. Compassion is part of what leads organizations to give back to the community through corporate social responsibility and philanthropy. They also understand that doing good is good for their overall brand.

Facing It, Then Acing It with Courage

"It is better to lead from behind and to put others in front, especially when you celebrate victory when nice things occur. You take the front line when there is danger. Then people will appreciate your leadership."
~ Nelson Mandela

Leadership is not for the faint of heart—it takes a lot of heart and courage to become a great leader. According to a report published by the global organizational consulting firm Korn Ferry International, "Managerial Courage" is a known differentiator when it comes to identifying great leaders.[80] Chrystel Martin, Managing Director and Editor-in-Chief at Manageris (a leadership think tank that gathers insights about management from international publications), offers a progressive definition of managerial courage. She argues that courage is a quality that distinguishes great leaders at all levels of an organization and even distinguishes high-potential employees.[81] Steve Farber posits that if you don't stretch yourself, leap out of your comfort zone, and feel fear every day, then you're not a true leader—hence his use of the term "extreme leadership.".

Courage cannot exist in the absence of fear.

Courage cannot exist in the absence of fear. Fear happens when we perceive a threat (real or imagined) to ourselves or those we care about. Fear holds us back and keeps us stuck in our comfort zone—it keeps us small. Courage comes into play the moment you decide to go forward toward your goal despite your feelings of dread. It is when you feel that what you and your team are about to do is so important that you decide to face your fear and then ace it!

---

80   J. Evelyn Orr and Kathleen Sack, "Setting the Stage for Success: Building Leadership Skills that Matter," *Korn / Ferry International,* accessed June 24, 2019, http://www.kornferry.com/media/lominger_pdf/LA_article_web.pdf.

81   "Create a Climate of Constructive Debate," *Manageris,* posted February 18, 2013, https://www.manageris.com/blog-management-nuggets.html.

Draw on your purpose and your passions to fuel your courage. When you and your employees are clear on the reasons why what you're doing is important, you'll be able to draw on your will and the courage of your convictions to push through and transcend fear. You and those who choose to follow you will leap toward your shared goals with vigor and fervor. As the Indigenous leader Chief Seattle said, "When you know who you are; when your mission is clear, and you burn with the inner fire of unbreakable will; no cold can touch your heart; no deluge can dampen your purpose. You know that you are alive."

Unless you're a first responder, a surgeon, a stunt actor, a soldier, or a heavy-machinery operator, you're not likely to run into life-and-death situations at work. So, what does practicing courage within an office environment look like? Building on themes covered in earlier chapters, here's a summary of practical actions that demonstrate courage in the workplace:

♦ *Exercise managerial courage* and boost the ability to navigate the approvals process efficiently and effectively by managing expectations, and by reaching out to colleagues from other parts of the organization.

♦ *Don't hide behind HR and other policies* and be prepared to stand behind your decisions. If you and your HR representative decide on a course of action (e.g., in cases dealing with progress discipline or not awarding an employee a bonus), don't say things like, "HR made me do it." That's a cop-out and an indication that the manager/director is not taking full accountability for their decisions or actions.

♦ *Step up to defend recommendations* based on your team's work, even when challenged by members of senior management.

♦ *Set healthy boundaries* and prevent your team from being overworked by having the guts to flag workload issues to senior management, set priorities, and negotiate more reasonable timelines or more resources at work.

♦ *Have the courage to trust your employees and take calculated risks.* Shift your mindset from "risk avoidance" to "risk management." Be bold and be a model for courage, step outside your comfort zone to innovate and put ideas forward, and challenge managers and colleagues at all levels to do the same.

♦ *Commit to respectfully and authentically communicating the "Why"* behind decisions and challenging situations, even if it's uncomfortable to do so.

♦ *Seek help.* Hire a coach, see a psychologist, read books, and push yourself out of your comfort zone to boost your confidence if fear is holding you back from reaching your full potential at work.

Most importantly, it takes great courage to be vulnerable and authentic within a professional setting. Yet your imperfections and fears are what convey your humanity. When you allow others to glimpse your truth, your struggles, and how you're working to overcome them, they can relate to you better. When your employees see you trip and get back up—while maintaining your class and dignity—they'll be inspired. And when you let your true self shine through, it'll ignite their courage.

A STORY OF SEPTEMBER 11TH— A STORY OF COURAGE
By Brenda Silverhand-Garriss, Writer, Lecturer, Life Consultant, and Former COO[82]

The most challenging leadership event experienced in my lifetime took place following the horrendous acts of 9/11.

On Tuesday morning, the 11th of September, at 8:54 a.m., terrorists hijacked American Airlines Flight 77 with the intention to plow into the Pentagon, Military Headquarters of the United States, and destroy as many operations and as much human life as possible.

At the time, I was Chief Operations Officer of a highly regarded professional staffing firm located just outside Washington, DC, where we had many consultants employed by various divisions of the government, including the Pentagon. That bright sunny morning of 9/11, my schedule included meetings

---

82   For more information on Brenda Silverhand-Garriss, author of the upcoming book *Fire in My Bones,* please visit http://www.brendagarriss.com.

with our consultants and management teams assigned there. I was less than a quarter of a mile from my destination when the terrorists' attacks became reality. As smoke and fire began to ascend, all eight lanes of traffic were immediately shut down as we sat motionless in disbelief. The Twin Towers had already been hit moments before. Shock and fear began to arise throughout the United States and the world, as no one knew if friends and family members had been affected or where the next hit would take place.

Traffic remained at a complete standstill while sirens from police cars, fire engines, and ambulances blasted through the atmosphere and rescue workers made their way through thick, curling, black smoke to the Pentagon. My thoughts turned to all the employees trapped inside, not only ours but all those who were working there. The radio in my car was blasting its own brand of terror as it began reporting what was happening in New York, Pennsylvania, and Washington, DC.

Fortunately, we did not lose any of our employees; however, the same cannot be stated for others. Sixty-four people on Flight 77 died instantly as well as 190 employees at the Pentagon. Hundreds of others were injured. Terrorism had attacked the United States, and the world would never be the same. Our employees would never be the same. I too, would never be the same.

Most employees assigned at the Pentagon—and in other government agencies as well—were severely traumatized. Many left their jobs, several took sick leaves, some moved away, and others remained. The greatest assignment in my entire career had just begun. This was not the time to focus solely on managing the workload, which had just increased dramatically, but also on leading our teams toward healing and wholeness—not just for the ones who remained but for all those with whom we had been fortunate enough to have worked. Managers everywhere were quitting their government jobs because they could not process the fear and stress these events had left in their wake.

Those at the management level need to know how to lead their people through chaos and transition no matter how large or small, for it is by our own actions that we set the recovery for others who are watching and learning. We do not have the luxury of getting lost in the drama. We must focus very quickly on everything positive we can find, for we cannot allow ourselves to become part of the chaos but rather the solution. When a crisis like this takes place, people need something to believe in, something to hold on to in their time of despair. We were still alive, and we were strong individually and collectively as a nation. We would not only survive but thrive because that was who we were, or at least who we were in the process of becoming.

True leaders in the workforce do not allow themselves to fall into the negative; instead, we must first lead ourselves and then our people out of the darkness of fear and depression into a place of safety and positivity. If we do not feel it, believe it, and act on it ourselves, we will not be able to lead anyone anywhere. We have to be balanced and centered, no matter what our situation is, because there are many who depend on us at every level. We do this by taking the high road as a role model and being patient and compassionate with others because everyone reacts differently, while at the same time shifting into high gear in positive thought and action. In private, we give ourselves the space we need to breathe, "gear up," focus on the end result, and bring individuals on our teams through the negativity presenting itself at the time. We are humans working at a high level of business accountability, yet we must be empathetic and caring to those who are struggling. Praying for understanding, wisdom, and strength was very high on my personal priority list, realizing the degree of physical and mental difficulty in accomplishing the ongoing task at hand. There was no quick fix to be made, but rather a long, arduous journey ahead.

For the next full year, we embarked on a powerful healing journey together. For some, it took much longer than for others. As leader of the pack, it was important to work diligently on myself, not allowing my words or actions to fall into the low vibrations of stressful conversations, worry, and sorrow. Being an example, whether we want to or not, is our job. It defines us and our message. We still had to get the work done and heal at the same time.

Washington, DC, became a heavy place to live in, and often we would see armed guards on top of government buildings. Life had changed forever. We began to set up regular phone calls, meetings, and private consultations with those still on our teams, both in house and outside. And those who had left were not forgotten; we stayed close to them while they worked through their own adjustments. We remained accessible for all, realizing everyone does not heal in the same way or within the same amount of time. We did not know the future, but we prepared as best we could, realizing we only have this moment to live our lives fully and in a positive manner. We were all one family, lifting each other up and dedicated to healing and prospering. We knew it would take time, and we were willing to do whatever it took to become whole again.

True leaders don't create followers; they create more leaders. During the healing of 9/11, many new leaders came into being. There is a quote by Nikos Kazantzakis that I live by in regard to leading: "True teachers use themselves as bridges over which they invite their students to cross; then, having facilitated their crossing, joyfully collapse, encouraging them to create bridges of their own."

There is no greater challenge or deeper reward.

Brenda's poignant story of how she stepped up to lead during an extremely difficult time shows that true leaders demonstrate their courage by providing comfort and restoring a sense of normalcy when others are too distraught or too scared to carry on. The way I interpret the Kazantzakis quote that Brenda applies to leaders is that great leaders understand that they need to guide their employees and support them until employees learn and gain confidence. Once a leader sees that an employee can handle more responsibility and become more autonomous, a great leader will give them the space they need to become leaders in their own right.

Catapulting to Success with Competence

Managers and employees at all levels need to be given the time and support to develop their leadership abilities just as they would to develop their technical abilities. Development needs to be a healthy balance of technical and leadership abilities, for it is only through effective leadership that the highest level of technical abilities can be expressed.

In other words, as a leader, you need to consciously take steps to increase your own competencies as well as those of employees. To this end, you can involve employees during meetings and reduce the role of hierarchy in decision-making. Engaging people to provide input and participate in the decision-making process, especially for decisions that directly affect their work, demonstrates faith in their talents and takes their experience into consideration. It also shows that you trust them, which goes a long way to increase employee engagement and their understanding of the business context in which decisions are made. It boosts their political sensitivity and sharpens their ability to position ideas based on audience needs so that they are clear and concise and support decision-making at all levels. When employees watch you succeed and you recognize them for their hard work and contribute in the process, they're powerfully inspired.

BE A SOURCE OF MOTIVATION AND INSPIRATION FOR YOUR TEAM
An Interview with Michel Rodrigue,
Vice President of Operations at the
Mental Health Commission of Canada

To demonstrate how competence can lead to greater connection with employees, I will share insights from my interview with Michel Rodrigue, former Press Secretary for the provincial Government of Ontario, President of several boutique management consulting firms, a former CIO, and now Vice President of Operations at the Mental Health Commission of Canada. Michel describes himself as a strategic and compassionate leader, someone who deftly navigates change and engages employees and motivates them to contribute their best.

Public speaking and delivering compelling presentations, and then supporting the people you lead to do the same, are important leadership challenges. Michel used public speaking as an example to demonstrate what it means to inspire your team by having them watch you excel and demonstrate a high degree of skill and competence.

Michel shared that back when he was the founder of a firm, his team of five consultants had worked very hard for months on a fairly large proposal bid. Michel brought the whole team with him when it came time to make a presentation to the members of the prospective client's management team. He said,

"I thought it was important for my employees to see me in action so that they could learn through observation. I made it clear to them that although I was the one making the pitch, I was representing the whole team." Not only did they win the contract, Michel knew from his employees' reactions that he had wowed them with his ability to deliver a winning speech.

"As a leader, you need to deliver results and 'walk the talk.' You need to bring your employees along when you are about to do something big on their behalf, like successfully and masterfully delivering a presentation to senior management. Finding ways for your team to watch you in action is a powerful way to inspire them, as they then begin to picture themselves following in your footsteps. Then, most importantly, you need to create opportunities for your employees to shine as well. Set them up to succeed by providing them with the necessary resources and support that they will need to increase their own degree of competence so that they too can masterfully and successfully deliver a presentation to senior management."

Fast forward several years, and now Michel is a vice president who heads the management team responsible for operations within his organization. Michel and his team were asked to make a presentation to the board of the Mental Health Commission of Canada. The objective of the presentation was to convince the board that Michel had the right team of employees in place to deliver the right strategies. Thanks to his public-affairs background and extensive experience, Michel could have delivered the presentation himself. However, Michel decided to take this opportunity to help three members of his team, a director and two managers, to shine. Michel recounts how he delivered the news to the members of his team that he wanted them to deliver the presentations:

"When I first announced to the participants that they were going to make the presentation instead of me, there were two of my employees in particular who were visibly nervous. One had never even been in front of the board and didn't know what it felt like to present to them. The other went infrequently. I had seen them present to the executive committee before and saw they were showing obvious signs of anxiety. Kudos to them: they took on the challenge to present to the board anyway. I saw this as an opportunity to help them grow their skill set and develop their leadership abilities."

Michel said that he finds it helpful to reassure employees when they are anxious and nervous by creating a safety net for them. Reassure them that, "In order for you to succeed, I will make great support available to you."

For example, Michel hired a renowned expert public-speaking coach to help prepare the director and managers to boost their confidence and help them excel. For several weeks leading up to the presentation, Michel interacted with them to see how they were doing with their preparation and to provide guidance. He also followed up with the coach on a regular basis to discuss where his employees needed the most support and to provide insights.

When it finally came time to deliver the presentation to the board, each of the presenters was well prepared to shine. "The board members were extremely impressed by the director and the managers and their message," Michel said. "They were also impressed that I parked my ego and didn't feel the need to interfere and do a big closing. They could see that I trusted and had confidence in them. It felt great that, thanks to the excellent presentation delivered by my team, the board had seen that we had the right people delivering the right strategies."

In addition, Michel got word that the board members had noticed that he had not intervened when board members asked his team tough questions: "I let them work it through, and they did a great job. The board saw that I had full confidence in my team. The sense of pride and intrinsic reward I felt when I watched my employees shine and be recognized for their performance far outweighed how I would have felt had I been the one making the presentation."

Michel also remarked that, "When you respect and help employees grow their own leadership, you will earn their respect and they will *want* to help you achieve your vision."

Here are additional tips that Michel shared for ways to help your employees succeed:

- Meet with them and explain the challenge.
- Set the bar high while also being encouraging and nurturing.
- Create a safety net by committing to getting them the support they need, such as hiring an external expert to coach them and help them develop the confidence and the skills they need to excel.
- Help them prepare, provide guidance, and work through the material with them.

♦ When they're writing or preparing for a presentation, make sure they craft the message using the proper tone, aimed at the right level based on the audience (e.g., when presenting to the board, you need to be more strategic than when presenting to your direct reports).

♦ Provide encouragement as well as the mentorship, support, and resources they need to develop their skills and competencies.

Michel concluded, "What you'll get in return from employees in terms of respect and commitment is off the scale."

One of the biggest take-aways from my interview with Michel was the importance of modeling competence to your employees and then equipping them to grow their own competence. He said, "If they respect you and see that you are energized, they will want to follow you." In addition, Michel reinforced the idea that great people leaders can experience a sense of accomplishment and reward by helping their employees grow their own leadership abilities and to succeed.

Boosting leadership capacity and competence supports the integration of all three connection values of compassion, courage, and competence in everyday work life—and leads to improved performance and results. Numerous studies highlight the crucial role leadership plays in boosting productivity and achieving success through highly engaged employees and well-managed processes. Here are some examples of concrete actions for living these values:

♦ *Invite managers and employees* to meetings with senior management to discuss their files, make recommendations and obtain direction.

♦ *Let go of perfectionism, increase tolerance for errors,* and recognize that making mistakes is an important part of learning and gaining confidence (if mistakes are handled as lessons learned) and boosting long-term capacity.

♦ *Place emphasis on continuing to build one's own leadership competencies* through formal and informal means and encourage managers and aspiring leaders to do the same, which will help build a leadership pipeline and support succession management (e.g., training, mentoring, one-on-one coaching, peer coaching).

♦ *Have a strong commitment to fostering inclusion and feelings of belonging* and zero tolerance for gossip and vexatious behaviors.

♦ *Properly align resources*—such as people, processes, and technology—to allow managers more time to engage with and develop their staff and build their competencies.

♦ *Be a source of motivation and inspiration for your team.* Share with them your stories of times when you experienced challenges and made mistakes and how you persevered to overcome. Let them see you in action, tap into your own talents, and shine so that they can be inspired to do their best work.

Applying the 3 C's of Connection

Kathleen (Kathie) Donovan is a coach and TV personality with over thirty years of experience in broadcasting in Canada. She is the author of *Unconformed: Harnessing the Radical Power of Courage* and *Inspiration in Action: A Woman's Guide to Happiness.* The following interview highlights how to apply values consistent with the 3 C's of Connection to be a great leader.

CONNECTING THE DOTS WITH THE 3 C'S OF CONNECTION
An Interview with Kathleen Donovan

During my interview with Kathie, she highlighted the importance of fostering kindness and authenticity, provided real-life examples of positive values in the workplace, and shared what she believes are the five most effective leadership behaviors and qualities:

♦ *Be a Visionary*—Someone who can explain ideas in a way that easily converts the team to jump on board and contribute to the end result.

- ◆ *Be Honest*—Someone who can offer excellent input and feedback or who can provide direction in a way that any team member can accept and respect.
- ◆ *Be a Good Listener*—Someone who appreciates input and is eager to learn from others.
- ◆ *Be Curious*—Someone who is constantly learning, asking questions, and taking an interest in others.
- ◆ *Be Supportive*—Someone who wants the best outcome for the greater good and understands that humans come with all sorts of interesting situations and paradigms. A supportive and compassionate leader knows when to say yes and when to say no to benefit the team member and the greater good.

When I asked Kathie what methods leaders should use to inspire people to do their very best, she said, "I believe in what Gandhi said when he expressed, 'Be the change you want to see in the world.' I tell people in my community that I, like them, am a work in progress. I love to ask questions; I love to share my stories and hear their stories of courage. I believe we learn from each other and teach each other by sharing our experiences. I love to surprise-reward people with some sort of recognition. It really is the little things that make a big difference."

Being a great leader requires a multi-pronged approach when it comes to engaging employees and building solid relationships with colleagues and clients. Once you've connected with your employees, then you need to ignite their engagement and motivate them to show up and do their best work. The next chapter outlines "The 8 P's of Ignition."

"Authenticity is a daily practice. Choosing authenticity means cultivating the courage to be emotionally honest, to set boundaries, and to allow ourselves to be vulnerable; exercising the compassion that comes from knowing that we are all made of strength and struggle and connected to each other through a loving and resilient human spirit; nurturing the connection and sense of being that can only happen when we let go of what we are supposed to be and embrace who we are."

~ Brené Brown

Chapter 20
ENGAGE WITH THE LIGHT A FIRE PRINCIPLES: "THE 8 P'S OF IGNITION"

"Everyone has been made for some particular work, and the desire for that work has been put in every heart."

~ Rumi

What sets a great leader apart is their authenticity and their ability to connect with their employees at the human level. In addition, not only are great leaders clear about their own passions, they also help employees to connect with theirs—and to link employee passions to the overall mission and mandate of the organization. They help people in the company see a shared vision for a better future for themselves, the company, their community, and the world they serve.

There are leaders who fall into this category, though when we consider the Gallup State of the Global Workforce Survey results discussed earlier in the book, we could safely say that there are too few great leaders within organizations. Instead, I would argue that too many highly talented subject-matter experts are promoted to positions of high authority solely because they are good at delivering high-quality work on time and pleasing their bosses. Just because someone is amazing at building a widget, coming up with brilliant ideas, or even preparing the most intricate analytics framework, it doesn't mean they will make a great people leader. They may even make a terrible leader who's unable to engage and inspire others and who may kill whatever passion and enjoyment employees may have had to begin with.

When the majority of workers are disengaged, there are far-reaching implications for public health, the economy, the environment, and the evolution of humankind.

How people feel about their work impacts not only their own health and productivity but that of the entire organization. This should be of concern to employers, governments, and society because when the majority of workers are disengaged, there are far-reaching implications for public health, the economy, the environment, and the evolution of humankind. So, what is the antidote to the problem of disengagement? Based on research and experience, the following principles emerge to form the basis of the Light Your Leadership© approach for igniting engagement, which features "The 8 P's of Ignition":

- Profundity
- Passion
- Purpose
- Perseverance
- Professionalism
- Play
- Philanthropy
- Prosperity

How to Integrate the 8 P's of Ignition into Daily Operations

While tapping into my network to seek suggestions for courageous, compassionate, and competent leaders to interview for this book, Karen Baker-Anderson came highly recommended.

As an executive director, Karen led a team of over thirty-five employees who are running the Inuuqatigiit, a multi-service Inuit organization that provides cultural, educational, recreational, and social support services to children, youth, and families of Ottawa's growing Inuit community. Karen is the recipient of the Children's Aid Society of Ottawa's Service Providers Award and the Success by 6 Family Friendly Workplace Award. Under her leadership, Inuuqatigiit was awarded the United Way Community Builder Award for the "Growing Up Great" category.

During my interview with Karen, I learned a little more about her approach to leadership and how she embodies the 3 C's of Connection and the 8 P's of Ignition.

CREATING A WORKPLACE THAT IS SAFE, SECURE, REFLECTIVE, AND FUN
An Interview with Karen Baker-Anderson, Past Executive Director of Inuuqatigiit

Karen's philosophy is that leadership is all about relationships and connecting with the various parties. "As a leader, I built relationships with staff, funders, community, and kids and parents," she told me. "As a leader of an agency, it is important that I establish relationships with both internal and external stakeholders, including the Inuit children in Ottawa and their families."

Characteristics of a Great leader and Advice for Aspiring Leaders

Karen identified the following characteristics of a great leader. "Great leaders are passionate about what they do and the cause or organization they represent. I wouldn't be an executive director for just any agency—I need to be passionate about it. I couldn't be a leader if I didn't care about the issues: helping kids and youth; that is why I took on this leadership role." She also said that great leaders need to be comfortable being the decision-makers and taking responsibility.

She offered advice for current and aspiring leaders: "Ask, 'What relationship will I establish this week that is meaningful?' Leaders need to remember that everybody wakes up in the morning and wants to belong; people want to be assured by their leaders that they are valued and a part of something bigger than they are: 'You are here, you are safe and secure, you belong, and we follow a set of core principles.'"

She also offered this advice on how to become a better leader:

- ◆ Meet with other leaders and learn from one another.
- ◆ Check in with employees often.
- ◆ Read constantly.
- ◆ Take downtime when you need it.

She added, "I set myself up to be successful because I am doing something that I am passionate about. Visiting and hearing from my community inspires me."

Applying the 3 C's of Connection and the 8 P's of Ignition

Karen believes that a leader needs to work at maintaining good morale and boosting engagement. The following are specific examples of actions that Karen has used to boost employee engagement. I've indicated which of the 3'Cs of Connection and the 8 P's of Ignition apply to each activity:

- ◆ Everybody wants to belong, so find ways to ensure that all employees feel included and like they are part of the team and organization. You want your employees to feel like, "I belong, and I know that I made a difference." (Connection)
- ◆ If someone is sick or experiencing challenges at home (for example, they have a sick child), give them the space they need to take care of their health or their situation. They will return to work and be grateful for it and will want to contribute their best. (Compassion)
- ◆ Demonstrate the ability to make tough decisions, coming from a place of principles and core values. Even during tough times, you need to be direct and honest. Be positive and work toward a solution. Let employees know, "I have a plan," and let them know that you will be there for them. (Courage)
- ◆ Engage employees in problem-solving. (Competence)
- ◆ Many people don't know how to be reflective and are just doers. As a leader, you can show them how to be reflective (e.g.,

reinforcing values by being reflective about why we do what we do). (Profundity)

♦ During meetings, ask employees to highlight their work rather than just focus on the statistics. You can ask, "What filled your bucket this week? What did you see this week that inspired you?" (Passion)

♦ Be a good visionary and be reflective. Employees need to understand the vision of why and where, and how it will feel like when we achieve it. Share the stories of the impact of the work we do and how the organization is making a difference. (Purpose)

♦ Do not blame. Allow people to learn from their mistakes and to try again. (Perseverance)

♦ Model and expect honesty, dignity, and respect. Treat people fairly, work hard, and expect a lot from your employees. Be honest, have honest conversations, and recognize that people need to leave if they don't fit; otherwise, they will bring the others down. (Professionalism)

♦ Have BBQs, lunches, and potlucks. Encourage employees to decorate and to celebrate birthdays, holidays, and other special occasions so that people can really get into the spirit. And if some people say they are not having fun doing a certain piece of work they must do, whenever possible, help them find ways to make it more interesting and meaningful for them. (Play)

♦ Model what it means to be a good citizen and show that the organization is socially responsible and supports important causes. (Philanthropy)

♦ Recognize and thank people when they least expect it—for instance, by sending a bouquet of flowers or giving an unexpected day off or a gift card to the spa. It is best to give this type of recognition in private so as not to put the person on the spot or make others feel left out. Encourage employees to appreciate one another. (Prosperity)

Karen really does put people first in all aspects of her work. For instance, in many instances during periods of retrenchment and emphasis on fiscal responsibility, organizations often clamp down and stop investing in training and employee recognition. Karen's response to suggestions that money for recognition or celebration should be cut back is, "People are much more important than pens and paper, and yet we still spend money on that!"

As I have seen with other great leaders, Karen understands servant leadership and doing what is right. She says, "Leadership is not about being more powerful—it's about having greater responsibility; there is no power in it. Everybody in your organization can go to bed knowing that they have a job, and the shareholder can go to bed knowing that their interests are also being looked after by the leaders and their employees."

To further assist leaders in applying Karen's advice and learning to light a fire in the hearts of employees, the following sections break down the 8 P's of Ignition.

1—PROFUNDITY

> *Profundity* is defined as "deep insight; great depth of knowledge or thought."[83] Applied to leadership, it is the ability to dig deep and figure out who you really are as a person and a leader.

This principle is based on the notion that leadership surges from the inside out. For this reason, most great people leaders I've met or studied have

---

83   "Profundity: Definition of Profundity in English by Lexico Dictionaries." *Lexico Dictionaries* | English. Accessed October 3, 2018. https://www.lexico.com/en/definition/profundity.

practiced profundity rituals such as self-reflection, meditation, journaling, spending time in nature, praying, or creating vision boards as a regular part of their success routine.

Mindfulness practices offer numerous benefits. For instance, here are just a few examples of how they can help you:

♦ Raise your self-awareness and expand your emotional intelligence to deepen your understanding of yourself and those around you.

♦ Gain greater clarity about your passions, purpose, mission, and vision.

♦ Identify what's most important for you, both personally and professionally.

♦ Identify and remove blocks that prevent you from achieving your vision.

♦ Boost your resilience and courage to step out of your comfort zone.

♦ Practice self-care to boost your physical, emotional, mental, and spiritual health.

♦ Gain deep insights and bring useful information to the top of your mind so that you can innovate and solve problems.

♦ Tap into your intuition and equip you to make more aligned decisions.

♦ Increase your focus so that you can reach your goals at home or at work.

When you take time to stop, get quiet, and reflect, you're able to access a deeper level of inner wisdom that can help you take inspired action. This is also the profound wisdom you need to access in order to connect with your employees, your colleagues, and your clients—it is what it takes to ignite employee engagement and to create better workplaces. With greater under-standing comes empathy, which in turn leads to adopting more compassionate views and behaviors. This "knowing" leads to more meaningful and sound work experiences for all.

When we stop to reflect on what truly calls us and what really moves us, sometimes the answers come to us easily and other times it's more challenging. To reach our inner truth, we often have to get through all the inner "muck":

negative programming, self-judgment, other people's expectations, and what we think we "should" be doing. The good news, however, is that there is a sea of modalities to help you gain greater clarity and raise your consciousness, ranging from traditional methods (such as praying, meditating, practicing yoga or quiet contemplation, or seeking advice from a coach, therapist, or spiritual teacher of your chosen faith) to the more esoteric (such as energy healing, going on spirit quests, and even being coached by horses).

That's right, you read it correctly—being coached by horses through Equus Coaching™ founded by Koelle Simpson, Koelle Institute of Equus Coaching. Given that this is a relatively new modality, I'll use it to illustrate the power of profundity.

Equus Coaching is a unique and highly effective Corporate and Life coaching service offered by two of my friends, renowned Ottawa motivational and leadership coaches Marlene Armstrong and Maureen Donoghue, that can help leaders raise their self-awareness and work through blocks that hold them back.

Horses are highly intuitive and deeply tuned in to their environment. It's said that they can sense our energy fields, subtle nonverbal cues, and stress levels. In fact, researchers at the Swedish University of Agricultural Sciences showed that an increase in a human's heart rate affects the heart rate of the horse they are leading or riding.[84]

Horses always react in an extremely authentic and intrinsically honest way—without judgment. Participants in Equus Coaching step into the round pen with a horse. Given how sensitive horses are to shifts in our energy field, physiology, and nonverbal cues, they have immediate visceral reactions to the participant's state of being. This is the moment the human coaches begin to ask you powerful coaching questions about your life and leadership. The horse acts as a lie-detector of sorts. The horse behaves in different ways, depending on how transparent, authentic, and open you are with the coaches and, most of all, with yourself.

If you're struggling to get clear, the horse will immediately reflect that back to you, most times by not wanting to be near you. If you're clear and confident, standing in your truth, then the horse will relax and will want to be next to

---

84   Nancy Zacks, "Horses React to Human Heart Rates, Study Finds," *The Horse*, posted July 1, 2009, https://thehorse.com/121855/horses-react-to-human-heart-rates-study-finds/.

you. Horses are looking for a leader who will keep them safe—after all, that is how they have survived on the planet as a prey animal for over 60 million years. The whole experience highlights your strengths and brings to light your growth areas as well as your overall effect on others. Your energy, body language, and tone speak volumes with the horses as they do with the people you interact with every day in your personal life and at work. Through Equus Coaching, you will become more aware of the effect you have on others and the emotions that drive it. With these profound new insights, you will be better equipped to show up as a leader at work and in your life in general.

Certified Equus Coaches Marlene and Maureen worked within corporations in both formal and informal leadership roles before launching Unbridled Coaching. In addition to coaching individuals to help them get clear, transform, and gallop forward with the life they want, they also offer services to organizations. Therefore, they are quite familiar with workplace and leadership dynamics. I asked them to share their perspective on leadership based on their experience with horses.

LEADERSHIP LESSONS FROM THE HERD
By Marlene Armstrong and Maureen Donoghue, Certified Equus Coaches at Unbridled Coaching

Leadership in the Round Pen explores the interactions between a human and a horse within the enclosure. While engaging in a variety of experiences with the horse, the person's personal awareness is heightened, leading to greater clarity about their intent, the energy they put out into their environment, their ability to communicate, and their leadership abilities.

As mentioned, the basis for Equus Coaching is that the horse, as a prey and herd animal, looks for leadership for the purpose of remaining safe. Horses have evolved with the knowledge that their safety depends on the leader having the capacity to be aware of the environment, decode that environment, and signal what action needs to take place in order to be safe. From the horse's perspective, all this information is communicated energetically.

Just as with leading people within an organization, the horse and human are having an "energetic" conversation in the round. We call this Relationship Intelligence,™ which has two pillars: Emotional Intelligence[85] and Conversational Intelligence.[86] In this model, conversations (verbal and nonverbal) create relationships, which create the culture in an organization. The development of Relationship Intelligence creates trust, which is the key driver for all highly innovative, collaborative, and accountable organizations.

Leadership in the Herd: What can leaders learn about leading by observing the herd?

In her book *The Power of the Herd*, Linda Kohanov writes brilliantly on this subject. She states that the horses trade leadership and dominance roles according to who is the calmest, clearest, most committed, or most invested in the outcome. She refers to this as a form of more consensual or situational leadership.[87]

Equus Coaching participants tend to deepen their self-awareness about how they show up as leaders at work, including what are ineffective and effective behaviors when it comes to leading horses in the round pen as well as leading people at work. Ineffective behaviors include:

♦ *Acting without clarity*—When a leader is not clear on their intention, it confuses those trying to follow them.

♦ *Lacking compassion*—A leader who gets easily frustrated is intolerant, overly critical, and likely to assign blame for errors; they put out negative energy that is sensed by those they are trying to motivate.

♦ *Controlling*—Micromanaging others and trying to force them to do things "the right way" and hovering over them will break trust and quash innovation and creativity. People and horses are likely to resist being backed into a corner.

85   Daniel Goleman, *Emotional Intelligence: Why it can matter more than IQ* (New York, NY: Bantam Books, 1995).

86   Judith E. Glaser, Conversational Intelligence: How Great Leaders Build Trust and Get Extraordinary Results (Brookline, MA: Bibliomotion, 2014).

87   Linda Kohanov, The Power of the Herd: A Nonpredatory Approach to Social Intelligence, Leadership, and Innovation (Novato, CA: New World Library, 2012).

- ◆ *Being unavailable*—When leaders are distracted, rushed, inaccessible, or not listening (to both verbal and nonverbal cues), then they aren't present to provide followers with the proper guidance they need to achieve goals.
- ◆ *Lacking courage*—When leaders lack courage and confidence in their actions, horses and people will notice and will in turn lose confidence. As a result, the followers will disengage and act based on fear.

Thanks to their interactions with horses, leaders in the round pen will raise their awareness about the way their behaviors, actions, and nonverbal cues are being perceived by others. They will also learn to tune in to and follow their intuition. With this increased knowledge, participants can be more mindful and adopt effective behaviors such as: being clear in their intention and communication, being compassionate, being more trusting when delegating (rather than micromanaging), being available and accessible for employees, and building their courage and confidence.

The participants learn that they're much more effective leaders, both in and out of the round pen, when they have clear vision and values, and when they use compassion and courage in their interactions.

The key lesson of profundity is that as a leader, it is very beneficial for you and your employees to embark on a journey of getting to know yourself, early on. Not only will this bring you greater clarity about how you want to show up as a leader, it will also help you grow your leadership abilities and your ability to connect with your employees. There are many tools available, ranging from sitting quietly to self-reflect to journaling and Equus coaching. A wise practice is to experiment until you find the tools that are right for you to gain greater clarity about your authentic self and to practice authenticity. Listen to and follow what lights you up and be courageous. Become a master at knowing what you want, have the courage to pursue that, and get the answers you need from within in order to lead others toward a shared goal.

2—PASSION

Passion is a strong feeling of enthusiasm or excitement for something or about doing something.[88] It is like a burning desire that, when tapped into properly, is like diving into a deep well filled with golden and vibrant energy that we can draw from to manifest what we want.

This principle highlights how helping people at work to tap into their passion is a powerful tool to ignite employees' engagement and to light a fire in their hearts.

In order to be happy at work and in life in general, it is essential to gain greater clarity regarding one's own passions, which enhances the ability to understand what is important to employees and motivates them to do their very best. Leaders can tap into the power of passion to transform their organizations. Skilled leaders help individuals link their passions to achieving the team's vision or the overall mission and vision of the organization.

Turning Maslow's Hierarchy on Its Head

As a psychology major in university, I was fascinated with Maslow's Hierarchy of Needs. Maslow's model has had a major impact and influence in every field, from psychology to marketing, commerce, and organizational behavior. His model purports that before a person can reach self-actualization, they first need to satisfy their basic needs, beginning with physiological needs, safety needs, belonginess and love needs, and esteem needs. I still love this model for its simplicity in explaining motivation at the basis of human behavior. Having said that, I believe that, as with any behavioral model, it needs to be adapted

---

88   "Passion." Definition for English-Language Learners from Merriam-Webster's Learner's Dictionary. Accessed December 6, 2018. http://www.learnersdictionary.com/definition/passion.

as our human consciousness continues to evolve. I conducted research to see whether there were like-minded people out there and was glad to see that others agree with the need to modernize Maslow. For instance, Nick Nielson wrote an article entitled, "Inverting Maslow's Hierarchy," which elaborates on this idea.[89] In fact, Maslow himself revisited the hierarchy. While he did not suggest turning the pyramid onto its head, he did add "aesthetic," "cognitive," and "transcendence," to his original model.

It is time we recognize that we've moved past the Industrial Age. Knowledge workers in free countries with developed economies typically have their basic needs for food, shelter, and security met. Yet members of our society continue to fixate on "job security" and live with a scarcity mindset that thrusts us into a loop of "never enough." The common fear that keeps people stuck is well expressed by energy healer and coach Cindia Carrere, who specializes in removing people's abundance blocks based on false beliefs such as: "I never have enough money or security to guarantee my basic needs. Therefore, I need to stay in this job or career I have, even if I hate it, because if I do anything to jeopardize it, my basic needs to put food on the table, have a roof over my head, and have job security, go out the window."

This mentality is tied to a broader phenomenon: when we have never gone without food and shelter, we begin to confuse our needs with our wants. This loop keeps going and gets tighter and tighter until it feels like we're running out of breath and are going to burst. Many of us are so focused on needs and wants that we're never able to climb Maslow's pyramid, toward self-actualization. Our spirit is left starving for joy and fulfilment.

Rather, we need to begin looking at Maslow's Hierarchy of Needs from a twenty-first-century perspective. As we continue to evolve human consciousness in the Passion Age, people who are committed to getting out of this loop begin to turn their attention to what is most important to them in life, beyond the basic needs. The shift that is happening is that we are beginning to pay attention to our passions and purpose earlier, as a way to meet our basic needs while finding meaning and fulfilment through our work.

Whereas older and outdated leadership models encourage employers to retain their employees by convincing them how great their pay, benefits, and culture

---

89   Nick Nielsen, "Inverting Maslow's Hierarchy," *Medium*, posted May 26, 2016, https://medium.com/@jnnielsen/inverting-maslows-hierarchy-b2c32156f091.

are—all external motivators—modern leaders understand that the most powerful retention strategy is to inspire their employees to connect with their passions. They then help their employees paint a vivid picture of how they can manifest their passions by contributing to the organization's vision, mission, and mandate.

To demonstrate how progressive Passion Age leaders can help their employees discover what's most important to them and then live these passions at work, I interviewed Beth Lefevre. Beth is a Master Trainer for the Passion Test and has collaborated with the creators of the Passion Test, *New York Times* bestsellers Janet Bray Attwood and Chris Attwood, to adapt their model to be used by leaders to tap into the passions of their employees.

WE NEED GREAT LEADERSHIP, ASAP!
An Interview with Beth Lefevre, Master Trainer
and Coach at Enlighted Alliances

The Passion Test for business is referred to as ASAP—Advanced Solutions for Activating Passionate Engagement. ASAP Engagement focuses on "work passions"—the things that matter most at work—and then drills down to determine why those things are so important to the individual.

There are major benefits to helping employees connect with their work passions. Companies that go through the ASAP process experience the following:

- ♦ Greater commitment
- ♦ Greater openness to new ideas and innovations in change management
- ♦ Increased likelihood that employees respond positively to ideas and suggestions from their co-workers
- ♦ Stronger tendency to create a friendly, more productive work environment
- ♦ Increased ability to positively affect customers

Beth and other Passion Test for Business facilitators are helping progressive leaders by taking them and their employees through a process where the company's passions and the employees' passions are mapped out and aligned to realize greater meaning and fulfillment, which has resulted in greater engagement and productivity. For instance, Listen Up Español is a $50-million-a-year call center that implemented the Passion Test for Business programs. According to CEO Craig Handley, here's what focusing on passions has done for them:

"As the company grew from a few hundred people to over a thousand people, I saw a lot of little things, negative things that have no place in the culture we wanted to create. The Passion Test for Business helped us turn things back in a positive direction.... Since its inception, the people we hire are better and more aligned, turnover has gone down, and the energy on the floor is up, which means the results have improved. I believe that the Passion Test for Business has improved our company tremendously, and it may have literally saved our company. Having the Passion Test for Business seemed to be about a $1.5-million revenue generator in our business."

As demonstrated by Beth's work with Listen Up Español, the power of passion can be harnessed to create a success culture where employees' motivation is ignited and they're ready to perform and contribute their best.

3—PURPOSE

Purpose is the reason for which something is done or created or for which something exists. It a person's sense of resolve or determination.[90]

---

90   "Purpose." Dictionary.com, accessed November 05, 2018. https://www.dictionary.com/browse/purpose.

This principle underlines that it is important for a leader to clearly articulate the "Why" of an organization as well as the "Why" behind roles and key decisions. This is crucial to engagement. People need to understand how their hard work fits in to the overall vision and with the *raison d'être* of their role, their team, and the organization. Clear roles and responsibilities, combined with a healthy sense of purpose, increases engagement, courage, and resilience. It supports innovation and aligns decision-making. It's the ingredient that calls someone to leap outside their comfort zone and have a positive impact on the lives of others. When a leader helps people connect with purpose, they can motivate them to give of their talents and find meaning while they contribute to something greater than themselves.

> *"How are you going to keep your workplace engaged, retained, active and motivated? It all comes down to what kind of meaning and purpose can you provide."*
> ~ Marc Kielburger

When I asked my Light Your Leadership Community on Facebook what "Light a Fire in Their Hearts" means to them, one response eloquently expressed the sentiment of living your life on purpose and integrating that feeling into your work:

> To me, this means that when I "show up" for work, I am doing so with passion, purpose and intent so I can be my best self to be of my best service to others. I loved what you said in your interview, that people want meaning in their work, not (just) money. So many people are searching for that meaning, and when you find it, it is pure gold! When an employer is able to connect what is meaningful for their employees, an environment of purpose and passion is ignited. And so, sets one's heart on fire. ~ Erin Crotty

I completely agree with Erin, and I also have the honor of witnessing this firsthand as a member of the Advisory Board of KLIQ.ca, a new Canadian start-up. KLIQ.ca is an exciting new platform that simplifies the life of senior high school students, their parents, guidance counselors, and youth counselors in the community. This new state-of-the-art platform is being developed by a passionate team of entrepreneurs. The founding members—Kashif Siddiqui, Hana Ameera, and Issam Elajhe—have a strong sense of purpose and a "Why." Here's a glimpse of what they had to say.

KLIQ.CA—A START-UP WITH PURPOSE
Featuring Kashif Siddiqui, Hana Ameerah, and Issam Elhaje

When I asked Kashif about the vision for KLIQ.ca, he responded, "Our vision is simple and clear—we want an educated and prosperous Canada. We want students of all ages to be able to model their educational journey to a successful career that is relevant, in demand, and fulfilling. We know how vague, confusing, and frustrating picking a program and career can be—we were once there ourselves—so we decided fix it!"

The KLIQ.ca team believes that anyone who has a dream of going to college and university to manifest a bright future should have access to accurate, up-to-date information about post-secondary institutions and potential career paths. They are so passionate about ensuring that all youth and adults be able to access this information that their big bold mission stretches beyond our borders: to help people around the globe make more informed and better-aligned decisions about their career and education.

As Issam said, "One day, you will be told it is impossible or you cannot make it! On that day, you are either going to choose your path and follow your dreams or accept the fact that you will be told what is yours. Success is not impossible. Success is what you believe."

The KLIQ.ca platform is still in its early days. Its primary focus at this stage is to help high school seniors to quickly and easily access information about post-secondary institutions, including available programs, tuition fees, and potential career paths.

Hana elaborated on the KLIQ.ca vision and her own "Why" for supporting it: "I'm a strong believer in empowering youth to have a bright future for our nation. KLIQ.ca is empowerment. KLIQ.ca gives the kids the confidence to make critical decisions at a very young age (their career and program of study). It helps them make their way to a successful life using real data with simple steps. We've been in their shoes and are determined to fix it."

Thanks to Kashif, Hana, and Issam's idea, fueled by a sense of purpose, gone will be the days when concerned parents pulled their hair out and high school seniors rolled their eyes in exasperation while spending hundreds of hours googling individual colleges and universities to narrow down their list and figure out where to apply. KLIQ.ca's vision and "Why" are so compelling that I said yes on the spot when Issam asked me to become a member of the Advisory Board and again when Kashif officially offered me the post. I look forward to supporting the organization as they continue to grow and open up a world of possibilities to youth and anyone else seeking to enroll in post-secondary education. As KLIQ.ca's motto says: there are "Many Paths. Choose Yours."

4—PERSEVERANCE

Perseverance is the continued effort to do or achieve something despite difficulties, failure, or opposition.[91]

---

91   "Perseverance," Merriam-Webster, accessed June 24, 2019, https://www.merriam-webster.com/dictionary/perseverance.

I believe that perseverance is where patience intersects with persistence. In other words, where one has the ability to wait for good things to happen or things to line up, while continuing to resolutely and stubbornly move toward their vision, goal, or objective—even in the face of obstacles.

Seen through the leadership lens, this principle recognizes that learning, creating, and succeeding can take a lot of time and many failed attempts and lessons learned before things click into place. A great leader knows how to pick people up when they fail, help them learn from and fix their mistakes, and guide them toward success. Perseverance is crucial for sustainable long-term success and is inherent when it comes to resilience. The ability to pick oneself up and bounce back in the face of adversity is a necessary part of achieving one's vision.

If I may indulge for a moment, like many authors will tell you, writing a book is an exercise in perseverance—especially if it tackles big issues and comes from the heart. This book is no exception. It has taken me five years. In those five years, I have experienced so many tests and distractions. My son faced health challenges, and several other family members—including my husband, my mother, and myself—got pneumonia. Because my mother's case was so severe, my sister and I devoted most of 2018 to nursing her back to health. (I'm happy to report that Mamma is back on track!) My aunt, our beloved Zia Zinute, who was like a second mom, passed away, along with two other relatives, all in the first three days of 2019. On top of the health issues, we had a flood and lived in our basement for a month and had construction workers in our home for over four months. Our sweet dog and fur-baby, Shadow, was covered in itchy patches called hotspots—we were so sad to watch him suffer and lose most of his fur. Thankfully, after two years, the vet finally figured out what Shadow needed.

With all the curveballs thrown our way, we experienced serious financial challenges and our future success seemed very uncertain. And this is just scraping the surface. All these things happened while I was building my skills and building a business, meeting high levels of client demand, and working on completing some of the most challenging consulting work I've ever done.

The long and short of it is that if I hadn't had such a strong and clear sense of purpose, an inherent stubbornness that kept me going, an irrationally optimistic outlook, and amazing friends, family, clients, healers, and coaches surrounding me—as well as a deep sense of trust—I would have given up on this book a long, long time ago. Above all else, this project required that I continue to call on a strong faith and my perseverance.

As a leader, you can count on the fact that you and your team and organization will face any number of challenges, at both the personal and professional levels. Perseverance represents the strength and courage leaders need to cultivate in others in order to persist through thick and thin to achieve any vision and goal.

Over the last decade, there has been a great deal of talk about the importance of "grit" to achieve success. Angela Lee Duckworth, the renowned psychologist and author of *Grit: The Power of Passion and Perseverance*, developed the Grit Scale, a five-point scale that measures perseverance and consistency of interests. Research conducted by Jesus Alfonso Datu, Jana Valdez, and Ronnel King tested the Grit Theory within collectivist societies such as the Philippines and found that perseverance was the strongest predictor of success.[92]

Perseverance as a Superpower

At an event that took place on December 5, 2014, I shared the stage with Doug Smith, a former NHL player whose story personifies the phoenix rising from the ashes.

"I was told I would be paralyzed for life. Now I teach others that life is not about trying to be the best in the world but trying to be the best for the world." ~ Doug Smith

The following recounts part of his inspiring journey and his message of perseverance. Doug is an amazing example of how perseverance is a superpower that can be called upon to get through life's most difficult and dire circumstances.

---

92   Jesus Alfonso D. Datu, Jana Patricia M. Valdez, B. King Ronnel, "Perseverance Counts but Consistency Does Not! Validating the Short Grit Scale in a Collectivist Setting," *Current Psychology* 35, no. 1 (March 2016): 121-130.

THE MAN WHO PERSEVERED
AND BEAT THE ODDS
Featuring Doug Smith, Trauma Expert,
NHL Star, Author, Presenter, Lecturer

Doug was drafted second overall into the NHL, at the age of eighteen years and two weeks old. He became the youngest player to ever play for the Kings at the time. In professional game 607, at the age of twenty-nine, his professional sports career ended instantly when he went headfirst into the boards and shattered his spine.

Just one week after the birth of his second daughter, Jamie, Doug found himself paralyzed from the chest down. Doctors told him that he would never walk again. He became suicidal. Doug credits his wife Patti for saving his life and getting him back onto his feet and walking again. Working as a team against all odds, Doug and Patti persevered, and Doug was able to manage the trauma and learn to walk again.

Today, Doug Smith is a published author who wants others to get better. He teaches people about the effects of trauma and how to better manage emotional trauma. Not only can he do this at the individual level but also at the organizational level. When you use a system to manage the mental aspect of life, you build in security and predictability.

"I was told I would be paralyzed for life. Now I teach others that life is not about trying to be the best in the world but trying to be the best for the world."

In his book The Trauma Code, Doug teaches the reader how to cultivate a higher level of awareness of the value of change. He does this by making you aware of the only four types of trauma, the three priorities of our subconscious (which controls you), and the eight behaviors that feed the three priorities. (See www.dougsmithperformance.com for a video and for the four types of trauma and the three priorities of our subconscious).

The following eight behaviors effectively feed the three priorities of our subconscious brain easing the management of emotional trauma. With the "438" process (i.e., 4 types of emotional trauma, 3 priorities of our subconscious brain, and 8 behaviors to effectively address them), Doug teaches a system that is anchored in neuroscientific research and mainstream medicine.

1. *Awareness*—Reduce the pain of change. (Feedback is the lubricant for awareness.)
2. *Purpose*—Be the best *for* the world, not the best *in* the world. Why are you here?
3. *Motivation*—Raise your risk tolerance.
4. *Focus*—Reduce your risk.
5. *Belief in Self*—You become what you are around.
6. *Trust*—Rapidly internalize other people's belief in you.
7. *Asking for Help*—Work better with other people.
8. *Emotional Control*—Stop yourself from hurting other people.

In conclusion, Doug has documented a simple, manageable process to continuously improve mental performance in individuals, teams and organizations. Doug has used "System 438" in his life to better manage emotional trauma and continuously improve mental and physical performance. This is a path anyone can explore.

Doug Smith not only inspires with his ability to persevere and to overcome incredible personal mental and physical challenges, he also shares important steps to help leaders and employees overcome trauma experienced at work. When I think of perseverance, I think of Doug Smith.[93]

---

93   "Break Through Adversity to Reach Your Goal," Doug Smith Performance, accessed June 24, 2019, http://www.dougsmithperformance.com/

5—PROFESSIONALISM

Professionalism is the conduct, aims, or qualities that characterize or mark a profession or a professional person.[94] *This conduct is characterized by how we conform to the technical or ethical standards of a profession, follow appropriate etiquette, and exhibit courteous, conscientious, and businesslike behavior in the workplace.*[95]

The principle of professionalism involves integrity, respect, professional presence, and continual learning to grow one's competencies. It is essential for boosting credibility, having influence, and creating respectful, civil, and inclusive workplaces.

Enhancing your professionalism as a leader will result in enhanced communications and more trusting relationships with clients, colleagues, and senior management. It is tied to upholding ethics and integrity. It is about investing time, effort, energy, and resources to grow both your technical abilities and your competencies.

THE POWER OF PROFESSIONAL PRESENCE
By Erin Crotty, Founder and Director, BloomStra Consulting

Anyone who aspires to a position of leadership within the workplace needs to understand the power of professional presence. Professional presence is a necessary life, business, and leadership skill. It broadcasts who you are and determines how you are seen, heard, and respected by others. It consists of both an inner mindset and the outer skills needed to create an authentic, confident, and consistent self-pre-

---

94   "Professionalism," Merriam-Webster, accessed June 24, 2019, https://www.merriam-webster.com/dictionary/professionalism.

95   "Professional," Merriam-Webster, accessed June 24, 2019, https://www.merriam-webster.com/dictionary/professional.

sentation. It is a dynamic combination of leadership qualities, communication, and engagement that impacts your ability to inspire, influence, and connect with others.

Professional presence is a significant differentiator within the highly competitive business arena because it affects one's promotability in the workplace, effectiveness with colleagues, and relationships with clients and stakeholders, as well as the perception of others. You cannot simply tell people you're a leader and expect them to treat you as one. You must show people your leadership in a way that motivates them to follow you, believe in you, and, most important, place their trust in you.

Those who possess a strong professional presence are highly aware of their impact upon others, create alignment between their intentions and how they want to be perceived by others, stand true to their core values with grace in all situations, and project a demeanor that exudes positivity, civility, decorum, and respect in any business or social situation.

The true power of professional presence is that it enables you to leverage your greatest potential as a leader, form deep connections with others that foster trust, and drive business, loyalty, and career success.

Top Six Tips to Enhance Your Professional Presence

1. *Manage your image.* Communication experts believe that 55% of the total message presented by a person during a first meeting consists of their personal appearance. How we dress does have an impact on people's perception of us. People respond to and give more respect to those who are dressed appropriately and professionally within the business arena.

2. *Be aware of your posture and facial expressions.* Good posture instantly creates an impression of confidence. In addition, the best way to make others comfortable and at ease when you meet them is by giving them a genuine smile. It helps create a friendly environment which encourages conversation.

3. *Master your handshake and introduce yourself to others.* A handshake is the ultimate business greeting and the physical connection that goes with our words. Make sure you have a firm-but-friendly handshake. A firm handshake is a sign of confidence, credibility,

and professionalism. Shake hands when you introduce yourself to another person. Never wait to be introduced. Take the initiative. It is how you make your presence known and demonstrate to others that you are engaging, personable, and caring.

4. *Make direct eye contact.* Direct eye contact is very important in the business arena because it tells the other person that you are listening to them, and it actually makes you a better listener. In addition, it makes the person with whom you are speaking feel that they are important, valued, and heard.

5. *Let your people skills shine through.* Let the other person be the center of attention. Ask them questions about themselves. By doing so, you will demonstrate that you are interested in others and what they have to say. Once the conversation has finished, they will leave thinking that you were a very attentive, gracious, and good conversationalist. Never end a conversation without saying "thank you" or "it was a pleasure to meet you." Ending a conversation graciously and professionally with another person will leave a positive impression.

6. *Follow up.* Honor any promises that you have made to another person during a conversation, such as connecting with them for coffee to learn more about their business or promising to send a great article via email. If someone has taken you out for a business lunch or provided a random act of kindness, send them a thank-you email along with a handwritten thank-you card. By doing so, you will enhance your credibility and create an opportunity to continue building upon that professional relationship.

Professionalism, integrity, and mutual trust are keys to establishing and maintaining strategic partnerships. Professionalism in leadership requires core competencies such as strategic thinking and good management practices, written and oral communications, relationship building, project management, business acumen, and the ability to lead and influence at all levels. Professionalism also demands that people behave their best and be held accountable if they gossip or behave in ways that are not aligned with the values of the organization.

If you are the head of the organization, you need to respect your employees by ensuring that policies and regulations are written in a respectful manner—a topic elaborated on in the following piece by policy expert, Lewis Eisen, whom we met in an earlier chapter.

TREAT YOUR EMPLOYEES LIKE ADULTS IN EVERYTHING YOU DO—EVEN IN THE WAY YOU WRITE CORPORATE POLICIES
By Lewis Eisen

As leaders, we know we need to make rules and set boundaries. When we put them on paper, we might label them "policies" or "directives." Too often we take so much care about what we're saying that we forget to look at how we are saying it. We tend to be oblivious to how our policies and dictates sound to our employees.

Some years ago, I headed one of the corporate services teams in a large government department. Management was continually frustrated with the low level of compliance with some of the policies. The rules were all written down, but no one appeared to be following them.

So, management went back and redrafted the policies, buffing up the language to make them sound scarier and more official. They inserted tougher wording, like "Employees must always…" and "Employees should never…" Then they added lots of boldface, italics, underline, and capital letters to make sure everyone OBEYED THE RULES!!!!!

Of course, the harsher wording in the policies did nothing to increase compliance. If anything, it caused more friction between management and staff.

Policies and compliance are supposed to be a cooperative effort, not a power struggle. When rules sound like they were written by angry parents scolding naughty children, they send a subtle but clearly perceptible message to people that management prefers to exercise control with sticks rather than carrots.

A jobseeker named Karen once told me that whenever she's a candidate for a job, she first asks to see the corporate policies. She wants to know how management at that organization speaks to its employees. If she finds the language lacking respect, she moves on.

Good employees are hard to find. Someone who cares enough about her employment situation to do her due diligence around the prospective corporation is exactly the kind of employee you want. But you will lose Karen by not paying attention to this issue. Moreover, you will lose her without ever knowing why.

All your communications with employees must be written in a respectful manner, not just the email messages and memos you send to individuals. Your policies and other rules documents deliver the same kind of messaging in their undertones, conveying your respect for the people they are intended to govern—or the lack of it.

One of the key messages from this piece is that all interactions and communications with employees need to be professional and respectful. In this example, Lewis discusses the need to write respectful policies. In addition, as a leader, you need to ensure that any written or verbal communications follow the same principle, including memos, emails, performance evaluations, speeches, and interactions during meetings.

6—PLAY

A common definition of play is to "engage in activity for enjoyment and recreation rather than a serious or practical purpose; engage in a game or activity for enjoyment; performance,"[96] and synonyms include to take part in, participate in, be involved in, compete in, do. It also includes to amuse oneself by engaging in imaginative pretense.[97]

The word "play" has a long list of definitions—some positive, as they are linked to enjoyment, and others negative, as we saw earlier while discussing "Playing the Game." But when we talk about the principle of play at work, it means engaging in work we love and enjoy to the point where it feels like fun and recreation rather than work.

Pauline Fleming, the master coach who trained me to become a Certified ProActive Coach, taught me a great deal about the importance of play at work. She linked it to a number of positive leadership behaviors, such as innovating, practicing self-care, and creating energy at work through leaders finding ways to make work more fun. Before that training, Laurin Kyle (one of my sister's high school friends and the person who introduced me to the Passion Test) built a consulting and training company focused on improving morale and performance through corporate play. Both of these women were ahead of their times, as now play has become a central theme for many start-up and tech companies, such as Facebook, Google, and Shopify. However, more traditional workplaces seem to struggle with the concept and in some cases lag far behind.

Don't be the leader in the workplace that fun forgot and employees can't wait to leave because they loathe their work. For instance, look around your

---

96   "Play," Lexico, accessed June 24, 2019, https://www.lexico.com/en/definition/play.
97   "Play," *Gale Encyclopedia of Children's Health: Infancy Through Adolescence*, 2019, accessed November 15, 2019. https://www.encyclopedia.com/literature-and-arts/performing-arts/theater/play.

office—listen to people's conversations and observe their nonverbal messages. Realize that, as the leader, you set the tone. For example, are you one of those leaders with a calendar on their desk, counting down to their last day of work? I remember one client happily declaring, "I have only five thousand days left before I retire!" Really?! Do you know how hard it is for the new people who join the team to get excited about work when their boss and more tenured colleagues are counting down to retirement?

Similarly, it's difficult to feel passionate about going to work on a Monday when all you have to look forward to is entering a sea of long faces gripping their coffee mugs with both hands, greeting you with blank stares. It's virtually impossible to feel fire in your belly when your favorite director got burned out and is on sick leave due to impossible demands from senior management, when there is little appreciation from your team members for working long hours within a toxic environment that lacks compassion, courage, and passion.

A great leader is skilled at turning those frowns upside down by creating healthy, professional, and inclusive fun at work so that people feel like they're playing while they're working and producing excellent results. In her Huffington Post article "Great Work Cultures," Michelle Burke quotes Dr. Stuart Brown, the author of Play and the founder of the National Institute for Play: "When employees have the opportunity to play, they actually increase their productivity, engagement and morale." [98] Dr. Brown goes on to say, "Not only does having a playful atmosphere attract young talent, but experts say play at work can boost creativity and productivity in people of all ages. There is good evidence that if you allow employees to engage in something they want to do…there are better outcomes in terms of productivity and motivation." Given the evidence in favor of play, Burke wonders why all companies aren't insisting on more playtime at work.

Other research shows that bringing play into work can decrease absenteeism, stress, and healthcare costs. When employees take time out to play, it lessens the stress of work, which leads to less sickness, a more positive attitude, and a more energized work environment."[99]

---

98   "The Power of Play at Work," HuffPost, updated December 6, 2017, https://www.HuffPost.com/entry/the-power-of-play-at-work_b_12011462.

99   Great Work Cultures. "The Power of Play at Work." HuffPost, December 07, 2017. Accessed May 05, 2018. https://www.HuffPost.com/entry/the-power-of-play-at-work_b_12011462?guccounter=1.

This is the basis of integrating play into the work environment: employees learning to integrate fun into everyday work activities, recognize and appreciate one another, and celebrate achievements and milestones together. Appropriate levels of fun breaks the tension and fosters positive collegiality among employees and levels the playing field. Appropriate use of fun and play at work can help boost morale and resilience during challenging times, and it can take engagement to the next level during good times. Leaders can use play to help put employees at greater ease and bring humanity and greater authenticity to the team.

People let down their guard and are more themselves when presented with the opportunity to share in some fun at work. It's like the glue that can bring people from diverse backgrounds together in a fun and friendly manner. It's also an excellent backdrop for learning. People retain better when learning activities are fun rather than boring and pedantic.

At the end of the day, playing is fun, and my mantra is that "Fun is fuel!" Having fun at work creates the energy that employees need to accomplish their work effectively and efficiently while remaining healthy and energized.

A great leader is constantly coming up with new ways to make day-to-day work more interesting and meaningful and to take the pressure off wherever possible—and encourages employees to do the same. This makes coming into work more fun.

For example, for anyone working in an office with a regular work Monday–Friday workweek, Sunday evenings and Monday mornings can feel downright dreadful. I know that when I was having a particularly rough time with overwhelm in my late twenties and early thirties, on Sunday nights I would sometimes curl up in the fetal position on the floor and "ugly cry." I'm pretty sure I'm not alone.

As a leader, think of ways to help your employees look forward to coming in to work. On my Light Your Leadership Community, I have a feature where I post about "Magnificent Manic Mondays." One time I posted, "What is one action you can take to make your Monday at work a little easier and healthier for yourself and for others?" Andrea Dubin, my niece who's a Senior HR Business Partner at a Crown Corporation (I'm a very proud auntie), had an excellent suggestion to help make the members of her team settle in to the workweek and make Mondays more fun: "I send my team a meeting invite to block our calendars on Monday mornings so that we can spend time prepping for the week ahead instead of in meetings. It helps to start the week off on the right foot."

That is such a simple idea that I am certain her employees appreciate a great deal.

Believe it or not, measuring results can create a sense of friendly and fun competition, provided it is done masterfully, with good intent, without blame, and while fostering a fun environment. It can be like playing a game of baseball with a group of people who value good sportsmanship, such as at a family reunion where there's competition, but everyone cares for one another and wants to help one another's skills improve; there's lots of high fiving and a little tasteful taunting that strikes the right balance, is light and inclusive, and doesn't get too personal.

MAKING WORK FUN HELPS TO GET THINGS DONE!
The Story of Mary McDonnell, a Master Motivator

In the 1960s, Mary McDonnell* was raising five children in a remote village in eastern Canada that had running water only in the warmer months. When the water froze each winter, the people in the village had to travel to a larger town or melt snow in order to have water for drinking, bathing, and cooking. Being a busy mother and not wanting to make the trip into town over the treacherous winter roads, Mary decided to melt the snow—plus she didn't see the logic of purchasing water when they had fresh, clean snow piled up all around them.

Mary would send her kids to fetch the best snow, which was down by the creek. However, the kids weren't too fond of this chore and would push back from time to time. One day, Mary decided that she would try to find ways to make fetching the water fun. So rather than have the children look at it as a chore, she decided to turn it into a fun game. She got the toboggans out and turned it into a race! This way the children didn't complain; in fact, they were having tons of fun, so there was always plenty of water to last them the whole winter.

When the neighbors saw what was happening, the other moms joined in the fun. Before long, all the other children in the neighborhood were racing to fetch snow down by the creek to see if they could do it faster than the McDonnell kids.

Mary's eldest, Elizabeth,* fondly remembers how Mary and the other mothers in the neighborhood had tapped into the spirit of play to motivate their kids to do work while they had a great deal of fun. Now all grown up and an executive leader, Elizabeth looks for every opportunity to make assignments fun and interesting for members of her passionate team of hard workers—to ignite passion and engagement. And the results have been every bit as good as they'd been during her childhood toboggan races: the engagement levels for her team have gone through the roof!

Another way to make work fun is to model how to host and participate in well-run meetings. The truth is that the vast majority of employees really can't stand boring and useless meetings. A simple tip is to avoid having meetings just for the sake of meeting. When you do have a meeting be sure that you have an agenda and that you train your employees on how to give status reports. Facilitate the meeting so that it is a conversation rather than just a monologue by you, the leader, and a handful of vocal members. Ask questions and allow others to answer. Listen. Have ground rules to ensure that everyone behaves respectfully. And most of all, inject a little fun and don't make it super serious. Ask people to talk about what interests them and what lights them up. Learn and use structured brainstorming exercises so that the meeting is meaningful and everyone has a voice.

In addition, when assigning work, try to find out what everyone likes to do, then give them more of that. Use the 80/20 rule or even go as far as 90/10—90% of the work you assign a person is something they enjoy and 10% is the stuff that has to be done but drains energy. Make sure your team is balanced. Fortunately, different people enjoy different tasks and activities. One employee might be a blue-sky thinker and loves to do strategies, whereas another might prefer to delve into the details. To the extent possible, assign work according to preferences, and it will increase the chances that your team members will rise to the occasion and get the work done.

The first order of business for me was to get to know each of the members better: what were their talents, passions, and interests? Then, I assigned tasks accordingly.

For example, when I was leading a team to develop a corporate accommodation policy for people with disabilities, I mobilized a cross-functional team of dedicated representatives from across the organization. The first order of business for me was to get to know each of the members better: what were their talents, passions, and interests? Then, I assigned tasks accordingly. For instance, I knew that one team member had a particular interest in conducting best-practices research, so I took her with me to meet with the VPHR at the national headquarters of large banks on Bay Street in Toronto. Another enjoyed conducting research on the internet, and a third liked to conduct interviews. All the team members were highly engaged and produced high quality work on time, and together we drafted a solid business case. To leverage the excitement and momentum, I made sure that after taking a few minutes to open meetings, I asked each team member to debrief on the work that they were most excited about. The energy during meetings remained high, and people showed up for meetings and took ownership. We had fun working together and established very positive relationships.

7—PHILANTHROPY

> *Philanthropy is the desire to promote the welfare of others, expressed especially by the generous donation of money to good causes.*[100] *At its root is the Latin via Greek word for "human-loving."*

Nurturing a spirit of philanthropy will bring out the best in people. It will help them tap into kindness and compassion and create an atmosphere where everyone feels like they belong and are supported.

Companies that practice corporate social responsibility by supporting important causes or charities, reap the benefits as employees tap into intrinsic *feel good* emotions that emerge when we do something good for another.

---

100 "Philanthropy," Lexico, accessed June 24, 2019, https://www.lexico.com/en/definition/philanthropy.

Once people experience this, they are more likely to extend this love, kindness and compassion towards one another in the workplace. Thus, positive feelings associated with philanthropy go a long way toward boosting employee morale and engagement. For instance, volunteering can help employees to experiment, build new skills, and grow their leadership abilities. It strengthens community and collaboration among all members, regardless of role or position in the hierarchy. It also fosters a sense of social responsibility and of giving back and can even counteract feelings of anxiety, anger, and stress.

According to Stephanie Watson, Executive Editor of *Harvard Women's Health Watch*:

> Studies have shown that volunteering helps people who donate their time feel more socially connected, thus warding off loneliness and depression. Volunteering has positive implications that go beyond mental health. A growing body of evidence suggests that people who give their time to others might also be rewarded with better physical health—including lower blood pressure and a longer lifespan… The Greek philosopher Aristotle once surmised that the essence of life is "To serve others and do good." If recent research is any indication, serving others might also be the essence of good health.[101]

This sentiment is echoed in the National Philanthropic Trust article "Giving is Good for Your Health," which reports on an Americans Changing Lives [ACL] study on volunteerism:

> ACL is the first—but certainly not the only—study to determine that volunteerism and giving is good for your physical and mental health. Making charitable donations triggers the brain's reward center, the same way food and sex do; researchers call it a "helper's high." Some findings from ACL and other studies found that volunteers experience:

---

101   Stephanie Watson, "Volunteering May Be Good for Body and Mind," *Harvard Health Publishing,* Harvard Medical School, posted June 26, 2013, https://www.health.harvard.edu/blog/volunteering-may-be-good-for-body-and-mind-201306266428.

- ♦ lower rates of depression (University of Texas)
- ♦ lower blood pressure (University of Michigan)
- ♦ lower rates of heart disease (Corporation for National and Community Service)
- ♦ longer lifespan (UC-Berkeley)[102]

When it comes to igniting employee engagement, practicing philanthropy represents a true force for good. If as a leader you can tap into it, it can become a source of strength, purpose, and meaning for your employees that will not only help those in need but also bring out the very best in your team members. The intrinsic reward of giving and helping others is said to be born out of a strong evolutionary impulse for the continuation of our species. Beyond that, philanthropy feels good and creates positive feelings. It brings people together and counteracts feelings of separation. Leaders who rally their troops to get behind a cause are both making a positive impact and enhancing team dynamics through closer bonds.

When as a leader, you're able to create workplace initiatives that help employees and colleagues open their hearts through philanthropy, you're helping them flex their compassion muscle and connect with their truth.

When as a leader, you're able to create workplace initiatives that help employees and colleagues open their hearts through philanthropy, you're helping them flex their compassion muscle and connect with their truth. For example, rather than host random team-building exercises that have a very short-term effect, get the team involved in an activity that helps a worthy cause. Involve them in selecting which causes have meaning for them, and have your employees take turns organizing activities that support these causes. In addition to team building, your team/company can do outreach,

---

102 "Understanding Social Inequalities in Health and Aging," *Americans' Changing Lives*, accessed June 24, 2019, https://acl.isr.umich.edu/; and *National Philanthropic Trust*, "Giving is Good for Your Health," posted September 16, 2013, https://www.nptrust.org/philanthropic-resources/philanthropist/giving-is-good-for-your-health/.

institute volunteer days, or organize and host community events or fundraisers. Be sure to communicate the positive impact of your employees' actions on the lives of others and watch their hearts swell and their sense of purpose go through the roof.

One philanthropist who has lit a fire in my heart and the hearts of people from around the world is Peter Beckenham. Peter, who calls himself the Thai Village Coach, is a true champion of authentic marketing. At seventy-four years young, he broadcasts his Facebook Lives to inspire people around the world almost every day. (At the last count, he had made over 500 Facebook live videos, not counting his webcasts and podcasts.) He has a very generous heart and shares his wisdom willingly.

Peter is my marketing coach and a valued mentor. After we'd had a couple of coaching calls, he shared with me that he was donating my coaching fees to help fund a school playground for the children in his village. I was so touched by this that I was moved to tears. Given my desire to one day launch a Better Workplace Foundation to boost leadership and make workplaces better all around the world, it was such a pleasant and meaningful surprise to realize that I was being coached by a real-life philanthropist.

Peter moved from Australia to Thailand because he had found love in a wonderful woman, Amnuai. While in Australia, Peter left his job as a school principal to become a life-insurance salesman. While recounting the story, Peter chuckles that when he first got into sales, he didn't know the first thing about life insurance. What he was really good at was sales—specifically, the type of sales that's authentic and grounded in core beliefs that put clients' needs above all else. Instead of trying to learn everything himself, Peter with his natural leadership abilities, engaged two students to work with him and asked them to learn about all the ins and outs of the products and the forms they would need to complete the transactions. Then Peter would be able to focus on clarifying the clients' true needs so that his two interns could find the best product to meet the clients' requirements. Peter brought the interns to all his meetings, and together they built a very successful business. By observing Peter, his interns learned how to connect with clients. The inspiration didn't end there. Being a philanthropist at heart, Peter made it part of his mission to help communities of Aborigines in Australia by donating part of the proceeds from his team's sales. This ignited even more passion and purpose in the hearts of the two interns and the clients as well. It gave more meaning to their work and to the business transactions, knowing that every time they made a sale, money would be put to good use to accomplish something greater.

Thanks to love, Peter brought his big heart to Thailand and met his match in Amnuai. Together they grew a beautiful family (his sweet granddaughter makes frequent cameos on his Facebook Lives). They also launched a silk-making business to create employment for the people in their small Thai village, which made a very a positive impact in their community. Further, with a background as a principal, Peter understood the importance of education. When he saw that he could improve the lives of the children of the village by supporting their education, Peter got to work on his soul mission. His desire to make a positive difference for the children is so strong that it's tangible. Here is Peter's beautiful story about philanthropy written in his own words.

A FEW PENNIES OF KINDNESS
By Peter Beckenham[103]

I live in a remote Thai village and have a passion for teaching others about ethical sales practices, so it was a simple progression to end up with the taglines "The Village Marketer" and "The Village Coach."

And one of the wonderful aspects of providing online coaching services is the opportunity to connect with people from all around the world. Despite our Thai village power and internet connections being something of a lottery as far as reliability is concerned, my coaching clients have not just accepted but also embraced these limitations with their support of my programs.

Our little village, in far northeastern Thailand, has an average family income of less than $80 per month. Many children leave school in their early teens to work on the family rice farm because they can't afford the modest

---

103   Learn more about Peter Beckenham at https://peterbeckenham.com/.

school fees or expenses involved. People here are very proud but financially very poor.

So, it became my coaching mission—my "Why"—to help educate the children of my village, and I share this with all my online connections. What makes me really happy is the way many of my coaching clients have shown a real interest and desire to also help with my mission. They know my coaching fees go to this cause but for many, they want to go the extra step and contribute to the village and our school-development plans.

The philanthropic nature of many of the people I have connected with online has been one of the real reasons for my coaching enjoyment and success. There is no doubt my mission was one of the factors in their decision to join my coaching programs. In fact, I have even received requests from folks who could not afford my coaching but believed in my mission and just wanted to help.

Just a few dollars can go such a long way in my village, and the village people are constantly talking about the kind and generous support they receive from people and countries they have never heard of before. And the kindness of people goes a long way to ensuring all the kids in this village get the chance to at least finish high school and improve their chances of employment, away from the traditional, debt-burdened life of rice farming. This help also restores my belief in the innate goodness of people.

To understand and appreciate the importance of this philanthropic nature of people, one only has to see the proud looks on the parents' faces when their children excitedly go off to school in new uniforms and backpacks.

This is priceless.

Tapping into the power of philanthropy together as a team will help you, your employees, and your clients get in touch with a deeper part of themselves and with a greater purpose that goes beyond and is more powerful than any company mission. They will feel the many valuable intrinsic rewards that accompany altruism, giving of oneself, and helping others. Once your team members get a taste of that, they'll want to access those feelings and bring the good vibes back to the workplace with them. They'll tap into a love that will stay with them and let the kindness flow into all aspects of their lives, including at work. You can help them make the link that the good feelings we get when we help others through charity can be accessed at work by being kind and compassionate toward one another at work.

Incorporate philanthropy and social responsibility as a core business value, hire people with philanthropic hearts, and then watch your people light up and the positive team dynamics soar to new heights.

8—PROSPERITY

> *Prosperity is defined as the condition of being successful or thriving, especially economic well-being.[104] The word has its roots from the Latin word "prosperous," which means "favorable" and "fortunate."*

As a great leader, prosperity is about you and your employees reaping the rewards of success that result from excellent work, management, decisions, investments, and leadership that connects at the human level to ignite passion and engagement. These rewards are both intrinsic and extrinsic and come in all shapes and sizes. They may include financial compensation and benefits for meeting and exceeding goals, the mighty "high" we experience for work well done, or the joy we feel as we serve our clients and our community—especially when we get to see how our labor and gifts help others and make the world a better place.

---

104   "Prosperity," Merriam-Webster, accessed June 24, 2019, https://www.merriam-webster.com/dictionary/prosperity.

This expanded view of prosperity is nicely summarized by Daniel Truran in an article featured in the website for the *Escuela de organizacion industrial*

> Most workplaces today operate with a driven-by-objectives mentality that misses a much stronger driver of motivation, of innovation and of success which is to become a purpose-driven organization. A growing number of companies, new purpose-driven companies, show us the growing influence of these organizations that we can learn from, companies that use innovation to create purpose and a wider sense of prosperity, [from] Second Muse to Ben & Jerry's, from Warby Parker to Patagonia.
>
> These new companies often enjoy a culture of freedom of thought where open conversations are encouraged, a sense of service where individuals support each other [and everyone helps] others to succeed.[105]

This circles back to the notion that, in addition to money, the modern worker is looking for meaning. In fact, I have had clients that when faced with the choice of staying in a higher-paying job they didn't like because it lacked meaning versus a job that offered less pay but more meaning, they chose the latter. This is very good news for the future of humanity, given that increasing numbers of people will hopefully continue to gravitate toward work that makes a positive impact on their clients and their communities and makes the world a better place.

The ideal situation is when great leaders leverage the desire to make a difference into creating prosperity for their organization, its employees, and the people they serve—a win-win-win situation. Organizations and social entrepreneurships that espouse "The 3 P's of Sustainability" and "The Triple Bottom Line: People, Planet, and Profit" (described earlier in this book) are well on their way to realizing that creating prosperity can be about much more than greed; it can be about helping people and saving the planet. Lead-

---

105 "What Innovation Creates Prosperity-Fostering Organization?" *EOI*, posted August 31, 2015, https://www.eoi.es/blogs/meaningfulinnovation/2015/08/31/what-innovation-creates-prosperity-fostering-organization/.

ers can help employees understand that it is a positive quality to seek prosperity when it's backed by the intent and actions to do good within your teams and organization, your community, to help people and other living beings around the globe.

Great leaders willingly share prosperity with employees so that they can take ownership, feel valued, and feel like an integral part of the team.

The following account is a demonstration of how being kind with your employees and your community and providing the best customer service can help your organization succeed. In other words, it is living proof that putting people first truly does pay off and bring prosperity.

PUTTING PEOPLE FIRST PAYS OFF AND BRINGS PROSPERITY
A Daughter's Story About Her Inspiring Father, John Albana Bursey
An Account by Nadine Bursey

In the 1970s and '80s, John Albana Bursey was inspired by W.K. Kellogg's approach to leadership, "Help people help themselves," and adopted these strategies for leading people to be successful in business.

John came from a small village on a fishing island of 1200 people called La Basse Côte Nord (St. Augustin River) on the banks of the Gulf of the Fleuve Saint Laurent—an isolated spot that's only accessible by boat or by plane. Nonetheless, by following his passion for the people working with him and the communities they served, he became an extremely successful entrepreneur at just forty-four years of age.

There were sixteen little islands in the area, all of them settled by fisherman. John owned the main general store in St. Augustin River, where he and his team went above and beyond the call of duty to provide services to the fishermen. For example, if a fisherman called him at two o'clock in the morning and said, "John, we need more fishing supplies," he would jump out of bed and go down and open the store to ensure they could get what they needed.

John was also an extremely good listener for employees. Everyone loved working for him or being his client because he made people feel very important—and everyone truly was very important to him, no matter what their role was. He would say, "Without your employees or your clients, there is no business." While running a business, John treated all those he encountered with the same degree of kindness.

His greatest passions were his customers and his employees. Throughout his entire career, he always surrounded himself with very intelligent people, and he treated his employees like gold—that was the secret to his success. He would share the resulting prosperity with them. For example, in times of community hardships or family emergencies, he would provide them with the leave time they needed and offer free groceries and sundry items from the store to those in need. He considered his employees to be part of his family, and in return, they contributed their best to making the store a success.

John's great leadership was also apparent in how he and his team served the community. For instance, there was an Indigenous community called Les Montagnais just across the river from John's store. Not only did John serve them, as his daughter explains, "My father would allow them to carry a line of credit in his store and would deliver the groceries to them by boat. My dad treated them like any other customers, regardless of the distance." John believed that customer service is a critical part of helping people in need who otherwise would have no access to the supplies required to live. Regardless of the situation, his philosophy was that you cannot turn away from people in need, and you need to do all in your power to improve their situation and affect positive change. John knew that this builds lifelong customer relationships—the support you give them translates into customer loyalty.

In the 1980s, as Nadine puts it, although her dad's store was in the "middle of nowhere," by creating prosperity for his employees and for clients, he still managed to sell his business to the Hudson's Bay Company of Canada for a great return. Yet even after he sold the business, John's leadership journey continued when he was voted mayor for the community of St. Augustin River. He had been up against competitive candidates with strong track records. However, the fact that he had been a successful businessman who was very involved in helping the community, and putting people first, had resulted in a favorable outcome for John. There were many ways in which he had helped the community. In addition, he had sponsored hockey teams in the area, and he even succeeded to bring hockey legend Bobby Orr to visit the village!

When he ran for mayor, virtually all the Montagnais people who could vote came over by boat. Nadine recounted her very fond memory of that day, "It was a real sight to see. Boats filled with Montagnais people came across the water to vote for my dad because he always provided them great service and showed he cared about them."

When I asked Nadine how it impacted her to have a dad who was such an amazing leader, she said, "I am exactly like my dad. He taught me well because I started working with him when I was just twelve years old, side by side."

Nadine continues to apply her father's lessons about giving back and helping others, which she does through her philanthropic work. "My best friend Jo-Anne Landriault, the founder of 'Women's Expressions,' and I started a volunteer project, Women Goddesses Initiative, to raise money for women's shelters," she told me. "We discovered that creating beautiful Goddess costumes for women and giving them the photos of their dreams was a very powerful experience for them. We are empowering women through positivity and by helping them connect with Goddess residing in their *being*. We raise money for sponsored shelters through the sale of calendars, Goddess photos, custom-built costumes, oracle cards, and fashion shows."

In addition to doing wonderful philanthropic work, in past years Nadine had made a significant contribution to establish a company called NATTIQ Inc. Today, she continues to follow in her father's footsteps by integrating her excellent leadership and customer service skills in all she does.

Practical Ways to Integrate
The Light Your Leadership© Approach

"Storytellers, by the very act of telling, communicate a radical
learning that changes lives and the world: telling stories is a
universally accessible means through which people make meaning."
~ *Chris Cavanaugh*

When you read about values and principles that form the basis of organizational culture, they may sound nice in theory, but they remain rather impractical and esoteric unless accompanied by practical examples of how they can be manifested in real life. The following suggestions provide practical ways to positive leadership behaviors into practice, ignite engagement, and light a fire in the hearts of your employees.

♦ *Light a fire in your own heart first.* Before you can get others excited about giving their best, you need to light your own heart. Get clear on your "Why" and your passions. Choose in favor of what is important and stay close to your vision. When you communicate from a place of truth, others will want to follow and share in your vision.

♦ *Be a visionary.* Help people at work get excited about a shared vision and show them how their work is a way for them to manifest their passions.

♦ *Tell stories from the heart* to illustrate lessons, apply values, celebrate people and accomplishments, raise awareness, and teach new things.

♦ *Encourage employees to keep their power* rather than to trade it with every paycheck. Others choose to follow you, so prove that you're worthy of their trust rather than expecting them to follow orders just because you're their boss.

♦ *Live a balanced life* and, by extension, don't thwart your employees' efforts when they try to do the same.

♦ *Invest time in connecting with your employees.* Send an instant message (IM) or a handwritten note to employees; connect with them over a cup of coffee. When you see employees in the hall or around the office, always smile, acknowledge them by name, and say hello. (And for goodness' sake, eat your lunch somewhere other than in your office. Get out and break bread with your employees once in a while!)

♦ *Show gratitude and say thank you.* Say "thank you" a lot, and mean it sincerely, from the heart.

♦ *Show what it means to "engage and inspire"* rather than "command and control."

♦ *Take ownership of the role you play in the performance of your team.* That is, if you have under-performing employees, take accountability for your role in the situation.

♦ *Give back to the community and model social responsibility* because you really believe it, not just because it looks good!

♦ *Be committed to inclusion and help people feel they belong.* True inclusion is setting aside stereotypes and seeing every single person on your team for who they really are and what they can bring.

♦ *Be fun, passionate, and enthusiastic, not flat and humorless.* Drop the cool airs and model what it's like to have fun at the office and to be excited about your work.

♦ *Celebrate all accomplishments,* from little to significant achievements—this is like fuel for the fire!

♦ *Quash gossip, bullying, and vexatious behavior.* Send a very clear message that you don't tolerate any mean-spirited words or behaviors.

♦ *Show that it's important to stand up for what is ethical and to uphold and model integrity.* Step up to the plate for your employees and followers and have the courage to be transparent and speak your truth.

♦ *Demonstrate that having fortitude does not mean winning at all costs.* It's okay to admit that others are right sometimes.

♦ *Be uplifting and give off positive energy.* Be uplifting rather than condescending.

♦ *Help all employees release their inner leader.* Let them shine! And feel proud of the role you played to help them grow.

♦ *Forgive them their mistakes and teach them to view errors as learning opportunities.* Help them feel safe to experiment with new ideas and let them know you'll have their back and will help them learn and guide them to fix their mistake.

♦ *Ask for forgiveness* when it is necessary.

♦ *Model what it means to be at once confident, courageous, and vulnerable.* Be a kind and confident person.

♦ *Model how to make difficult decisions and follow your inner compass.* Let your employees and followers go within for their answers. Expect the best from all of them.

♦ *View leadership and work as a manifestation of human nature and spirituality.* Put aside salaries and perceived status, and at the heart of it, you'll find that we all hold the same high degree of value as human beings.

Summary of Part IV

Part IV gave you insights, tools, advice, and wisdom of experts and great people leaders on how to ignite engagement and inspire employees to give their very best and boost the productivity of your team and organization while maintaining their health, feeling like they belong and are valued, having fun, and finding meaning at work.

While there are many valuable leadership-development programs out there that teach management and emotional intelligence, at the writing of this book, there is a gap when it comes to leading through the heart. Leadership development programs that teach about connecting at the human level and essentially bringing mindfulness and spirituality—love—into the workplace, are just beginning to become more mainstream. Those who will lead their organizations to thrive in the twenty-first century realize that this is the glue that holds the people of a profitable and sustainable company working together toward a shared vision. It is the foundation that is necessary for any type of organizational intervention, be it transforming organizational culture, managing change, or redesigning processes, to succeed. Without it, engagement levels tank, temporary increases in productivity wane over time, employees get sick, and the organization stagnates without ever fully realizing its talent and vast human potential.

Learning and implementing the 3 C's of Connection, and the 8 P's of Ignition will help you close the gap so that you can be a great people leader and contribute to creating a better, healthier, more prosperous and sustainable work environment for your organization.

"As we look ahead into the next century, leaders will be those who empower others."

~ Bill Gates

Conclusion
TOGETHER, WE CAN MAKE THE WORLD A BETTER WORKPLACE

"We need leaders not in love with money, but in love with justice.
Not in love with publicity, but in love with humanity."
~ Dr. Martin Luther King Jr.

Though the state of the workplace seems grim at times, there is a very optimistic outlook. In the past when experts spoke in front of large audiences or wrote about concepts such as servant leadership, kindness at work, and bringing love into organizations, there was a great deal of challenge, resistance, and even ridicule.

More recently, however, there seems to be a greater openness to these types of leadership philosophies and much less pushback. For instance, my friend and sister-author, Maria R. Nebres, wrote the book Love and the Highly Engaged Team, and it is being very well received by a new brand of progressive leader. We can be hopeful that organizations are changing for the better, especially with a surge of social enterprises, and a marked increase in organizations of all types that practice conscious leadership and corporate social responsibility.

Furthermore, the notion that people only work to make money is not as true as it used to be. People want to work for companies where they can do meaningful and creative work together with fun and interesting people within a healthy work environment.

Progressive leaders realize that to build high-performing teams and achieve success they need to live and work based on fundamental business principles that flow from a love for humanity and the desire for human connection.

As Steve Farber says, people want to work in organizations where there are "cool people, in a cool place, doing cool things," just like we saw with Karen Baker-Anderson's devoted crew at Inuuqatigiit, Michel's team nailing the presentation to the board, and Carol Novello's team of committed people at Humane Society Silicon Valley and Mutual Rescue, and the remote store owned by the widely loved mayor, the late John Albano Bursey.

Progressive leaders realize that to build high-performing teams and achieve success they need to live and work based on fundamental business principles that flow from a love for humanity and the desire for human connection. It is compassion, courage, and competence as a leader that inspires employees to do their very best and give the company a competitive edge. It is profundity, passion, purpose, and perseverance that helps leaders and employees to tap into what is important to them and to pursue their vision regardless of the obstacles they may encounter along the way. It is professionalism, play, philanthropy and prosperity that engages people to push their limits and to give their very best at work for one another, for clients, and for society. These are the secrets to attracting, retaining, and motivating a talented workforce in the twenty-first century—This is the wisdom that sets great leaders apart.

Be it in a bricks and mortar or a virtual office, in order to succeed as a great leader in this new era—in the Passion Age—you need to commit to fostering a positive and healthy work environment that advances collaboration and inclusion. Part of your job is to listen to employees and see what they need, find ways to help them love coming in to work, and at the same time ensure that they have enough time for themselves and to be there for their loved ones.

Another important responsibility is for you to devote time and energy to growing the next generation of leaders: You can mentor them and help them to grow their competencies and skill set so that they are well equipped to do their jobs—and then get out of their way by giving them the latitude they need to be creative and provide excellent service.

You need to light a fire in their hearts and ignite and nurture the flame that is their innate desire to do amazing things, to make a positive difference in the lives of others, and to contribute to something greater than themselves.

Together, we can make the world a better workplace.

Will there still be a need for leaders in the future? Certainly. To succeed, will they need to act differently from many of the people who are currently in power? Absolutely. The world is depending on it, as healthier workplaces will lead to a healthier planet.

My fundamental belief is that together, we can make the world a better workplace.

And it begins with you.

ACKNOWLEDGEMENTS

Thank you to the two people who brought me into this world and who were the first to teach me about leadership: My mom, Elvia Cattelan (née Vissa) and late dad, Corrado Cattelan. Thank you to my nonnas who modeled leadership and what it means to have faith for me.

So much love and gratitude go to my amazing husband, Andrew Palmer, and my wonderful son, Jake Palmer, for being there for me every single day on this journey. Thank you to my beloved siblings (and their spouses), who've encouraged me all the way and who have helped us get through some of the most challenging times: Emily Cattelan (Roger Lagace); Roger Cattelan (Isabelle Guay); my sister-niece Andrea Dubin (Dan Dubin), who read the very first draft of the first version of this book; and my niece Angelina for her great encouraging hugs. Thank you to my constant and loyal companion, Shadow, who lay at my side or at my feet while I wrote almost every chapter of this book.

Thank you to all my family, including my in-laws Philip and Sheila, Corey and Kimberley, and the rest of the Palmer family, with a special thanks to my niece Brandy (Dee) Lawson for her encouragement and for sharing her healing gifts with me. A big thank-you to all my many cousins, aunts, and uncles who have been encouraging me, praying for me, and sending me well wishes. A huge thank-you to my godmother, Giulietta (Juliet) Tonini, who invited me into her beautiful Montreal home for a writing retreat, and to my cousin Giorgio Tonini for helping me to proofread the manuscript.

A big thank-you to all my coaches along the way: beginning with The Passion Test family that lit up my heart to help me get clear on my passions (one of the big of which is now manifesting through this book): Beth Lefevre, Cheryl Burget, CeCe Homer, and the Enlightened Bestseller teachers and mentors: Janet Bray Attwood, Chris Attwood, Marci Shimoff, and Geoff Affleck. Thank you to Laurin Michelle Kyle, who was the first to introduce me to the Passion Test all those years ago—I am forever grateful. Thank you to Joel Roberts, "The Digger of Divine Deposits," and his amazing partner in life, Heidi Roberts, who were instrumental in helping me develop impactful messaging and have now become valued friends. Thank you to my more recent coaches, including Peter Beckenham, The Thai Village Marketer, who is a very special mentor and has become my friend from afar, for sharing his sage advice, wisdom, and encouragement. Thank you to Majeed Mogharreban for helping me become an expert speaker so that I can get the message about *Light a Fire in Their Hearts* out to the masses, and to M Shannon Hernandez for sharing her business savvy.

A big thank-you to the amazing team at Morgan James Publishing, including David L. Hancock and Jim Howard, Karen Anderson, Margo Toulouse, the sales and design teams, and so many others. Thank you for all your help and guidance to produce and launch this book and make it a success. A heartfelt Thank you to Jodi Chapman and Dan Teck for creating the Your Soulful Book Program and the YSB community, as they helped me to get through major writer's blocks and clear the last few hurdles to completion. I am so grateful to Dan, my super-talented editor, who has accompanied me on this last leg of a challenging book-writing journey.

I am so grateful for brilliant and loving friends and the first readers of the manuscript for giving me excellent feedback: Annette Dillon, Jill Sullivan, Dr. Teresa Janz, and Jan Riopelle. You were the perfect team to help me take the book to the next level and prepare it in for editing.

Thank you to my friends Lindsey Gibeau (photographer) and Leslie-Anne Barrette (make-up expert) for the headshot.

A big gigantic thank-you to all the amazing contributors, including Anisa and some whom I can't name as they shared their stories about the painful situations that they lived through in toxic workplaces—it is an honor to be able to give them a voice. A big thank-you to the great leaders, thought leaders, and experts I interviewed to shine a light on them so that they can be a model for the current and future generations of leaders (in alphabetical order): Hana Ameerah, Anisa, Marlene Armstrong, Karen Baker-Anderson, Peter Beckenham, Karen Bennett, Suzanne Bergeron, Rene Bibaud, Nadine Bursey, Carlo Cattelan, Erin Crotty, Dominique Dennery, Maureen Donoghue, Kathie Donovan, Dan Duguay, Lewis Eisen, Issam Elhaje, Steve Farber, Pauline Fleming, Dr. Marcelle Forget, Steve Kanellakos, Arthur Lacroix, Jacqueline Lawrence, Dr. Karin Lubin, Akshay Nanavati, Carol Novello, Jean-François Pinsonnault, Kashif Siddiqui, Brenda Silverhand, Doug Smith, Craig Szelestowski, Dr. Eleanor Sutherland, Michel Rodrigue, Anna-Karina Tabünar, Claudio Vissa, Mario Vissa, Lisa J. Weiss, and Stephen Whiteley. A huge thank you to Joanna Barclay, whose work I respect very much, for agreeing to read my manuscript and write a forward. Bios of contributors can be found on the www.lightafireintheirhearts.com website.

A big thank you to all my clients who continue to be a major source of inspiration for me. Gratitude to Martin Chenier of Grey Oak Consulting, LRO, Altis, and CLA that helped me to land very meaningful work that inspired me to focus on working with leaders. Thank you to Marc André Sirois and Ariadni Athanassiadis for contributing legal guidance. Thank you to Stefania Maggi of BYBS™.

In addition, thank you to those who introduced me to leaders I could interview, including Geoff Affleck, Nathalie Bloskie, and Kimberly Wilson. A big thanks to my wonderful friend Linda Caron for being the best listener, and to Linda and her sister-in-law, Ruma Bose, for making one of my vision-board dreams come true and introducing me to my hero, Sir Richard Branson!

A big thank-you to those of you who believed in me early on and invited me to speak and write about my book way before it got published on their shows/webinars, publications and at events: amazing community leaders, friends and change-makers Magdalene Cooman, Dominique Dennery, Carrie Roldan, Carol Davies, Cindia Carrere, Ashley Robson, Guillaume McMartin and Trish Taylor of GT Prosperity, and many others.

A big thank-you to all those who believed in me and contributed to my Go Fund Me campaign to help me cover expenses for this book and other related works, and to those who contributed to the early development of the Better Workplace Foundation that will support initiatives to advance leadership development in the twenty-first century.

I would also like to send a special thanks all my clients who continue to inspire me every day as they step into their leadership.

Most of all, thank God, Jesus, and Mary for all the divine intervention I received and continue to receive while writing this book. Thank you to the Angels and Ascended Masters. There were times when I didn't think I was ever going to make it due to health issues, illness of close relatives, financial challenges, a flood, death of a loved one, and the list goes on. Thank you to those people who were veritable earth angels and who showed up on my journey to help me.

I am infinitely grateful!

ABOUT THE AUTHOR

Lisa Anna Palmer loves her family and friends, is a proud mom and wife, and loves to help people live their best lives at work and at home. She holds a B.A. in Psychology, is a Certified ProActive Coach, Certified Passion Test Facilitator, and Cross-Cultural Competencies Facilitator. She is fluent in English, French, Italian, and Friulan. She started her career at the age of twenty-two as a consultant for PwC as part of the Organizational Renewal Group, where she led reengineering teams and conducted international best practices research on HR policies, teams, communications and other related topics.

Lisa draws on over twenty-five years of experience within a range of senior Human Resources & Organizational Development roles, leading teams responsible for HR Management, Talent Management, Talent Acquisition, HR Strategy & Policy, and transformation. In 2011, she launched Cattelan Palmer Consulting. She is now the Founder & CEO of the Cattelan Palmer Light Your

Leadership Institute (LYLI), which serves leaders and employees of organizations within the private, public, and the non-profit sectors. She has been on TV, radio, and podcasts in Canada and the United States. Lisa has also contributed pieces to four bestselling books of the *365 Days Series*, a collaborative book by Jodi Chapman and Dan Teck. She currently resides in Ottawa, Ontario.

You can access additional resources and learn more about Lisa at www. LisaAnnaPalmer.com and at www.lightafireintheirhearts.com.

Bibliography

American Institute of Stress. "Workplace Stress." Accessed January 12, 2018. https://www. stress.org/workplace-stress.

Americans' Changing Lives. "Understanding Social Inequalities in Health and Aging." Accessed June 24, 2019. https://acl.isr.umich.edu/.

Baratta, Maria. "Self Care 101: 10 Ways to Take Better Care of You." *Psychology Today*. Posted May 27, 2018. https://www.psychologytoday.com/ca/blog/skinny-revisited/201805/ self-care-101.

Beekun, Rafik. "Leadership and Islam: Effective Leadership Steps for Strategy Implementation in Islamic Organizations." *The Islamic Workplace*. Updated September 9, 2012. https://theislamicworkplace.com/leadership-and-islam/.

Blanding, Michael. "Workplace Stress Responsible for up to $190B in Annual U.S. Healthcare Costs." *Forbes*. Posted January 26, 2015. https://www.forbes.com/sites/ hbsworkingknowledge/2015/01/26/workplace-stress-responsible-for-up-to-190-billion-in-annual-u-s-heathcare-costs/#22a4d895235a.

Bonebright, Denise A. "40 Years of Storming: A Historical Review of Tuckman's Model of Small Group Development." *Human Resource Development International* 13, no. 1 (2010): 111-120.

Business Dictionary. "Leadership." Accessed June 24, 2019. http://www.businessdictionary. com/definition/leadership.html.

Business Dictionary. "Management." Accessed June 24, 2019. http://www. businessdictionary.com/definition/management.html.

Business Dictionary. "Peter Principle." Accessed November 19, 2018. http://www.businessdictionary.com/definition/Peter-principle.html.

Business Dictionary. "Retrenchment." Accessed June 24, 2019. http://www.businessdictionary.com/definition/retrenchment.html.

Cellucci, Rory, and Darlene Slaughter. "The 4 Ps of Change and Transition," *Linkage*. Posted April 2, 2014, http://blog.linkageinc.com/the-4-ps-of-change-and-transition/.

Charity Village. "The Changing Face of Volunteering in Canada." *Knowledge Centre*. Posted July 2, 2014. https://charityvillage.com/cms/content/topic/the_changing_face_of_volunteering_in_canada#.W_rUa6cZNQI.

Chief Executive. "Uncovering the Leadership Lessons of the Bhagavad Gita." Posted August 29, 2006. https://chiefexecutive.net/uncovering-the-leadership-lessons-of-the-bhagavad-gita__trashed/.

Chron. "Small Business." Accessed June 24, 2019. https://smallbusiness.chron.com/.

Ciampa, Dan, and Michael D. Watkins. "Right from the Start." *Harvard Business School, Working Knowledge: Business Research for Business Leaders*. Posted December 10, 1999. https://hbswk.hbs.edu/archive/right-from-the-start.

Cohen, A. *Everyman's Talmud*. New York: Schocken Books, 1949.

Datu, Jesus Alfonso D., Jana Patricia M. Valdez, B. King Ronnel. "Perseverance Counts but Consistency Does Not! Validating the Short Grit Scale in a Collectivist Setting." *Current Psychology* 35, no. 1 (March 2016): 121-130.

Deloitte. "The 2016 Deloitte Millennial Survey—Winning over the Next Generation of Leaders," p. 19. https://www2.deloitte.com/content/dam/Deloitte/global/Documents/About-Deloitte/gx-millenial-survey-2016-exec-summary.pdf.

Dennery, Dominique. "R.E.S.P.E.C.T in the Workplace: What Does It Look Like, Sound Like, Feel Like to You?" Posted November 28, 2016. http://dominiquedennery.com/uncategorized/r-e-s-p-e-c-t-in-the-workplace-what-does-it-look-like-sound-like-feel-like-to-you/.

Dictionary.com. "Purpose." Accessed November 05, 2018. https://www.dictionary.com/browse/purpose.

Doug Smith Performance. "Break Through Adversity to Reach Your Goal." Accessed June 24, 2019. http://www.dougsmithperformance.com/.

Economist. "Parents Now Spend Twice as Much Time with Their Children as 50 Years Ago." Posted November 27, 2017. https://www.economist.com/graphic-detail/2017/11/27/parents-now-spend-twice-as-much-time-with-their-children-as-50-years-ago.

EOI. "What Innovation Creates Prosperity-Fostering Organization?" Posted August 31, 2015. https://www.eoi.es/blogs/meaningfulinnovation/2015/08/31/what-innovation-creates-prosperity-fostering-organization/.

Fast Company. "Five Hidden Benefits of Gossip." Posted March 5, 2015. https://www.fastcompany.com/3043161/five-hidden-benefits-of-gossip.

Gallup. *State of the Global Workplace.* New York, NY: Gallup Press, 2017. https://www.gallup.com/workplace/238079/state-global-workplace-2017.aspx.

Gen Z Guru. "Gen X Parents Support Gen Z's Exploration of Alternative Education." Accessed November 25, 2018. http://genzguru.com/blog/gen-x-parents-support-gen-zs-exploration-of-alternative-education (site discontinued).

Gen Z Guru. "Gen Z's Willing to Work If the Price Is Right." Accessed December 4, 2018. http://genzguru.com/blog/gen-zs-willing-to-work-if-the-price-is-right/ (site discontinued).

Glaser, Judith E. Conversational Intelligence: How Great Leaders Build Trust and Get Extraordinary Results. Brookline, MA: Bibliomotion, 2014.

Goleman, Daniel. Emotional Intelligence: Why It Can Matter More Than IQ. New York, NY: Bantam Books, 1995.

Greene, Nick. "6 Essential Change Management Models to Help Innovate & Grow." *TallyFy*. Accessed June 24, 2019. https://tallyfy.com/change-management-models/.

Greenleaf, Robert K. "The Servant as Leader (1970)," accessed November 25, 2019, https://www.greenleaf.org/servant-first-servant-heart/.

Grant Thornton. "International Business Report: Women in Business 2018." Posted March 8, 2018. https://www.grantthornton.global/en/insights/articles/women-in-business-2018-report-page/.

Henein, Amal, and Francoise Morisette. Made in Canada Leadership: Wisdom from the Nation's Best and Brightest on the Art and Practice of Leadership. San Francisco, CA: Jossey-Bass, 2012.

HuffPost. "The Power of Play at Work." Updated December 6, 2017. https://www.HuffPost.com/entry/the-power-of-play-at-work_b_12011462.

IGI Global: Disseminator of Knowledge. "What Is Digital Generation." Accessed June 24, 2019. https://www.igi-global.com/dictionary/digital-generation/7631.

Intini, John, Martin Patriquin, and Ken Macqueen. "Workplace Stress Costs the Economy Billions." *The Canadian Encyclopedia*. Updated May 27, 2014. https://www.thecanadianencyclopedia.ca/en/article/workplace-stress-costs-the-economy-billions.

Intuit. "Intuit 2020 Report." Posted October 2010. https://http-download.intuit.com/http.intuit/CMO/intuit/futureofsmallbusiness/intuit_2020_report.pdf.

International Labour Organization. "Why Workplace Stress Is a Collective Challenge and What to Do About It." Posted April 27, 2016. http://www.ilo.org/global/about-the-ilo/newsroom/comment-analysis/WCMS_475077/lang--en/index.htm.

JKS Talent Network. "Managerial Courage Is a Winning Skill." Accessed March 10, 2016. https://jkstalent.com/managerial-courage-winning-skill/#.XABOLacZNQI.

Ken Blanchard Companies. "Situational Leadership II." Accessed June 24, 2019. https://www.kenblanchard.com/Products-Services/Situational-Leadership-II.

Kenton, Will. "Crown Corporation." *Investopedia*. Updated January 8, 2018. https://www.investopedia.com/terms/c/crowncorporation.asp.

Kohanov, Linda. The Power of the Herd: A Nonpredatory Approach to Social Intelligence, Leadership, and Innovation. Novato, CA: New World Library, 2012.

Lambrozo, Tania. "Why Do We Gossip?" *NPR*. Posted May 23, 2016. https://www.npr.org/sections/13.7/2016/05/23/479128912/the-origins-of-gossip.

Lencioni, Patrick. "Leaders Are Pushers." *The Hub*. Posted January 2018. https://www.tablegroup.com/hub/post/leaders-are-pushers.

Lencioni, Patrick. The Truth About Employee Engagement: A Fable About Addressing the Three Root Causes of Job Misery. San Francisco, CA: Jossey-Bass & Pfeiffer, 2016.

Leslie, Jean. "The Leadership Gap: How to Fix What Your Organization Lacks." *Center for Creative Leadership*. Posted September 2015. https://www.ccl.org/articles/white-papers/leadership-gap-what-you-still-need/.

Lexico. "Appreciation." Accessed June 24, 2019. https://www.lexico.com/en/definition/appreciation.

Lexico. "Philanthropy." Accessed June 24, 2019. https://www.lexico.com/en/definition/philanthropy.

Lexico. "Play." Accessed June 24, 2019. https://www.lexico.com/en/definition/play.

Manageris. "Create a Climate of Constructive Debate." Posted February 18, 2013. https://www.manageris.com/blog-management-nuggets.html.

McAndrew, Frank T. "The Science of Gossip: Why We Can't Stop Ourselves." *Scientific American Mind*. Posted October 2008. https://www.scientificamerican.com/article/the-science-of-gossip/.

McGregor, Jena. "In overworked Japan, Microsoft tested a four-day workweek.

Productivity soared 40 percent," *The Washington Post*, Accessed November 5, 2019: https://www.washingtonpost.com/business/2019/11/04/overworked-japan-microsoft-tested-four-day-workweek-productivity-soared-percent/

McLeod, Saul. "Maslow's Hierarchy of Needs." *Simply Psychology*. Accessed June 24, 2019. https://www.simplypsychology.org/maslow.html.

Merriam-Webster. "Passion." Accessed December 6, 2018. http://www.learnersdictionary.com/definition/passion.

Merriam-Webster. "Perseverance." Accessed June 24, 2019. https://www.merriam-webster.com/dictionary/perseverance.

Merriam-Webster. "Professional." Accessed June 24, 2019. https://www.merriam-webster.com/dictionary/professional.

Merriam-Webster. "Professionalism." Accessed June 24, 2019. https://www.merriam-webster.com/dictionary/professionalism.

Merriam-Webster. "Prosperity." Accessed June 24, 2019. https://www.merriam-webster.com/dictionary/prosperity.

Mind Tools. "Bridges' Transition Model: Guiding People Through Change." Accessed June 24, 2019. https://www.mindtools.com/pages/article/bridges-transition-model.htm.

Mitsuhashi, Yukari. "Ikigai: A Japanese Concept to Improve Work and Life." *BBC*. Posted August 7, 2017. http://www.bbc.com/capital/story/20170807-ikigai-a-japanese-concept-to-improve-work-and-life.

Nanavati, Akshay. Fearvana: The Revolutionary Science of How to Turn Fear into Health, Wealth and Happiness. New York, NY: Morgan James Publishing, 2017.

National Philanthropic Trust. "Giving is Good for Your Health." Posted September 16, 2013. https://www.nptrust.org/philanthropic-resources/philanthropist/giving-is-good-for-your-health/.

Nielsen, Nick. "Inverting Maslow's Hierarchy." *Medium*. Posted May 26, 2016. https://medium.com/@jnnielsen/inverting-maslows-hierarchy-b2c32156f091.

Nyberg, A, L Alfredsson, T Theorell, H Westerlund, J Vahtera, M Kivimäki. "Managerial Leadership and Ischaemic Heart Disease Among Employees: The Swedish WOLF Study." *Occupational & Environmental Medicine* 66, no. 1 (2009): 51-55.

Okubayashi, Koji. "Japanese Style of Teamworking." *In Corporate Governance*, ed. H. Albach. ZfB-Ergänzungshefte, vol 1. Wiesbaden: Gabler Verlag, 2000.

Orr, J. Evelyn, and Kathleen Sack. "Setting the Stage for Success: Building Leadership Skills That Matter." *Korn / Ferry International*. Accessed June 24, 2019. http://www.

kornferry.com/media/lominger_pdf/LA_article_web.pdf.

Ottawa Citizen. "Two Ottawa Recipients among Canada's 'Outstanding Principals.'" Posted May 20, 2014. https://ottawacitizen.com/news/local-news/two-ottawa-recipients-among-canadas-outstanding-principals.

Pofeldt, Elaine. "Are We Ready for a Workforce That Is 50% Freelance?" *Forbes.* Posted October 17, 2017. https://www.forbes.com/sites/elainepofeldt/2017/10/17/are-we-ready-for-a-workforce-that-is-50-freelance/#5f2997853f82.

Ravindran, Sandeep. "Feeling Like A Fraud: The Impostor Phenomenon in Science Writing." *The Open Notebook.* Posted November 15, 2016. https://www.theopennotebook.com/2016/11/15/feeling-like-a-fraud-the-impostor-phenomenon-in-science-writing/.

Safety & Health: The Official Magazine of the NSC Congress and Expo. "ILO: Global Cost of Work-Related Injuries and Deaths Total Almost $3 Trillion." Posted September 6, 2017. https://www.safetyandhealthmagazine.com/articles/16112-ilo-global-cost-of-work-related-injuries-and-deaths-totals-almost-3-trillion.

Sander, J. M. The Sharing of Traditional Aboriginal Knowledge of Pipe Carriers from Winnipeg, Manitoba and the Implications for the Health of Aboriginal Peoples Living in Urban Centers. Ontario, Canada, 2012.

SlideShare. "Freelancing in America, 2017." Posted September 28, 2017. https://www.slideshare.net/upwork/freelancing-in-america-2017/1.

UNC Kenan-Flagler Business School. "Engaged, Disengaged, Actively Disengaged. What's the Difference?" *Executive Development Blog.* Posted March 17, 2016. http://execdev.kenan-flagler.unc.edu/blog/engaged-disengaged-actively-disengaged.-whats-the-difference.

University College London. "Born to lead? Leadership can be an Inherited Trait, Study Finds." Posted January 15, 2013. https://www.ucl.ac.uk/news/2013/jan/born-lead-leadership-can-be-inherited-trait-study-finds.

Voices, Valley. "Don't Be Surprised When Your Employees Quit." Forbes. October 30, 2017. Accessed December 06, 2018. https://www.forbes.com/sites/valleyvoices/2017/02/22/dont-be-surprised-when-your-employees-quit/#726688d7325e and https://www.linkedin.com/pulse/employees-dont-leave-companies-managers-brigette-hyacinth/.

Watson, Stephanie. "Volunteering May Be Good for Body and Mind." *Harvard Health Publishing, Harvard Medical School.* Posted June 26, 2013. https://www.health.harvard.edu/blog/volunteering-may-be-good-for-body-and-mind-201306266428.

Weiss, Lisa J. "I of the Storm Coaching & Consulting." Accessed June 24, 2019. http://iofthestormcoaching.com/.

Vivian, Pat, and Shana Hormann. "What is Organizational Trauma?—Organizational Trauma and Healing." In *Organizational Trauma and Healing*. North Charleston, SC: CreateSpace, 2013.

William Bridges Associates. "What Is William Bridges' Transition Model?" Accessed June 24, 2019. https://wmbridges.com/what-is-transition/.

Winston, Bruce E., and Kathleen Patterson. "An Integrative Definition of Leadership." *International Journal of Leadership Studies* 1, no. 2 (2006): 6-66. https://www.regent.edu/acad/global/publications/ijls/new/vol1iss2/winston_patterson.doc/winston_patterson.pdf.

World Health Organization. "Burnout an 'Occupational Phenomenon': International Classification of Diseases." Posted May 28, 2019. https://www.who.int/mental_health/evidence/burnout/en/.

World Health Organization. "Mental Health in the Workplace: Information Sheet." Posted May 2019. https://www.who.int/mental_health/in_the_workplace/en/.

World Health Organization. "Stress at the Workplace." Accessed June 24, 2019. https://www.who.int/occupational_health/topics/stressatwp/en/.

Zacks, Nancy. "Horses React to Human Heart Rates, Study Finds." The Horse. Posted July 1, 2009. https://thehorse.com/121855/horses-react-to-human-heart-rates-study-finds/.

CPSIA information can be obtained
at www.ICGtesting.com
Printed in the USA
JSHW021931170723
44903JS00002B/266